Letting Them Go

Trusting God to Catch Them

Sharon M. Cluck RN

Contents

Dedication

I have dedicated this to my dad, Jeff Leopold. He was forever spouting his intentions to write a book someday but never got around to it; this one is for you Dad. To my husband, Joseph H. Cluck, who so willingly and lovingly took on my two older children as his own and fathered our last two. Joe has been a constant encourager of everything I chose to undertake for forty-one years. Of course, I'm including my four wonderful children, Jeff, Kelly, Rachel, and Samuel that have taught me myriads through the years, and to my God whose love propelled me to learn His ways.

Forward

When I started this journey, I intended my message to be to parents only. However, as this work unfolded, it was clear that the principles revealed in these pages can easily be applied to any stressed or even toxic relationship. Anywhere there are two people that love one another there are joys and heartaches along the way.

Whatever your situation is, even when parents are addressed, see yourself and your personal circumstances. Test your decisions and following actions with the challenging questions throughout this book. Perhaps you'll uncover motives hidden deep within your heart as well as in the hearts of those that you love.

I'm sharing my story with those who are working through the joys and the pains of *letting go*. Either you or someone you know needs this information, or you wouldn't even be holding this book in your hands. It's a book for those who desire to see their children become all that God has purposed for them to be, but you aren't sure if either one of you are on the right track. I've exposed my thoughts and actions which will reveal to you what I did right and wrong as I searched to find God's ways for me and my children.

I am first and foremost, a Christian. I'm the mother of four, grandmother of twenty and great grandmother of sixteen. In the past when I've shared some of my stories, the response has been, "You need to put that in writing to share with others." These comments came from people that were struggling with making tough decisions, especially where their children were concerned. Remarks like these motivated me to write this book. I certainly had plenty of ups and downs. I now have decades of insight, to go along with my perfectly clear hindsight, just waiting to be tapped into. I hope you'll see how I learned through trials and errors as I sought to hear God's voice more clearly. With each passing year I became a little better equipped to apply new truths. I found myself wishing I had known some of these things much earlier in life.

I've allowed myself to be vulnerable in hopes of helping you. My desire is to see you glean from my victories and defeats. That you'll learn lessons now that took me a lifetime to understand. I pray you will be able to relate to my story and view it in light of your own circumstances. You don't have to be a Bible scholar to apply the many questions, and self-examinations posed in this book. Hearing from God in the middle of your storm is difficult. The solution is to ask God for help first, instead of waiting till all else fails. Additionally, it's imperative to become familiar with how God speaks to you before the crisis hits.

There are plenty of books written on parenting and relationships. However, we just don't have the ability to see into the future. We don't see the webs being weaved. It's not until we or someone we love has been caught in a trap. You know the kind where nothing you do is ever going to be good enough to make things right. So, I've listed questions for you to ponder and help you to know yourself better. To help you know why you do what you do.

The introspections in this book will require being honest with yourself. They'll help you begin working through some of the hardest situations that you'll have with the ones you love. You'll encounter thought stimulating questions in most chapters. Please don't just read over these. Stop! Prayerfully and honestly give truthful answers to each question, before moving on. You'll learn a lot about yourself, your child, and your God along the way. My hope is that you'll have numerous "Ah Ha" moments as you read and reflect.

I understand that not everyone who reads this book will have the same spiritual understanding. However, it's healthy to consider your higher power as a loving, involved participant in the challenges your family is facing. I'm exuberant in my faith and I don't intend to offend anyone by that. I'm simply telling my story as things unfolded in my own life.

Happy reading, and much growth.

Sincerely,

Sharon M. Cluck

Chapter 1
What if?

What would life be like if you didn't toss and turn all night long? Is it possible to stop your mind from racing and worrying about what's going to happen to your child? What if your child could just grow up, live a normal life and you could actually look forward to a wonderful, carefree, relaxing retirement? What if you didn't have to keep bailing your kid out of so many situations and circumstances? How would life be different?

What if you could know that everything will be ok? What would be different if you could quit trying to fix things? What if you could stop trying to manage the outcome? What if you were so secure in your understanding of God's love and grace towards you and your child that you could just stop worrying? What if you could trust God knowing beyond a shadow of a doubt that He will protect and care for your children better than you can? What if you could just "*LET GO?*"

We all have doubts and fears. But those thoughts don't originate with God. Are you buying Satan's plan to distract you from the freedom that God has for you? Are you the great fixer? A Rescuer? The enemy tells you, "You can figure things out on your own." After all, God is simply too slow in getting things done. Or maybe He's just too busy to care about *your* little details. That's just not true. If He cares enough to number every hair on your head, He surely cares about what's going on in your everyday life, and the life of your child.

> And even the very hairs of your head are all numbered. Matt.10:30

Speaking of the devil, Jesus says:

> ...he is a liar and the father of it. John 8:44

I know there are times when it looks like your kids are going to fall flat on their faces. You find yourself wondering, "What can I possibly do to prevent this?" As parents, we instinctively want to make things better for them. We want to rescue them.

It hurts to see any of our children endure hardships. Consequently, there were times when I thought I could shelter my children. Unfortunately, my ideas weren't always the best. My experiences have taught me when I do anything without consulting God first, trusting Him for the outcome, I usually end up paying for it.

For those of you who know the Bible story of Sarai and Abram, it's a good example of what happens when we try to fix things on our own.

In Genesis 16, God promised Abram that he and his wife Sarai would be blessed with a child. After many years of waiting, it just didn't happen. The child wasn't conceived in the time frame Sarai thought he should be. She was aging and her biological time clock had seemingly run out. She decided to FIX things. So, she took the matter into her own hands. Her solution was to give Abram her servant girl, Hagar hoping to have a surrogate child through her.

> Now Sarai, Abram's wife, had borne him no *children.* And she had an Egyptian maidservant whose name was Hagar. So Sarai said to Abram, "See now, the Lord has restrained me from bearing *children.* Please, go in to my maid; perhaps I shall obtain children by her." And Abram heeded the voice of Sarai. Gen. 16:1-2

Sarai assumed it was God's fault that she hadn't had children. She had a solution; she'd override God's timing or delay with her own plan. It would give her what she thought God hadn't.

Hagar conceived, and it resulted in the birth of Ismael. Eventually, this would be an outcome Sarai wouldn't be happy with. She even blamed Abram for the difficulties she began to have with Hagar once she realized Hagar was expecting.

> Then Sarai said to Abram, "My wrong *be* upon you! I gave my maid into your embrace; and when she saw that she had conceived, I became despised in her eyes. The Lord judge between you and me. Gen.16:5

Ask yourself this: is it possible that decisions I make could change the course of history? Sarai's decision sure did. Do you think your decisions aren't that far reaching? How do you know?

The headlines in our daily news regarding the conflicts in the Middle East began with Sarai's idea on how to speed up the promises of God.

It's often tempting to think we already have the answers to our own problems, especially when it comes to our children. We don't consciously think we have a better plan than God, but that's how we act. We would never verbalize such a thing. Probably because we don't even realize we're thinking it. We just start acting it out. For those who don't know the rest of this story, Hagar bore Ismael. Then later Sarai, at age ninety, finally gave birth to Isaac. Isaac was the child God had promised. He arrived in God's perfect time. Because of all the conflict between Sarai and Hagar, Ismael and his mother were sent away.

Both of Abram's sons ended up being blessed and each became a great nation. However, even today, there is continuing conflict between these two nations, (Arabs and Jews). It all started from one presumptuous decision, not being able to wait on God and His timing.

There are benefits for those who learn the value of waiting on the Lord.

> But those who wait on the Lord Shall renew *their* strength; They shall mount up with wings like eagles, They shall run and not be weary, They shall walk and not faint. Is. 40:31 KJV

You and I are supposed to learn from these stories. We're to learn not to try to force the hand of God by making things happen in our time, instead of God's time.

> To everything there is a season, and a time to every purpose under the heaven. Eccl.3:1

Sarai's decision changed the course of history and if we're not careful ours can too. Especially when it comes to our children and their future.

As a Mom, I understand that it is difficult for any of us to stand by feeling helpless, and to watch one of our children go through difficult experiences. So, some of the questions I've learned to ask myself are these:

1. Is God in this trial?
2. Might this struggle be for the good of someone?
3. What if this trial is necessary for God to gain this person's soul?
4. Is this trial designed for my child to discover their destiny or purpose in life?
5. Is it right to bail a child out of every difficult situation?
6. Might they benefit if allowed to suffer consequences for their actions?
7. When should someone step in and rescue them?
8. Do you sometimes reward or comfort when discipline is what is required?

Perhaps we should ask ourselves, "Do I want an Ismael? Or do I want God's desired outcome for my children in his appointed time?" We can put God's truth for ourselves and for our children into practice when we learn to *let go*. If we can do that, we'll allow God to harvest seeds He has planted in our lives, and the lives of our children in His appointed time.

Don't just read through these questions. Pause, think back when you were the age your child is now.

9. Were there difficult things that you had to figure out for yourself?
10. Did it make you stronger or wiser in the long run?
11. What about your friends, did tough times ruin them?
12. Is it possible that hardships are a normal part of growing up?
13. Will it kill my child if I don't step in to "fix" things that might go wrong?
14. Will it kill me if my child gets angry with me? Or will he learn something, and get over his anger in time?
15. What exactly is it that I am afraid of?
16. What's driving the decisions I make regarding my children?

Taking time to think through these questions was all part of the process of getting to know myself and my children better. I didn't even realize I was working through these questions when I was in the midst of the conflict. Looking back, I can see that's exactly what I was doing.

An American Cultural Epidemic

There were times when I stressed over decisions my children were making. It made no difference how I tried to redirect them. It fell on deaf ears. Sometimes I felt their choices would destroy their life. There were other times I fretted over who they associated with. I wished I could persuade them to end those relationships before their lives were totally misdirected. There were activities they indulged in that I didn't approve of. I never stopped loving or encouraging them to do better, but I didn't have to support their decisions.

I would have to learn that I wasn't their banker. It's an even harder lesson for the kids to learn.

*According to a recent poll, 34.5% of young adults (18-34 years old) in the U.S. live in their parent's home. It's one of the highest percentages in recent memory. These are statistics before the 2020 pandemic. We still don't have an accurate count of this number under the current circumstances. Young adults continue to depend on their parents for financial support way beyond their high school and college years. That's because as parents we haven't required them to stand on their own. Some parents actually enjoy this dependency.

Even young children are permitted to *run the house.* At times it's hard to tell who the parents are and who the child is. Does this describe your home or someone you may know? Often adult children complete their education, paid for by Mom and Dad, and just move back home and live in the basement. They have an expectation that Mom and Dad will continue to pay their way for the rest of their lives. Wonder where they got such an idea?

At times parents are eager to help and *fearful* of seeing their child fail. They just fall into a pattern. They don't know how to break the cycle. It usually begins as a short-term solution to help and ends up going on forever. There's no exit plan.

Have you ever seen a child learn to walk without falling? What about learning to ride a bike? I don't think I've seen anyone learn to ride a bike without a few spills. It often results in at least a few scrapes and bruises. This is all part of the learning process. Somehow, it becomes much harder for a parent to handle the hard knocks of the learning process when it's no longer the bicycle. When

13

your child is now in control of the family car, it's important to realize who's in charge. You or them. Who's calling the shots?

I thought the goal was for the child to become an adult and to become self-sufficient. Or is that just old school?

I realize that all of us have difficult situations. One of the reasons I wanted to write this book is because I have friends and acquaintances that have children that are adults and have never learned any kind of responsibility. The parents don't know how to say "NO". The child hasn't yet discovered who they are, and what they're supposed to do with their life, beyond existing from day to day.

We have listened to the philosophies of men rather than the Word of God. We spend more time listening to the ideas of men on how to raise children than looking to what the Creator of the Universe has to say about it.

When we put God to the test by trusting in His Word and what He speaks to our heart, He'll do what He says He'll do. God doesn't lie. We just need to learn how to listen. He's faithful to speak; it's us that aren't listening. You can rely on your own wisdom and that of so-called experts, but God has a warning about that:

> Beware lest any man spoil you through philosophy and vain deceit, after the tradition of men, after the rudiments of the world, and not after Christ. Col. 2:8

Empty deceit, philosophy of men, is that what we have learned to depend on? When we do things God's way, the path is narrow. It isn't usually the easy way, but it IS the right way. The results are by far the best and lasting. Hopefully as we learn to trust God with our children, we can stop the craziness, the sleepless nights, worrying, fretting, planning, manipulating, controlling and the rescuing. I pray you are blessed as I share how I learned to *let go*.

STOP! Ponder

Here are more questions to provoke you to do some introspection. It's good to look over these questions now, give them some honest thought and record your answers. Then review them at the end of the book to see if some of your precepts have changed. These questions will be addressed throughout the text for your consideration:

1. Does God have a plan for my child that might not be mine?
2. Am I getting in God's way?
3. Do I have preconceived ideas of how God should be answering my prayers?
4. Do I know my own heart?
5. Why can't I let go?
6. Am I a rescuer?
7. How do I respond when things are totally out of my control?
8. Can I trust God with my child's future?
9. Does letting my child face a hardship build character?
10. Do I insist on being in control of most everything?
11. Do I try to force God's hand? (or manipulate the situation?)
12. Am I willing to let my child fail?
13. Do I believe it's a reflection on me personally if my child is not successful?
14. Is there anyone who can do things as well as I can?
15. Can I say I am sorry when I am wrong?
16. Can I say I am sorry even if I am not the one in the wrong?
17. Will a struggle strengthen or destroy my child?
18. What is the long-term goal?
19. Does God love my child more than I do?
20. What are the benefits and pitfalls of promoting independence?

You may have to resort to a pros and con list to be honest with yourself on the last question.

As you read my story, you'll realize I had to answer these questions for myself. Many are also good for your children to answer as well. However, if we find the answers to these questions for ourselves, many of the issues with our children will also be resolved.

This is a journey to healing. STOP NOW! Think. Be truthful with yourself. Write down your answers. There's a resolution for every situation. It'll be found in the Lord if you're willing to listen. Problems with your children won't be magically fixed by holding this book in your hands. Hopefully, it will encourage you along your way, so you won't have to stumble into the same pitfalls that I did.

Chapter 2
What Have We Come To?

Have you heard it said that the definition of insanity is doing the same thing over and over and expecting a different outcome?

Recently I visited an old friend and I ended up staying long enough to need to do some laundry. She directed me to the steps that lead down to the laundry room on the ground floor. I'd been down these steps before when her children were growing up. It used to be a busy, colorful place with lots of things for kids to do. This time it was hugely different. As I approached the bottom of the stairs, carrying my basket of clothes, it was very dark. I could feel the dampness and smell a musty odor. It was an eerie feeling. After groping around a little, I found the light switch.

In the light I could see this wasn't the happy place I remembered. There used to be three bedrooms with a nice private outside entrance, and a large lovely bathroom. I sure couldn't tell that now. Since the children were now adults, I expected guest bedrooms or maybe even storage rooms but not this. As I looked around, I could see just the bare studs of what used to be walls. Most all the drywall was gone, and there were water marks on what was left. The walls had huge holes bashed in them. I could see right through one room into the next. I thought to myself, what in the world happened here? A good part of it looked to have been done intentionally, as if a demolition crew had come through.

I moved around the area until I found the laundry room and tossed my cloths into the machine. As I shook my head in disbelief at what I was seeing, it felt like the whole ground floor screamed of destruction. I wondered why my friend hadn't said anything to me about this. Had she grown so used to the disastrous mess that she just didn't think to warn me of what I might see? Was it no longer an embarrassment to her? Had she grown so used to this crazy mess that she just accepted it as her new normal?

Normal? Really?

Questions kept flashing through my mind, who does this to a place? What happened here? I slowly made my way to the top of the stairs and found Sue in the kitchen. I ask, "Sue, what in the world happened to the basement? Did you have a flood?"

She calmly replied, "Oh No, that was Billy. When we told him that he had to move out, he went through the whole house and stuffed all the toilets with towels on both floors. Then he just started flushing them until they ran over and flooded the entire house. We had a huge mess to clean up."

I pressed her further, "So what are all the holes in the walls?" She answered, "Oh that's where he punched all the walls with his fist. He was so angry with his dad." Sue's answers were so matter of fact, without a bit of emotion even reflected in her voice as she told me the story.

I think I was right. This was Sue's "New Normal".

Her son had intentionally vandalized his own home. He had no concern of what it might cost to restore, or what conditions his 70-year-old parents would have to live with. I felt violated for my friend's sake.

"Oh my gosh, Sue, why would anyone do a thing like that?" Her answer was that he was angry, after all his Dad was forcing him to move out. She acted like that kind of behavior was what one would expect of an angry person. Billy was not a child. Billy was already in his thirties. He had been arrested for drug possession, lost numerous jobs, and finally ended up living in his Mom and Dad's basement. Why not? There was no rent to pay, no food to buy and he could get by without doing anything to contribute to the family.

Over the next few weeks, I learned from another family member that this youngest son had attacked Sue. Her husband stepped in to save her, physically commandeering Billy and throwing him out of the house.

I questioned if this experience might be a wake-up call for Sue. I wondered if the craziness made her finally realize she had to quit enabling Billy. It seemed that being threatened physically would cause her to change how she approached things with her son. But it hadn't. There were no real lasting consequences for his actions.

> Be not deceived; God is not mocked: for whatsoever a man soweth, that shall he also reap. Gal. 6:7

The danger in not bringing correction is that the protection from a loving God may be lifted. The consequences are that doors are opened for an assault from the enemy. That's a scary thought!

Instead, Sue continued to help Billy not only financially, but she did all his leg work for him. She searched all over town, trying to find just the right apartment. Then she furnished it and paid the rent. Once he was settled, she made frequent trips to see him. Her routine visits often started with a morning stop at the Quick Trip for a pack or two of cigarettes. From there she headed to the drive through for his favorite fountain soda and on to the restaurant to pick up an order of pancakes for Billy's breakfast. Finally, she made the climb to his second-floor apartment with her painful, creaky knees, to deliver all this stuff personally to his door. In the meantime, the basement was left untouched. What money could have been used for repairs was spent on keeping Billy's apartment up.

More questions than answers:

1. Does any of this make sense?
2. What's her motive?
3. What's the payoff?
4. Why would a mother allow this kind of behavior and then reward it?
5. Was she blind?
6. Did she think her responses would be helpful to Billy in the long run?
7. Had she thought this through at all?
8. Was this just her knee jerk response, was she living only for today, not considering the consequences or his future
9. Was she afraid of him? Or was she just afraid of having him withhold his affection from her?

My friend Sue is a Christian woman, she knows some of what the Bible says about parenting. She knows it's not productive to reward bad behavior or disobedience, and yet that's exactly what she was doing. I love my friend and I was troubled about her situation, I asked Sue, "What will happen to Billy if something happens to you?" Her reply, "I don't do that much for him. Sharon, He can't make it on his own." Then a pause, "I have to help him." Then she paused again and declared, "This is my husband's fault! He cursed the kids by speaking negative words over them when they were young. I *blame* him for this. So, if I die, I just die. The kids will have to figure out how to make it on their own once I'm gone".

Wow! Shocked with her response, I asked, "if they can do it then, why can't they do it now?" She angrily blurted back at me, "I just don't want to talk about it. I'm tired of people criticizing me about my kids all the time."

Sue was too blind to see I was genuinely concerned. Billy seemed to be just existing, with no future. Sue once told me a story about how someone had slipped a drug into Billy's drink at a party years before. She believed that might be what was causing this behavior now. Family members disputed this and felt Sue's story was an excuse for Billy's actions. Even if Sue's story was accurate, she wasn't doing anything to find a solution. Billy wasn't held responsible for anything he had done. Instead she chose to blame Billy's actions on something her husband said, once upon a time.

It's true, words hurt and can affect a person for the rest of their life. However, at some point, if we claim to be believers, we must learn to trust God with our kids. We must learn to *let go*. Our desire to rescue becomes enabling and prevents our children from ever finding out who they are in God's scheme of things. It keeps them from confidently knowing God on a personal level. Think about it. Why do they need Him as a provider? They have you.

People quickly learned not to speak to Sue about her children because she immediately became defensive and angry. She couldn't see that her solutions were only temporary answers to long term problems. Her interventions took care of today only. Billy wasn't her only problem. She had other children with similar circumstances. How was she ever going to spread herself thin enough, to put out so many fires burning all around her?

Hard Working Great Granny

Sue's story is not an isolated incident. I've known other parents so captivated with what's going on in their children's lives that they can't have lives of their own.

Rosemary was a seventy-eight-year-old widow in Texas. When I last spoke with her, she was still helping her adult children with everything. They seemed to have ongoing financial needs that required her pocketbook on a regular basis. She cleaned their house and worked their large garden in the hot Texas sun. When the produce was ripe, she did the canning, a labor intensive, thankless job. She often worked her tiny, frail body into exhaustion. She did all that after she cared for her own property and another rental house. I have no idea where she found the strength.

When I asked her why she was doing that, her answer was, "I just can't say no!" Her children were in their fifties at the time.

When a tenant moved out of one of her rental homes, she spent days alone cleaning the place. She climbed up and down ladders painting and repairing the property for new occupants. When she was finished, she headed over to her son's house to take care of his property as well. I just shook my head in disbelief. Rosemary was tired and looking for answers. She wanted to know how she could change things. How could she stop all this running and labor, without upsetting her son? My question was, how can your son expect you to continue this pace?

Let me be clear; I realize there are parents that truly have no choice. They end up raising grandchildren, because the child's parents are not present, or they aren't capable of doing so themselves. There are a growing number of young adults that without a miracle will have permanently altered their future due to substance abuse. I have great compassion for these situations. Some grandparents aren't ever going to be able enjoy their golden years.

Many looked forward to retirement, but instead they're raising a second family. My prayer for them is that they'll have strength to endure and even excel. That they'll know the perfect will of God for the lives of the precious children that have been placed in their care. It's a huge responsibility, and it's one God has entrusted to them. They certainly didn't ask for this. They are selflessly doing the best they know how to do.

Mental disorders among young people, like bi-polar and schizophrenia, are also on the rise. For those families, I highly recommend the book "*A Promise of Hope." This book does just what it says. It promises hope for many disorders. It gives some answers for everything from ADHD to seizures and extreme mental disorders. It's written by a woman who suffered terribly with her own nightmare and was able to overcome. Her book gives amazing hope for all those in the awful prison of mental illness. There's hope, not only in the natural, but spiritually as well. Jesus came to heal and to set the prisoner free.

> The Spirit of the Lord is on me, because he has anointed me to proclaim good news to the poor. He has sent me to proclaim freedom for the prisoners and recovery of sight for the blind, to set the oppressed free, to proclaim the year of the Lord's favor. NIV Luke 4:18-19

I thank God that I didn't have to endure these situations with my children, but I assure you, I had my own nightmares. God was there to carry us through every trial.

Both Sue and this elderly woman are born again, spirit filled Christians. When we say, "We trust Jesus," does that include everything except trusting Him with our children? Doesn't He love them more than we do? Perhaps He needs our help to get it right. Ya think???

The prophet Isaiah warns us:

> "And I will give children to be their princes, and babes shall rule over them. ....: the child shall behave himself proudly against the ancient, and the base against the honourable. Is. 3:4-5

The word princes in this passage means one who rules, a head person, a lord or master.

Is this what I was seeing? Were the children ruling over the parents? Had the parents become servants to their children? Had the child become the master or ruler over the parents?

Certainly, the children I have spoken of had behaved proudly against their elders. Verses 10-11 continue....."It shall be well with the righteous but ill for the wicked." But this isn't what I was seeing. What had gone wrong? Were these Moms behaving righteously, and what exactly does it mean to behave righteously?

Without realizing it, parents sometimes usurp the position of God in the lives of their children. They don't trust God to develop their children into productive adults that reflect His likeness. They weren't made in the likeness of their parents, but they were created to be in the likeness of God. Is it possible that the circumstances our children find themselves in are ordered by God, or at least permitted by Him?

When we constantly intervene in our children's lives, *we* become their God. They turn to us for the miracles they need from their Heavenly Father. Who's on the throne of your child's life? Who have we made King? If we're the one who rescue them all the time, they never learn to turn to God. We have set ourselves up to be their provider. Once a child becomes an adult, they naturally want to become independent. One of two things can happen if you never learn to trust God with them. They'll either dethrone you or stay dependent on you for the rest of your life. Neither option is desirable.

YOU ARE NOT A MIRACLE WORKER. You cannot replace God in the lives of your children. Is it possible that they may never learn to turn to God because of your interference?

We are all individuals, independent of our children. Can we allow our children to be independent of us? We would exist even if our children didn't! If we focus on our relationship with God and set that example for our children to follow, that will be the greatest illustration of who Jesus is in their lives.

Continuing the previous quote from Isaiah:

> As for my people, children are their oppressors, and women rule over them. O my people, they which lead thee cause thee to err, and destroy the way of thy paths. Is. 3:12.

Is this the answer? Have we been taught wrong, led to err? Have the ancient paths of the scripture been so diluted, that even people who call themselves Christians can no longer know right from wrong? Have we listened to Dr. Spock and others like him for too long? Are we just too politically correct to put God's Word in the place of final authority?

As I met new people from all over this country, more stories of troubled families surfaced. I saw what kind of behavior was being rewarded and what wasn't. The Apostle Paul wrote to Timothy, saying:

> This know also, that in the last days perilous times shall come. For men shall be lovers of their own selves, covetous, boasters, proud, blasphemers, disobedient to parents, unthankful, unholy. II Tim. 3:1-2

It sure looks like we have come to that day.

Dejected Alice

A young widowed friend of mine recently told me how disappointed she was because she and her guy friend were no longer seeing one another. His twenty-six-year-old daughter decided she didn't want to share her father with anyone else. So, the relationship ended based on his daughter's influence. She was a young woman in her twenties dictating to her fifty-five-year-old father who he could and couldn't keep company with. Two lonely, widowed, Christian people that wanted to be together are being controlled by the selfish desires of an adult child. There's something wrong with this picture. In time the child will have other interest and the Father will find himself alone, as will Alice.

So Exactly Who is in Charge?

Tammy had been abused forcefully in her first marriage. After many domestic violence calls to their home, the police told her, "If you don't get out, the next time we'll be taking you out in a body bag." Heartbroken, terrified, and alone she left for her own safety. It was a life and death situation. She ended up in a woman's shelter for a long time, with nowhere else to go and no one to turn to. She felt incredibly rejected and had to deal with the pain of being forced to leave her children behind. Tammy was an educated woman, beautiful and intelligent, but had been beaten into submission to the point of losing her own identity. Even though she was a licensed counselor, she was unable to apply what she knew to her own circumstances.

In her search for answers, she discovered a loving caring God that was just waiting for her to call on him. As her healing process began, she met and fell in love with a Christian man. Because she chose to remarry, her teenage children from her previous marriage refused to have anything to do with her. They used her love for them against her, to manipulate and control her. They demanded that she return to their abusive Father or they'd never speak to her again. Their demands magnified Tammy's guilt about leaving them behind, although she had no other choice.

Tammy was under great emotional stress when she found herself facing a surprise pregnancy at nearly forty years of age. She hoped the new baby would draw her other children closer, but instead it seemed to increase their demands. It was a difficult pregnancy even in a loving relationship. She couldn't shake the pain of being separated from her children. What should have been a happy time for her, became miserable. She went into a deep depression and cried often.

It's sad that children can have that kind of power over parents, by withdrawing their affection and their approval. Many parents are so afraid of this that they end up being controlled and manipulated by their own children and never even realize it.

I know I have lots of questions in this book, but I am a counselor at heart. If I were privileged to have a one on one session with you, I wouldn't give you answers, I would ask questions to help you get in touch with your own heart and motives.

So, I ask, why do believers in the Most High God of Heaven and earth (in whose image we are created) permit someone (especially their children) to control their emotions. There must be a reason. Is God so distant from us that we can't see He is working all things for our good, if we will just listen to him?

> And we know that all things work together for good to them that love God, to them who are the called according to his purpose. Romans 8:28

The Bible tells us when a child rules it is a curse. If that's true, then I fear that many of our Christian homes are under a curse. The time to teach your child to live by biblical principles isn't when they are thirty, forty, or fifty. It should have started at birth. If we haven't done that, start now. God is merciful, and He rewards those who come to him and seek His face. If we do all things through Christ who strengthens us, we can still find God's best solution for our situation. However, we must have faith that God will reach our adult children in His time and in His way.

I can do all things through Christ. Phil. 4:13

It is Not All Bad:

To be fair, I will share one more story.

I am not suggesting this next example is how you should run your household, and it certainly isn't how I ran mine.

This is a brief overview of how one family chose to allow hardships to mold their children and the results. Rescuing wasn't on the agenda. Because this was such a large family their approach didn't leave room for much flexibility. Each child was expected to not only take responsibility for their own actions but that of their siblings as well.

With a dozen children, there wasn't an opportunity for one of them to be in control. They all had their jobs. They were each expected to do their part as a member of the family. As soon as they were old enough, they were required to earn their own money. Some had lawn mowing jobs, others worked paper routes or did babysitting. In addition, they had household chores, dishes, mopping, laundry, cleaning and caring for younger brothers and sisters.

Some found fault with these parents. They felt the children were over worked and never really got the chance to be just kids.

I suppose the proof is in the pudding. Nearly every one of these children have grown up to be productive, responsible, God-fearing adults. Several of them have a professional degree, others are good parents and good providers for their households. Even with all the criticism of this family, the goal wasn't to make them happy as children. The goal was to produce productive, happy, successful adults.

These children never expected something for nothing. They have all found their place in this world. Even those who are still a trifle bitter about the way they were raised are successful, either because of, or despite their parents. They are adults that any parent would be proud of. This may sound like it is something out of the 1940's but it's not. The oldest child is only thirty-two years old.

I'm not suggesting we all put our kids to work as children. I admit that at times I was one of those critical of this family's parenting skills. This was a poor struggling family that somehow taught their children what was valuable in life. Those who have the love of God instilled in them from their youth and are expected to pitch in and do their part, are better equipped as adults.

Almost all these kids found a way to pick themselves up when they stumbled. They realized life is full of difficult situations, and they're living through those circumstances positively. As adults they continue to encourage and champion one another.

I've never seen such a tight loving family. They seem to have the ability to forgive no matter how often they're offended. They have each other's back all the time regardless of the circumstances.

In contrast we have generations of adult children that think if they have hit a bump in the road of life, it must be Mom and Dad's fault. Therefore, Mom and Dad should pay to get them out of whatever mess they get into. There's nothing wrong with a helping hand occasionally when climbing out of the mud puddle. However, you mustn't heed the constant accusation that somehow everything is your fault, while children lack acceptance of responsibility for their own actions. As Christian parents we need to learn to hear God's voice and to know when it's right to say "Yes," and when it's right to say "No".

Happiness in life isn't making sure you child gets into the finest schools or even to the best pre-school. Happiness isn't playing first string on the football or basketball team. It's not about being on the cheerleading squad. Happiness isn't being voted as Prom King or Queen or being the most popular in school. It's not even finding the perfect soul mate. Happiness is from within. It's knowing God, knowing who you are, and why you have been created. It's finding God's destiny for your life and living it out.

When we mess up, as we are sure to do, if we allow God to have the final say in our children's lives, somehow, He will reach them. He loves them more than we do, and He can take the biggest messed up situation and turn it for his glory.

Chapter 3
Expectations and Disappointments

> Train up a child in the way he should go: and when he is old, he will not depart from it. Pr.22:6

This was one scripture promise I learned early in my Christian walk. As a new believer, I thought this meant exactly what it said. All I had to do was to teach my children the Word of God and do my best to live it out before them. They'd learn by example. I thought I'd never have to worry about any of them going astray. I knew there was a devil, but I didn't realize I'd be in a constant battle with him over my kids. Satan knew God had a purpose and a destiny for each one them, and he'd do whatever he could to interfere with it.

I was twenty-six and had two children before I surrendered totally to The Lord. I didn't realize that my life before I knew God would have such a lasting impact on my family.

I took God's Word to heart. I held on to it, and still do. Over the years I have learned the character of my God to the point that now I know what He says is true even when it doesn't appear to be so. You'll see this as my story unfolds. I still expect this scripture to hold true for every child and grandchild of mine.

> God is not a man, that he should lie; neither the son of man that he should repent: hath he said, and shall he not make it good? Num.23:19

God simply doesn't lie. He has our best and highest good in His heart.

> For what if some did not believe? Will their unbelief make the faithfulness of God without effect? Certainly not! Indeed, let God be true but every man a liar. Rm. 3:3-4

I pray for comfort and confidence to be built in your heart as you follow my journey. That you'd know God is in complete control no matter what it looks like. If I could put what I've learned in a word, it would be "surrender." If He is the one in control, then *we* must *let go*. You *AND* God can't both be at the controls at the same time, so it must be one or the other. Is it going to be *HIM* or *YOU?*

For we walk by faith and not by sight. 2 Cor. 5:7.

It takes faith to let go, but the Holy Spirit will comfort you along the way and encourage you as you grow.

Blessed be God, even the Father of our Lord Jesus Christ, the Father of mercies, and the God of all comfort Who comforts us in all our tribulation... 2 Cor.1:3-4

Some of the greatest struggles of my life have been related to my children. Through the trials, conflicts, and victories, I've become intimately acquainted with The Great Comforter: The Holy Spirit. I've learned I can't live this life and do it well without His guidance. Without Him in the center of things it's easy to become overwhelmed. He gives hope when you bring Him your confusion, trouble, darkness and even despair. Just *surrender* it to The Father.

At some point in each of our children's lives, we must *let go* and trust God to oversee what we can't. It'll be different for each child. You may be disappointed to find that you don't get to choose their careers, their friends, or their spouses. Perhaps you'll have input into those decisions, but in the end, they make those choices for themselves. Contrary to what you might think, many children don't really care what their parents think. On the other hand, there'll be some who are afraid to make any decision without you. They're still too dependent on your influence in their life. Even their relationship to God is based upon you and what you think.

When we continue to hold on to our children, or enable them, it hinders them from becoming the men and women of God that they were destined to be. Of course, there's the possibility that you don't even realize you're in the way. I didn't.

We were given oversight of our children, not ownership. They're on loan from above. If they need to be rescued, there's One who will always be there to catch them when they fall. Our job is to nurture, and to train them, uphold them in prayer and trust God with their lives. He knew them before they were in the womb (Jer. 1:5). He has a purpose and a destiny for them. It's possible that we'll get in the way of God's perfect plan when we have an agenda of our own.

It's not unusual for a parent to become a rescuer, but to establish a constant pattern of that behavior is dangerous. I've fallen into this trap at times myself. Not just with my children but even with my spouse. It takes an open heart to trust God with those we love. It can be quite scary. It's not easy to let go. You'll see that some of my choices were difficult, I had to know for sure that I was hearing from God. This I know, God will always honor our obedience.

> Trust in the LORD with all thine heart; and lean not unto thine own understanding. In all thy ways acknowledge him, and he shall direct thy paths Pr. 3:5-6

People tend to look at what they see right in front of their eyes, and assume this is the final outcome, the end picture. Or at least we think we can guess how this is going to turn out. The truth is we can't see what God sees. Just like the Hebrew children going into the Promised Land. All they could see were giants, but that's not what God saw at all. God saw a land flowing with milk and honey, a gift to His beloved Israel. But they rejected His gift and saw it as a curse instead.

The book of Hebrews says of this people:

> "Let us therefore fear, lest, a promise being left us of entering into his rest, any of you should seem to come short of it. For unto us was the gospel preached, as well as unto them: but the word preached did not profit them, not being mixed with faith in them that heard it. For we which have believed do enter into rest.....Heb. 4:1-3a

If we don't take God's Word and truly mix it with our faith, we'll fail to enter God's rest. The story of Billy is about a son who God had a plan for. However, it's easy to see, that up to this time Billy hadn't found his purpose in life, even though he was raised to know God. What happened? God meant for Billy to be a blessing. Why isn't he?

There's no way to experience rest when we see it as our job to *fix* everything in our children's lives. There's no rest in that at all. No rest when we insist on rescuing and being in control. When there are no consequences for our children's actions, we create monsters, instead of blessings.

Even with all my children grown, I continue to learn some tough lessons in this area. It's hard at times to remember that God loves them more than I do. I know I say that a lot. It's a truth we need to burn deep in our souls. God can be trusted with our children. There's not much more in a parent's life that can either bring such pain or such joy as our children.

Here's another caution. Do you have "a best friend" relationship with one or more of your children, instead of a parent/child relationship? When separation comes, as God has planned, it can leave a big hole, emptiness in somebody's heart. God intended for a child to leave their Mother and Father, and eventually connect with a lifelong partner. A loving spouse that they cleave to for the rest of their lives.

> Therefore shall a man leave his father and mother and shall cleave unto his wife, and they shall be one flesh. Gen.2:24

This leaving is more than a physical separation. It's a financial and emotional leaving as well. It's supposed to be the start of a new life, separate from that with mom and dad.

So, what happens if you don't agree with their choices? It may feel like your opinion just doesn't matter.

That's a painful reality and you may even feel rejected. You find yourself crying out to the Lord, "They just won't listen." Why is that so very important? It's probably because you can see them making mistakes that might take a lifetime to correct. Perhaps they're the same mistakes that you made at that age, and you know the price they'll have to pay. Because we love them, we want to prevent their pain.

If you already have a pattern of rejection in your life, like abandonment from a parent, or spouse, then a child's rejection is doubly difficult to deal with. It's like the same old record playing over again, but this time with your child. After all, this is your precious little baby that was supposed to love you forever, no matter what.

Rejection from anyone hurts, but rejection from your children can blindside you. It seems no one can hurt you quite like your children can. Caution, don't let fear control your thoughts and decisions. That's exactly what the devil wants you to do. Don't allow fear to become a theme or pattern in your life, controlling your thoughts, worrying that the rejection from one child will repeat with another. Thinking, here we go again! This could cause you to be overly protective and more determine to be in control. *Letting go* is painful for many. The reason is it usually requires some kind of death to self, and a surrendering to God to let Him manage the situation.

Your fears will make it easier for you to be manipulated by people as well as the devil. Learning to hear the voice of God speaking into our lives counteracts fear. It brings faith and resolve and keeps you from being sucked into a manipulative controlling spirit. Insisting on your own way will cause you to end up making terrible decisions.

> For God hath not given us the spirit of fear; but of power, and of love, and of a sound mind. 2 Tim. 1:7

> There is no fear in love; but perfect love casteth out fear: because fear hath torment. He that feareth is not made perfect in love. 1 John 4:18

If your home has become a battlefield, you may be saying, "That sounds pretty good right now, power, love, and soundness of mind." If you're feeling torment, according to this scripture fear is at the root of the torment, and love is being silenced.

These little creatures, our children, come into our lives and we have dreams and expectations for them. Sometimes children just mess up, but so did we. They're wayward, they have minds of their own, and plans of their own. At times they may ignore you completely. They may even disregard God, everything we believe in, and everything they've been taught. The years we have influence over our children, while they are living under our roof, fly by very quickly.

> Whereas ye know not what shall be on the morrow. For what is your life? It is even a vapor, that appears for a little time, and then vanishes away. James 4:14

In the beginning, I know, those first few years seem to crawl by very slowly, but the years after that really pass quickly. The years where you have lost control of their environment, and your influence seems to matter less and less.

One of my lifetime goals was to be a great Mom. I guess it depends upon who you ask if I made it or not. The enemy knows how important these desires are for us as moms and dads. Since the devil is a bully, he likes to attack us in our most vulnerable spots, our children. He never plays fair. He'll attack our children at the youngest possible age, anywhere he can find an open door.

In raising my children, I faced some unfulfilled expectations. These were difficult times, but through them I learned important truths from The Holy Spirit. These truths have taught me how to survive the pain and disappointment that many of us go through on this parenting road. They also taught me how to stand in the evil day, until the victory came, and if *you* will stand, victory *will* come.

> Wherefore take unto you the whole armor of God, that ye may be able to withstand in the evil day, and having done all, to stand. Eph. 6:13

It's indeed an evil day when you see your child do things or associate with people that you think may destroy their lives.

So, my story isn't about complete victory and everything working out every time. Since one of my main goals in life was to be a "good" mom, to feel like I'd failed in that area was just not acceptable. I'm sure there are many of you who feel that way as well, even if you've never actually said those words out loud. It's probably true. I had a specific idea of what a good mom looked like and so I strove for that as one of my life's goals.

God has seen me through and sustained me in the midst of every struggle. It's about surviving, doing it well, and coming out stronger on the other side of every trial. Each challenge I've faced resulted in a closer walk with my Creator. This story isn't about each one of my children finding success, although I have some of those stories. It's about God's faithfulness to me. Regardless of how carefully we plan, life just doesn't seem to go according to our expectations. Sometimes we need grace to extend God's mercies, when we'd rather call down His Fire.

> For my thoughts are not your thoughts, neither are your ways my ways, saith the Lord. For as the heavens are higher than the earth, so are my ways higher than your ways, and my thoughts than your thoughts Is.55:8.

Unfortunately, I never became the perfect mom, and I don't have perfect children. I am, however, the mother of four uniquely different individuals, each with their own story.

The revelations in this book were spoken directly to my heart from a loving, caring God. He's the greatest parent of all. Each revelation has been an "AH HA" moment. They were thoughts and concepts I'd never even thought of before. In an instant they just popped into my head. They are things I was never taught by another teacher. I hadn't been pondering these truths when they came. They were just dropped directly into my heart by God. Just like the still small voice that came to Elijah in 1 Kings 19:11-13, we too can hear the voice of our God, speaking to our hearts. His love towards us is so amazing, and He desires that we are comforted with His comfort. The Psalmist tells us:

> In the multitude of my thoughts within me thy comforts delight my soul." Ps. 94:19

Thoughts can seemingly come out of nowhere. The truth is that if they line up with The Word, they are thoughts from God. Learning how He speaks to you is vital. It's always good to test the spirit and ask, are these thoughts mine? Are they God's? Or are they from the devil?

Hearing God is learned by practice, by listening. It may take a little time, and everyone will make mistakes along the way. In time, as you become familiar with the scriptures and experience the character of God, you'll recognize His voice and know Him more intimately.

This doesn't mean that God doesn't speak to brand new believers. He does. Sometimes louder and more clearly than He is able to speak to those who have had time to cloud their hearts with religion instead of relationship. The Apostle Paul told Timothy:

> Let no man despise thy youth; but be thou an example of the believers, in word, in conversation, in charity, in spirit, in faith, in purity. 1 Tim.4:12

We all start somewhere.

I have learned a valuable lesson about "*letting go,*" with each one of my children. I wanted to fix things. I wanted to make it all better. I didn't want them to experience the pain I did growing up, or for them to make the same stupid mistakes I did. Somehow, I thought I could control that. I had to learn how to "*let go*" and trust God with my most cherished possessions, my children.

Remember this, your children aren't the only ones that have a destiny and a purpose, so do you. Each heartbreak and victory is permitted to draw you closer to God. You can either let that happen, or you can fight it for the rest of your life.

Chapter 4

Once I was a Kid

When you read this chapter, you'll understand why I had to learn to *let go*. It is pretty clear that I had no intention of allowing my children to go through the same things I did. If there was any way in the world that I could prevent it, I would. I believed that God gave me my children, but in the beginning didn't bother to ever ask him for help. Not with my kids, or anything else.

> God is our refuge and strength, a very present help in trouble. Ps 46:1 KJV

Right! I certainly wasn't aware of this! I just made a habit of doing things on my own. Even if I had to bulldoze my way through whatever it was. Quitting or surrendering was never part of who I was, even as a kid.

I was born in a large metropolitan city, the third of five daughters. I was the middle kid. My parents were not church going people, except for the annual Christmas and Easter services. These were always big events in my family. For Easter, Mom dressed us to the hilt. We all had frilly new dresses. I can still see that light blue chiffon fabric with tiny pink flowers and a pink sash around the waist. We had all the accessories, gloves, new shoes and even a little purse and an Easter bonnet. Often, my sisters and I were dressed alike. The Sunday service was followed by the Easter egg hunt at the park each year. These were fun times to remember. But they were just traditions. We knew Christmas was Jesus's birthday, and Easter was when He died on the cross. Beyond that, and a memorized prayer at the dinner table, that was my understanding of who God was.

For our bi-annual appearance, our family arrived, in stair step fashion, oldest to youngest. We attended a large Lutheran Church with a beautiful, massive altar. The pastor wore a white robe and was elevated over the congregation in what looked to me to be a small castle like structure. At the front of the church was an incredible architectural facade that surrounded a picture of Jesus praying in the garden. There were lights directed right at his face, and they gave the appearance of light flowing straight from heaven. Sometimes the site of this beautiful picture would bring tears to my eyes.

My dad had a wonderful boisterous voice, and we all loved to hear him belt out, "Up From the Grave He Arose." He always sang this with such conviction. He truly had a heart for God though he had never had what Christians call the "born again" experience. He'd been raised in a Catholic orphanage. As an adult, he had no desire to continue in that religion.

Mom was a follower. Wherever, and however Dad led, Mom followed. At Christmas we attended the midnight service as a family. Even after we were adults and married, we gathered at Mom and Dad's house with all the grand kids. As the Leopold family entered the church it looked like a small invasion. With much to do, we took up several long pews to fit all of us in together. It was the only time our husbands participated in church activities.

When we were little, there was a time Dad felt we might need to learn more about God. So, he agreed to have a teacher from the Jehovah's Witness church come to the house to teach Bible stories. As you can guess, that didn't last long. This was the first time I realized my Dad lied. He hated liars, but when the Bible teacher came to the door, Dad said to tell him that he wasn't home. I'm sure Dad didn't realize the impact that had on me.

Sometimes I attended Sunday School with the neighbor boys that lived behind us, across the alley. This is where I was told for the first time that I was a sinner. I was only five or six, and the concept offended me. I didn't know what it meant, but I was sure it couldn't be good. I argued with the teacher back and forth as she tried her best to convince me that I was a sinner. She kept asking me if I ever told a lie. Did I ever disobey my Mom? No matter what she said I denied it. I was NOT going to admit I was a sinner. It just couldn't be a good thing.

> For all have sinned and come short of the glory of God. Rm. 3:23

I would be fourteen before I had any understanding that I needed to confess or acknowledge sin. At five, I had no realization that someone else had redeemed me.

> But God demonstrates his own love for us in this: While we were still sinners, Christ died for us. Romans 5:8

On occasion, especially in the spring, two or three of my sisters and I would enjoy taking the long walk to Sunday school. We'd skip, sing and lollygag along going to and from church. In our neighborhood, the houses were situated side by side, row after row, allowing for us to run up and down the terraces in front of the houses. We'd do that all along the way and have fun just being with one another. Sometimes we picked the colorful spring flowers through someone's fence. They were just so pretty.

Dad only had an eighth-grade education, but he was very well read and held his own in nearly every circumstance. No one could tell Dad hadn't graduated from High school. When he was a teenager, he ran away from the orphanage often, "hoboing" across the country, and jumping freight trains. He was a colorful kind of guy and had a story for every conversation, even if he had to invent one.

With this kind of background, you might understand my parent's reaction when I started attending the Baptist Church at age fourteen. After a traveling missionary visited our church, my little sister and I decided we wanted to be baptized. It wasn't an event that Mom and Dad took seriously or even attended. I believed that I had a genuine encounter with the one true God. One Sunday night after hearing the missionary speak, I felt I was also called to be a missionary. I didn't understand what that would require, but since I was in a Baptist Church and women weren't permitted to preach, what I must be feeling was a "call" to missions.

God is faithful, who has called you into fellowship with his Son, Jesus Christ our Lord. 1 Cor.1:9

I was so excited, I'd been called, chosen by God to do his work. I remember walking home from church that night alone. I was talking out loud to God as I approached the house. We'd moved and lived only a few short blocks from the Baptist church, where I was attending. I couldn't wait to tell Mom and Dad about my new-found ambitions. It was the first time in my life I'd ever really given much thought to the future or what I might want to do with my life.

There were a lot of cars parked outside my house, but that wasn't unusual. We were living in a lovely home in the suburbs and we had what they called a rathskeller. That was a fancy name for a basement that was fixed up for partying. It had an amazing horseshoe shaped bar, stocked like a night club, and shuffleboard tiles on the floor. Dad had thousands of records, which hung in racks on the walls like pictures on display. Mom and Dad entertained there often, and the four of us girls hung out there with friends during the week. Our house was "The Place to Be." It was sort of a hangout for some of the more popular high school kids.

This night, I didn't consider all the other people that would be surrounding my parents when I ran down the steps to announce to them that I was going to be a missionary! They'd all been drinking. They found the thought of one of Jeff Leopold's daughters becoming a missionary to be hilarious. Apparently, I was just a joke.

I went up the steps and headed to my bedroom, feeling very discouraged that no one thought what I was experiencing was of any value.

A few months later I attended the Baptist Youth Camp. My parents didn't pay for me to attend. Instead, a family in the church which had taken an interest in me offered to cover the expenses, as a gift to me. I have never forgotten their generosity. It compels me today to do the same for others.

> Remember this: Whoever sows sparingly will also reap sparingly, and whoever sows generously will also reap generously. Each of you should give what you have decided in your heart to give, not reluctantly or under compulsion, for God loves a cheerful giver. And God is able to bless you abundantly, so that in all things at all times, having all that you need, you will abound in every good work. 2 Cor 9:6-8 NIV

While at camp one night in the general assembly, there was a question and answer session. I raised my hand, was recognized, and stood. I asked, "Can women be preachers?"

Again, my question was laughable. I could hear the chuckles from those all around me. The answer from the podium was an emphatic "No, the only place women are permitted to preach is on the mission field." I wondered how can I be feeling like I am called to preach, when that is against God's Word? At least that's what the teachers said. It seemed strange to me that as a woman I could go to the dangers of the mission field in the depths of the jungle to preach, but it was a sin to do the same thing in America. I was told, if I wanted to preach, it would have to be done on the mission field. I didn't understand the draw in my heart to preach.

Within a year, my family moved away from my church which was the only spiritual support group I had. It would be nearly ten years before I would find my way back.

Derailed

My family moved back to the inner city into a huge three-story home in a very affluent part of town. Dad was incredibly involved with the Dixieland Jazz movement there. He eventually became the founder and President of a Jazz lovers club. One of Mom and Dad's friends was the secretary of the club. She had a son who was completing a three year stretch in the military, and he would be coming home from Germany soon. She had recently moved to the city herself, and was concerned that her son, who would be living with her, wouldn't know anyone in the area. He was twenty years old.

I had just turned sixteen when Mom and Dad introduced me to Wayne, at one of their club meetings. They didn't realize; I had just been thrown to the wolves. He was four years older than me and had already been married once, which ended in an annulment. I would later learn that he had lived with another woman while stationed in Germany. She had a child while they were together, but he claimed it wasn't his. I was naïve enough to believe him.

Wayne was extremely good looking, and he knew it. He looked a lot like the movie star, Robert Wagner. Wayne saw himself as an experienced world traveler, spouting off his limited vocabulary of German words. I didn't know any better, I just assumed he could speak a second language.

In Mom and Dad's defense, they didn't know all this stuff about Wayne. Dad never had a father around, so he just did the best he knew how to do as a dad. They liked this young man, and no matter how bumpy my road was with him, my parents always cared for him. Even till the day they died.

I had only dated one other boy, and he was my own age. Compared to me Wayne was a very experienced fellow. To top off his great qualifications, he proclaimed to be an atheist. Not exactly a glowing resume for a young man wanting to date your teenage daughter. Sometimes I still wonder, what were my folks thinking? Were they thinking at all?

This is where I want to tell you, who you introduce into your child's life is of vital importance, male or female. Once they begin to date someone, or associate with them, it can have an influence that will last a lifetime. We have a perfect example in King Solomon:

> They were from nations about which the LORD had told the Israelites, "You must not intermarry with them because they will surely turn your hearts after their gods" I Kings 11:2 NIV

Christian parents make great efforts to give their children a Godly foundation. The enemy will use any tool he has to steal that.

Even just a casual date can develop into a life-long connection, or marriage. Marriage produces children, which are your grandchildren. What starts with just one date, or even a chance meeting, can change the course of someone's life, and that of your entire family. Trust me, I have had to learn this lesson for myself and it has been a truly painful one. Just one sudden, poorly thought out decision can change generations to come.

> Then, after desire has conceived, it gives birth to sin; and sin, when it is full-grown, gives birth to death. James 1:15 NIV

Once something is put into motion, it can be difficult to stop.

I was in my junior year at high school. Wayne would be waiting outside for me when the bell rang at the end of the day. He wanted to drive me home. I was too young and inexperienced to see what I was getting into. Looking back, I think he had one goal in mind. In time I would realize Wayne was obsessed with conquering women. Any woman!

Over a matter of months, I fell in love with Wayne. With my parent's permission, we were married. I was sixteen and a half.

My Mom and Dad had a very loving relationship, and I wasn't prepared to have anything less than they had. That was all I had ever seen. All I had ever witnessed. Wayne on the other hand, came from a broken home where his parents took turns putting each other in the hospital, after beating one another up.

I never considered that the differences in what we believed about God would matter so much. It did. I thought everybody believed in God. I didn't completely understand what it meant to be an atheist. When we talked about it, Wayne said he didn't believe Jesus walked on water or was born of a virgin. I thought that meant there were parts of the Bible he didn't believe, not that there was no God at all.

> The fool says in his heart, "There is no God." They are corrupt, and their ways are vile; there is no one who does good. Ps. 53:1 NIV

I was seventeen and a half when Jeff, my first son was born. For sure, he wasn't an unwanted child. When I discovered I was expecting, I was thrilled! Even though I wasn't living for God at the time, I instinctively knew that a child was a gift from God.

> Every good and perfect gift is from above, coming down from the Father of the heavenly lights... James 1:17 NIV

I believed that if I had a child, there would always be someone in my life to love me unconditionally. It didn't enter my mind that a child could be strong willed, hardheaded or ever reject his parents. I hadn't done that, so why would one of my kids? I was naive enough to believe that my children would always love me, and that none of them would ever withhold their affection from me. I was ecstatic about becoming a mother. However, I was so ignorant and unprepared, that as the due date approached, I was hesitant to even take a walk. I was afraid I would go into labor, and the baby would just fall out. No one had spoken with me about what to expect when labor began, not my Mom or even my grandma.

I know this is laughable in the society we live in today. Everybody knows how you have babies and that they don't just fall out, but I didn't.

When labor pains began, Wayne drove me to the hospital. After a little while he tired of the wait and left. He said he was going to take a break and get something to eat. Much to his surprise, my older sister walked into a local bar where Wayne had gone. He was there snuggled up in a booth with another woman. I was only seventeen and a half with a brand-new baby and a cheating husband.

My parents were at my side during the labor and delivery. I was dopey from the anesthesia and fortunately didn't realize that my husband wasn't there when the baby was born. Labor lasted twelve hours (so much for the baby falling out). This was plenty of time for Wayne to grab lunch and get back on time. I guess he got distracted. Unfortunately, he would stay that way throughout our entire marriage.

Forceps were used during Jeff's delivery. Consequently, his little head was pulled into an elongated shape, and the corner of his right eye was nicked. He looked like a little Martian. The first time I saw him, he had little mittens on each hand, so he wouldn't touch his face. The swelling from the forceps caused his right eye to stay shut. So, he actually looked like a one-eyed Martian. As the nurse handed Jeff to me, she chuckled and joked that he had been bitten by the stork. My Dad had no sons, so I wanted to name my son after him.

Every time I fed Jeff, I massaged his head, so eventually he began to look more normal. I didn't know anything about the bonding process, but perhaps Jeff's battle scars from birth kept his dad from connecting with him. It's hard for some people to accept others who aren't perfect in their eyes. Unfortunately for Jeffery, there would never be a close relationship with his Dad.

Jeff learned to walk when he was only nine months old. It seemed strange to see him go from crawling on his knees to walking in the same day. There wasn't any transition between the two. He stayed with a close family friend while I worked during the day. When I left for work in the morning, he was pulling up in the play pen and when I came home that evening, he wasn't just walking but nearly running at a slow trot. When I picked him up from the sitter, she said, "Jeff is walking." I thought she meant he had taken a few steps. She lived just a few houses away, so I carried him home in my arms.

Wayne and I were already separated for the first time, and I was staying at Mom and Dad's. As I came into the house, I set Jeff down on the floor and to my amazement he just took off. He was wobbly but went all the way around the circle of my parent's home. First the living room, into the dining room, then the kitchen and back around through Dad's office, returning to the living room again. There was probably a path worn in this circle at Mom's house, as each new grandchild found they could just keep running in circles around the main floor, taking in each and every room. Like any Mom, I felt I had missed a big event in Jeff's life. I was working when he took his first step. But at least he was with a wonderful babysitter, who cared deeply for him.

Jeff was a lovable child but not an easy child. He was strong willed. I was a young mom, and often it seemed he thought he was the one in charge. Even when he was just three and four years old, he did independent, crazy things. Once he took Wayne's lighter outside and found boxes setting in front of someone's house. They had just

46

moved in. Jeff played in the boxes with a friend until he set them on fire with Wayne's lighter. The burning boxes then caught the front of the people's house on fire. When I heard the fire trucks coming and looked outside, I was shocked to learn Jeff was the cause of the fire.

My marriage to Wayne was so rocky that we were separated about once every six months or so. During one of these reconciliations, my daughter Kelly was conceived.

There was always another woman. Wayne never fell in love with these women, he simply had a need to conquer them sexually. I have never been a quitter, and I wanted to believe it could be fixed. I am grateful that my parents were there to help me through these situations. They were good at throwing out a lifeline to help me get back on my feet again. However it never solved the real problem; which was my heart. Yes, I had issues with Wayne, but I had issues of my own.

Every time I tried to leave this awful marriage Wayne would talk me into coming back again. We tried marriage counselling, and he even saw a psychiatrist once. He was trying to understand his obsession with adulterous relationships. Mom and Dad must have felt like their house had a revolving door. Over and over, I believed Wayne's promises that things would be different. He had a kind of mystical, unnatural hold on me mentally and emotionally. I couldn't escape his control. I knew the relationship was toxic, but he always convinced me to try just one more time. He was very charming, and still is to this day.

I was descending down into a deep dark hole. It wasn't just the adultery; it was the lifestyle. Because it was so difficult for me to escape this captivity, I better understand the demonic hold that other women find themselves in.

This went on for six and a half years, before I could muster up the courage to get away for good. I always felt sorry for him. I didn't want him to be alone. In the end, it boiled down to him or me. I really began to wonder if I was even going to survive. I had begun to drink heavily. It was my way of coping. I felt like I was dying. I attempted to turn to God several times, but each time I would pay the price of ridicule from Wayne. I wasn't strong enough to handle his tormenting words.

The deciding factor for me was that I could see what all the turmoil and instability was doing to my children, Jeff and his baby sister, Kelly. We lived out of state and I had no idea how I was going to provide for myself and my kids when I got back home. I just knew the craziness had to stop if the kids and I were going to have any kind of normal life. The times I had gone home before, I didn't stay with my parents very long. Mom worked and had a busy social life. I knew it was best for everyone that I move out on my own as soon as possible. Mom was never a kid lover, and they really got on her nerves.

I may never fully know how this rocky start to my children's lives affected them. I wasn't thinking that far ahead. I was just trying to survive one day at a time.

The break-up was especially traumatic for Jeffery. He and I had been through many separations from his dad together. During these years of turmoil, it seemed it was Jeff and I against the world. He was my little man. He provided company for me during those long nights when I didn't know where Wayne was. Often, I worried all night wondering if he was ok, or if something terrible had happened to him. I'm sure Jeff felt my fear.

The final blow came when Jeff was in kindergarten. Wayne's behavior became blatant, obvious to everyone. I was at work one morning when the Post Chaplain came into my office. He asked to speak to me privately, but since I had no idea what he wanted, I told him he could speak freely. So there in the presence of both of my bosses, he demanded that Wayne leave his wife alone. He'd been calling the Pastor's wife at work, trying to hook up with her. Everyone in the office heard it. It wasn't unusual for Wayne to pursue married women. In fact, those were the ones he went after, never caring whose marriage he might destroy.

I planned my final escape. However, in the middle of loading my belongings into the moving van, Wayne came home for lunch. He had never done that before. I thought I would be gone by the time he arrived and would be able to avoid another awful confrontation. When he saw I was moving, he was enraged. He had grown up in a family of yellers, so he was loud and scary. He immediately started in on Jeff. He told him I was taking him away, that he would never see his father again. That it would be my fault. It was a lie and he knew it. Wayne was famous for using Jeff against me, only this time it was over the top. I can still see little Jeff clinging to Wayne's legs crying," No Daddy, No Daddy, No Daddy," Over and over again. He tormented our son, in his effort to control me. I begged Wayne not to say those things, but it made no difference. I was terrified that all this trauma was going to cause a lasting effect on Jeff.

> He heals the broken hearted and bandages their wounds. He counts the stars and assigns each a name. Our Lord is great, with limitless strength. We'll never comprehend what he knows and does. God puts the fallen on their feet again.
> Ps. 147:2-6

Thank God that He does. These are the kind of events the devil loves to use. Being a bully, he'll use any traumatic event to his advantage to wound or capture our kids. Fortunately, Kelly was too young to remember. Divorce is very ugly, and in no way is it God's design or desire for the family.

When I finally made the break, we were living in Kentucky. I put Jeff and Kelly into the car and headed back to Missouri where I could be near my family again. I had been working a part-time job and was able to purchase a car. It was the first time I ever had anything in my own name. I was only twenty-two years old with two kids, under educated, and getting a divorce. Many young people my age were just completing college.

Wayne had believed that once we had a second child that I was trapped. He thought I wouldn't be able to leave again, but he was wrong. My children were the reason I found the courage to strike out on my own. I had two children that I would now be completely responsible for, and I didn't know how I would provide for them. Today a single mom can apply for public assistance and get help from the state. There was nothing like that available at that time. I knew I would have to find a way to do this on my own.

I was drawn to reconnect to what I had experienced with God as a young teenager. I didn't know I could turn to God to help me in raising and providing for my kids. I didn't understand that God had never left me, even though I had left him.

"......: and, lo, I am with you always, even unto the end of the world. Amen". Matt. 28:20

Chapter 5
Finding My Way Home

Divorce was a heart-breaking failure which left me feeling empty. I had been so beaten down and rejected. I felt stupid for believing all Wayne's lies and for staying so long. I felt betrayed and deceived. Surely there was someone out there who would love only me.

It seemed the only thing I had going for me was my appearance. I wanted to be appreciated for so much more. There were times when I was dating that I resented being told I was pretty. I didn't do anything to earn that. I was born that way. I wanted credit for who I was inside. I wanted somebody to *see me!* I had no real feelings of value or worth. I wanted to be more than pretty, after all I was artistic, had a lovely voice, I was caring, creative, determined, and a hard worker. The truth was, I hadn't developed much character, except to know I had two great kids and I was going to do whatever it took to care for them.

I knew something was missing in my life. I wasn't sure what I was looking for or how to find it. It's like being hungry for something and never able to satisfy the craving.

I went through one relationship after another. I seemed to be gifted at picking what others would call "losers." I just wanted to be loved, not used. I didn't know how to even love myself. I believed I could find happiness in another person. The truth was, I was empty. No wonder no one could *see me*. I couldn't even *see* who I was; I was lost. I had left the most meaningful relationship in my life behind when I chose Wayne.

> But I have this against you, that you have left your first love. Rev. 2:4

That is exactly what I had done. I had been drawn away by Wayne's charm. I was determined to get back on track, and to make something of my life. Only Christ in me would satisfy my longings.

I have to say my parents helped where they could and where they were comfortable. Dad was there for me in many ways. He even borrowed money to help me to move back to Missouri. I knew I had to pay him back quickly. Not working or supporting myself was never an option. My parents always lived paycheck to paycheck, so I knew I couldn't leave my Dad hanging for the money he borrowed to help me.

I landed a job out near the airport and rented a nice duplex. It was far enough from Mom and Dad that I was pretty much on my own.

For Jeff's birthday that year, I purchased a manufactured treehouse fort that required some assembly. Dad was kind enough to make a trip out to help with putting it together. While he was there, we had one of the most memorable conversations of my life.

Wayne always despised watching anyone cry. So, I learned how to hold back tears for years. I didn't even cry when his mother died, even though I cared deeply for her. I felt like a failure, but I resisted crying over the divorce. It was a feeling of despair; my heart was breaking but I refused to give in to it. I told Dad, "I don't think I can ever love or trust again."

It must have sounded crazy to him coming from someone still so young, but that's how I felt. When he learned how long it had been since I cried, he made it his mission to push me over the edge until I broke into tears. It was like the dam broke. To this day, I can't remember what he said to get me to cry, but when I did, I cried like a baby as he held me in his arms. He said, "Sharon, that's what life is all about, you fall down, and you get back up. Then you fall and you get back up again, over and over again."

Those words were revolutionary to me. They went deep into my heart. They would sustain me throughout the rest of my life. I began to realize that life would be hard but worth living, and that failures would make me strong!

With that in mind this high school dropout, who struggled with learning to read and comprehend, enrolled at the university. I had completed my GED a few years earlier. I was on my feet all night waiting tables at a nice restaurant and went to classes during the day. It wasn't easy. There were days I felt so overwhelmed that I didn't even want to get out of bed. I was juggling school, work, kids, keeping house, laundry, and an occasional date. At times I felt depressed just thinking about how much reading there was to do;

tests, term papers, and class projects could be crushing. Failure wasn't an option. I had already had all of that I could bare. When I completed the first semester with a B average, I really felt like I had accomplished something amazing. Oh my gosh, I'm not a dummy after all!

I decided to move back to the inner city into my old neighborhood. There was a Baptist church with a bus ministry about eight blocks from our home. I had wonderful memories of the Baptist church from my teen years, and this church offered to pick up the kids, Kelly, and Jeff for Sunday School every Sunday morning. I thought it would be good for them. It's strange how even when we're not serving God, we still think it's good for our kids to learn about him.

> Suffer the little children to come unto me and forbid them not: for of such is the kingdom of God. Luke 18:16

The truth was this worked out great for me. I could stay out late on a Saturday night, get up and get the kids ready on Sunday, and once I shipped the them off to Sunday School on the bus, I could go back to sleep.

When summer rolled around the children wanted to attend Vacation Bible School. I figured it couldn't hurt and it would probably be fun for them both. At the end of the week, they had a graduation ceremony and an open house.

They really wanted me to see all the arts and crafts they had made, and to meet their teachers. Reluctantly I agreed. I had filled my life with the world by then and a relationship with God wasn't foremost in my mind.

I joined the children for their ceremony, and It was pleasant. It seemed once I had my foot in the front door that it wasn't so hard to think about returning. The bus continued to pick the kids up every Sunday morning, and Jeff started begging me to go with them. Even though I wasn't willing to admit it, my life was a mess, and I had no husband to blame. So, one morning I got ready with them and I drove the kids to church myself, instead of sending them on the bus.

> A man's heart devises his way: but the Lord directs his steps. Pr. 16:9

The kids went to their classes and I sat alone in the congregation.

I filled out a visitor's card and checked the box that said I was single. I wrote Mom and Dad's address on the card instead of my own.

Coming Back to Faith

The following Thursday night I was doing my laundry at Mom's when I heard a knock on the front door. Daddy had installed one of those great big door knockers, and it made a huge clang when the door opened or closed. I went to the door and when I opened it, there stood a short, very pregnant woman. Her hair was dark and pulled straight back tightly into a ponytail. She said, "Hi, my name is Diane. I'm from the Baptist Church and I came to visit you, are you Sharon?" What are the odds that she found me there when she came? I've often wondered.

I was polite, invited her in and offered her a seat. As she began to speak, she shared her life story with me. I thought I had problems until I heard Diane's story.

She had a son before her husband went away to war. After his return, she gave birth to a little girl named Tamara who was born with multiple birth defects. It was determined they were the result of her husband's exposure to Agent Orange while in Vietnam. Tamara's ears were down on her neck and she had only one eye in the center of her face. She couldn't swallow so Diane had learned to feed her with a tube through a port. Though not expected to live at all, Tamara lived to be two and a half years old. Now Diane was pregnant again. Somehow, she didn't seem to be concerned about the wholeness of this unborn child.

She continued to tell me that shortly after her daughter's death, her husband also died. When he returned from the war, he was having difficulty adjusting to civilian life. He was using alcohol to deal with the memories and trauma he had experienced. One night while drunk he had a terrible automobile accident that left him brain dead. When he arrived at the hospital, he was placed on life support to keep him breathing until family could be consulted. After weeks of no change in his condition, Diane was forced to decide. Should she continue the life support, or have it removed? She agonized over the gravity of being the one to make this decision. The worst part was her in-laws were fighting her in the public arena. Her story had been plastered all over the local newspapers, as she was made out to be a monster depriving her husband of life.

Life support was a big debate back in the seventies. Depending upon who you spoke to, Diane was either a villain, robbing someone of life, or she was a hero allowing a person to die with dignity.

She told me how she struggled in prayer about this. She finally felt as though she had heard from God and knew His will. She reluctantly got dressed to make her way to the hospital where she would agree to have her husband "unplugged." Before she got out the door the phone rang, it was the hospital. Diane's husband had died. Relief flooded over her soul; she was spared the agony of being the one to make the final decision. She was deeply grateful to God for intervening for her.

I sat listening intently to Diane's story, it was so overwhelming. She kept me on the edge of my seat as I wondered, how did she get through all this? She had a husband go off to war and come home an alcoholic. He died suddenly, right on the heels of the death of her daughter. He had left her pregnant and facing that all alone. She was completely confident that God had everything under control. As she rose to leave, I closed the door behind her. I leaned my back against door, and nearly slid down it, as I sighed in emotional exhaustion. I heard the knocker clanging on the door as I considered what I had just heard. I thought to myself, if this woman cares enough, after all she has been through, to come and talk to me about God, the least I can do is to show up at church this week. I didn't want her visit to be in vain.

> Therefore, my beloved brethren, be ye steadfast, unmovable, always abounding in the work of the Lord, forasmuch as ye know that your labor is not in vain in the Lord. 1 Cor. 15:58

Diane was in the married couple's class at the church. She shouldn't have even gotten my visitor's card which was marked as a single person. She came because I was supposed to hear her story.

I thought about Diane frequently that week. The following Sunday, I drug myself out of bed and managed to get to church on time. This time I sat in the pew with Jeff under one arm and Kelly under the other. The preacher began to teach on the Apostle Paul's shipwreck. He talked about throwing over excess baggage and cargo, things that would weigh a ship down when going through a storm. Then he said, "Are there things in your life that you need to throw overboard?"

I will never forget this moment in time. I sat in the pew pondering and struggling with decisions I should have made a long time ago. My eyes were opened to see myself more clearly. I was terrible at picking partners. I had made so many mistakes and I was only twenty-six years old. I was shaking under the power of conviction. I began to cry. A heavy feeling of remorse settled upon me as I realized that I had left the God of my youth behind. I was bathed in the Spirit of Repentance. I had been making all my own decisions, and never even acknowledging God in my life. When was I going to quit trying to do this alone? As I considered all of this, I knew the only thing in my life worth keeping were these two children. In my mind I threw over the "looser" boyfriend". He was gone, drowned in the sea of forgetfulness.

Acts 27:27-28:5 tells the story of the Apostle Paul's shipwreck. I had made a wreck of my life, but I was determined to turn it around. I was tired of being tossed around in the waves of my turbulent lifestyle. I needed a safe harbor.

> What a blessing was that stillness as he brought them safely into harbor. Ps. 107:30 NLT

At that moment, in my heart and mind, it was just me and the kids now. As we stood to sing the invitation song, I did a knuckle cruncher. I hung onto the pew in front of me with tight clenched hands as God continued to deal with me. I told God that I knew as a teen I had been called to ministry, but now I was just an old divorcee, and no one would ever listen to me. I began to confess, "God I can't do this alone. I need you, and I need someone in my life to help me. I need someone I can lean on. Every man in my life has leaned on me. I have never known a man that was Godly. I'm terrible at picking partners. So, if you have a partner for me, I want you to pick him. Nevertheless, I'll serve you for the rest of my life. I'll love you and I'll serve you, even if I've got to do it alone." I meant every word of it.

> And Jesus said unto him, No man, having put his hand to the plough, and looking back, is fit for the kingdom of God. Luke 9:62

I never wanted to look back again. I wanted to move forward with

Jesus as my guide. I finally had the courage to step out into the aisle and walk down to the front. The Pastor met me. I told him that as a teenager, I felt I was called to ministry. That I'd fallen away from God and now I wanted to serve Him again. Only this time it would be whole heartedly. It would be all or nothing. I was giving Him my whole life. This was the turning point of my life. I'd never be the same again!

The Pastor handed the microphone to me and said, "Will you please tell the congregation what you just told me?" I was crying, and my makeup was streaming down my face. My voice cracked with every word I spoke. "I want to live for God. I want to serve Him completely."

> Whosoever therefore shall confess me before men, him will I confess also before my Father which is in heaven. Matt. 10:32

Something miraculous happened the moment I stepped out into the aisle to surrender to God. It was an instantaneous answer to the prayer I had just uttered. There was a young man in the choir. As he looked up and saw me coming down the aisle, God spoke to him. "There she is! That's the one you've been praying for all your life."

His name was Joe. He was already thirty years old and had given up on finding the "Love of his Life." Hearing God speak to him this way shook him to the core. He'd been saved since he was twelve and praying for his wife ever since. He knew the Word of God said:

> Whoso findeth a wife findth a good thing and obtains favor of the LORD. Pr.18:22

Joe moved quickly on what God had spoken clearly.

The Baptist churches traditionally have a welcome line for people who have made decisions for Christ. So, I stood up at the front of the church as people filed by to take turns shaking my hand and welcoming me as a new member. Joe made sure he was the last person in line.

I was embarrassed because I was standing in front of an entire congregation crying. Kelly who was only four, left her seat and ran up front to embrace me. She hugged my waist as she inquired, "Why are you crying Mommy?" It didn't make since to her that I would cry when I was happy. As I attempted to reassure Kelly that I was ok, Joe introduced himself. He was a well built, good looking red head. He asked if I would join him for lunch. He was so young looking that I figured I must be quite a bit older than he was. I politely thanked him for the offer but refused. Then he asked if he could walk me to my car. He was confident that God had spoken to him and knew what he'd heard. He wasn't going to give up easily. I asked him how old he was. He told me he was thirty, but I didn't believe him. So, I asked to see his driver's license. I wasn't used to guys who told the truth, I needed proof.

Joe had been dating another woman in the church for some time, and the expectation was that they would be married. As he would say later, He knew there was something lacking in their relationship, "There just wasn't any fire, there was no passion."

She was a good woman and he had thought she would make a fine wife. He'd become weary of searching. I, on the other hand, was engaged to a pot smoking, beer drinking jerk. Another one I'd met at the club my parents were so devoted to. I should have known better. In my mind that day, I threw him overboard, from "my ship of life". He was the first thing to go. I'd made a commitment to live for God and he had no place left in my future. It was ungodly company that had led me astray in the first place, and I wasn't willing to go there again.

> For of this you can be sure: No immoral, impure or greedy person—such a person is an idolater—has any inheritance in the kingdom of Christ and of God. Let no one deceive you with empty words, for because of such things God's wrath comes on those who are disobedient. Eph.5:5-6 NIV

I'd experienced deceitful, empty words in every relationship up to that time. The one thing I didn't want was to be deceived again.

That evening, I returned to church. When the service was over, I was invited to join the single adult group. They were gathering at a local restaurant for fellowship. I took the kids with me. Joe sat across the table from me and we hit it off, talking and laughing the whole evening. He walked me to my car again and as we put the kids in the car, Kelly turned to Joe and said, "Will you be my Daddy?" I was so embarrassed, I wanted to crawl under the car. Joe just chuckled, after all he'd heard from God and already knew the plan. I hadn't. He and Kelly clicked right away.

It only took Joe ten days to propose. In that time, he broke things off with his gal and I ended my relationship with my former boyfriend. The very day that I committed to follow Jesus, I met Joe. It was like God had him hiding in the wings waiting for my complete surrender.

> "For my thoughts are not your thoughts, neither are your ways my ways," declares the Lord. Is. 55:8

Thank God because my ways sure weren't working for me.

Joe and I caught our Pastor off guard when we went to see him. Joe told him we wanted to be married. Like everyone else in the church, he had assumed we were both going to marry someone completely different. He told us we needed at least a six months engagement before he would perform the ceremony. He said, "If your engagement can't last six months, your marriage won't last a lifetime." He gave us excellent counsel in many ways and we were glad we took his advice.

I always felt Joe took a huge gamble on me. I was a looser at relationships. I'd lived without God in my life and he had been faithful. He never saw it that way. From the beginning he began teaching me God's Word. I knew nothing, but he could see my eagerness to learn, so he taught me how to witness and how to be a Godly woman.

> Husbands, love your wives, even as Christ also loved the church, and gave himself for it; That he might sanctify and cleanse it with the washing of water by the word. Eph. 5:25

That's what Joe did, washed me with God's Word. I thank God every day for Joe and for the forty-one plus wonderful years we've had together. In short, it was my children's influence, and Diane's amazing testimony of how God had sustained her, that prompted me to go to church. If not for them I might have been in one more dead-end relationship, falling deeper into sin. Diane and I have remained lifelong friends.

Chapter 6
Something More

As a new believer, I was astounded at how much I could sense God speaking to me. I began to feel that I should pick up where I left off as a teenager, before I fell away. When I was in high school, I took a field trip with our youth group to a Baptist college in Hannibal, MO. At the time I felt that I would one day attend there.

That never happened, but after completing a semester of college elsewhere, I was feeling that God was giving me a second chance. This school taught the Bible and I was desperate to learn. Joe and I had already put a down payment on a home and were making plans to marry, when I announced to him, "I want to go back to school". Joe was understanding and supported me in my decision. Over the years Joe never hindered me in any way when it came to the things of God. On the contrary, he pushed me. He was always happy to be the guy in the background, insisting I be in the forefront, even when I didn't want to be. He loved me deeply and thought I could do just about anything.

Fortunately, we were able to get out of the contract to purchase the house. Then I headed off to college, with my two young children. That put us two hours away from Joe. I didn't have the money to attend. I went by faith. I was so confident that God would work things out for me, that I didn't even give a thought to the cost. Incredibly, I ended up with a ministerial scholarship meant for preachers, at a Baptist College. I was a unique sight indeed on this campus. I was a divorcee, with two children, living in staff housing and a woman on a scholarship meant for preachers, in a denomination that didn't even permit women to preach. Being divorced was contrary to their doctrine, and yet I had been given this favor.

> For thou, Lord, wilt bless the righteous; with favor wilt thou compass him as with a shield. Ps. 5:1

No doubt I had been given favor. It was like all the rules had been bent to make a way for me to attend.

The Holy Spirit Comes

It was a cold January morning in the Midwest as I walked across campus. I could see my breath in the air since I was praying out loud. I said, "Father, I want *everything* you have for me." I didn't care what that might entail. I didn't know that would mean the infilling of the Holy Spirit.

After all, I'd never heard of such a thing. The following Sunday while I was visiting Joe, he told me about a lady at work that he greatly admired. He said, "She speaks in tongues". I didn't know what that meant either, but I was about to find out. He said, "She's really a Holy person, and I want to be like her." None of that made any sense to me.

Joe had been seeking the infilling of the Spirit for years. He'd visited many churches and denominations looking for something more. He just knew there was something beyond what he was experiencing in the Baptist church. He too, was very hungry for the things of God.

Back on campus the following week, I was destined to encounter yet another Diane. This one was a Dianna.

One morning between classes, I was stopped in my tracks. As I stood in the hallway on the second floor of the main college building, I looked out the window across campus. My eyes fell on what seemed to me, the most beautiful young woman I'd ever seen. I thought she was breath taking. There seemed to be a glow about her, almost like a halo. I was stunned by her appearance.

Late that afternoon, I walked into my Mathematics class and there she was. Dianna was sitting right next to me. Strange how God works these things out, isn't it? She had already heard about me from another student by the name of Kevin. He'd told Dianna, "There's a new gal in my speech class, and she's "on fire for God." She was already looking forward to meeting me. After class we spoke, and she invited me to a home Bible study on the following Friday night. I thought, what a fantastic place this is! People just invite you to a Bible Study and they don't even know you. I was two hours away from home and missing Joe, I was glad to be making new friends.

One of the dorm parents on campus kindly offered to keep my kids so I could go with Dianna. Had they known where I was going, they'd never have agreed. I'd find out later that Dianna was considered a troublemaker. Of course, I didn't know that. I'd just arrived on campus days before. Dianna picked me up for the Bible study which was being held at a doctor's home. She shared with me how God was moving in this group of people and that Dr. Bach believed in healing. I was so encouraged! I'd never met a doctor who believed in the healing power of God! That was awesome! Dianna lead as we entered the house where the meeting was held. I could hear people speaking in other languages. They were singing worshipfully, but not in English. We turned the corner into the living room from the foyer, and I could see a circle of people with their hands in the air, just loving God. They each spoke softly or sang in a language I didn't understand. Dianna and I joined the circle.

> And when the day of Pentecost was fully come, they were all with one accord in one place. And suddenly there came a sound from heaven as of a rushing mighty wind, and it filled all the house where they were sitting. And there appeared unto them cloven tongues like as of fire, and it sat upon each of them. And they were all filled with the Holy Ghost, and began to speak with other tongues, as the Spirit gave them utterance. Acts 2:1-4

I found this all very mystical and wasn't sure what to think. In my mind, I began to hum the theme from "The Twilight Zone." This was just so weird. I thought to myself, I'm pretty sure this was what Joe told me about just the week before. I trusted Joe so I figured this must be OK. He'd been a Christian since he was twelve years old and I knew he knew the Bible even though I didn't. He wouldn't ever steer me wrong spiritually.

There was a group of about twenty people at this meeting, and after beautifully worshipping God, we all sat down for a teaching. I heard things I knew nothing about, but they were being read from the Bible. When the teaching was over, people began to mill around and visit and enjoy refreshments. Dianna asked the speaker and several others if they would pray for me. He asked if I understood what he had taught? Admittedly, I didn't. So, he opened his Bible and had me read with him all the passages about being filled with the Holy Spirit. I was extremely glad I'd seen these scriptures with my own eyes. If it was in the Bible, it had to be true. As they prayed for me to receive the gift of the Holy Spirit, I had my eyes closed and yet I could see something like a movie reel passing before my eyes. On this movie reel were all the sins of my life. They were passing before my eyes as they were leaving my body through the top of my head. I thought this must be what it is like when you're drowning. I'd been told that drowning victims see their whole lives pass before them. That's what was happening to me. This was the first of many visions I'd experience through my life, and it nearly took my breath away. At one point I said to myself, " Oh My God, everyone here can see all my sins!" Truly I didn't really care. I was experiencing the presence of God in my life like never before. I just wanted more of God. Remember? Whatever you have for me God, I want it. Thankfully, no one there saw what I saw, but I knew I had been completely set free.

> If the Son therefore shall make you free, ye shall be free indeed. John 8:3

I didn't hear myself speak in tongues at the meeting that night, although others said that I did. I knew something wonderful had happened. When we got into the car to leave, Dianna was driving. I was in the middle of the front seat and Kevin was on my right side. It began to rain, and it rained so hard we couldn't see where we were going. Just then the windshield wipers stopped working. Dianna did something I'd never seen before. She started rebuking the devil. She commanded him, "Stop messing with my windshield wipers in the Name of Jesus." I was shocked! I said to myself, "Oh my God, she talks to the devil!" Kevin smacked me on my knee and said, "Agree with her, agree with her!" I quickly responded, "I agree, I agree." Immediately the windshield wipers began to work again, and we could see where we were going. It goes without saying, I was amazed. We dropped Kevin off at his dorm and headed back to my apartment.

Driving toward the house, I had lots of questions for Dianna. How does this work? Can you speak in tongues anytime you want or is it just special times? She explained to me that it's a prayer language that by-passes your thought process and goes right to God. That the Holy Spirit is praying through you in the perfect will of God.

With that she began praying out loud in her prayer language as she was driving. It sounded so holy to me that I started to cover my ears. I felt like I was ease dropping on a conversation with God.

After arriving home, I tucked the children in their beds, prayed with them, and kissed them good night. It was just a one-bedroom duplex and we all slept in the same room together. I laid down in my bed and began to pray, telling The Lord again, "I want everything you have for me. If this is of you, and you gave this gift to others, I know you'll give it to me as well." This was a supernatural knowing. I had no doubt at all. I was wholly convinced, so I said, "I know you love me as much as you love everyone that was at that Bible study this evening. I know if you gave them the gift on tongues that you'll give it to me".

> Then Peter opened his mouth, and said, Of a truth I perceive that God is no respecter of persons. Act 10:34

At that very moment of realization/faith, I began speaking in a heavenly language. I was so utterly amazed and astounded that I got up and went to the bathroom to look in the mirror. I watched my image reflecting back at me as the words flowed out of my mouth. I needed to see because it was so supernatural. Was this perfect beautiful language really coming out of me? I was speaking a fluent language that I'd never learned, and yet I was speaking it. I spoke in tongues the entire night. I was awe struck! My face actually hurt because I prayed all night without stopping one time. I didn't have just a few words but a full and complete language. My sins were forgiven, and I'd been baptized in His Holy Spirit. Wow! What a treasure!

As a child I used to try to make up languages to fool people into thinking I was from a foreign country. I couldn't make my mind think fast enough to make up words. This was vastly different, it just flowed out of my inner most being, and the more I did it, the more I sensed the presence of God. It was a glorious experience!

> But ye, beloved, building up yourselves on your most holy faith, praying in the Holy Ghost. James 1:20

That's exactly what I was doing! So many times, when I didn't know how to pray, the Holy Spirit would make intercession for me.

And he that searches the hearts knows what the mind of the Spirit is, because he makes intercession for the saints according to the will of God. Rm. 8:27

Likewise the Spirit also helps our infirmities: for we know not what we should pray for as we ought: but the Spirit itself makes intercession for us with groanings which cannot be uttered. Rm. 8:26

The next day Joe drove up from St. Louis to see me and the kids. He was picking us up for Sunday School. As I opened the door, I said to him, "Guess what happened?" He answered, "You don't have to tell me, I see it all over you. You received the baptism of the Holy Spirit." I felt so holy it was hard to let Joe even hold my hand. I didn't want him to kiss me or touch me. I was holy, and it was an incredible experience. Together, we headed on to Sunday school and I was silent most of the time. I couldn't talk, because my face hurt. Joe said, "This is the first time I've ever known you to be quiet."

I learned to call speaking in tongues "My Keeping Power." It would be my go-to spiritual tool every time I was in the middle of a test or trial. Every time I was tempted, confused, traumatized or fearful, I could open my mouth and literally hear the Spirit speaking through me. It would give me the strength to face everything from that moment forward. To God be the glory!

So, here I was, a divorced woman with two children, on a ministry scholarship. That meant the school was paying for me to be there and now I spoke in tongues, another doctrinal no no. I had become a topic of frequent controversial conversations on campus.

There were times of doubt during these early days, because other students told me that I'd let the devil touch me! Once a Professor spent hours with me in the cafeteria trying to explain why all this "spirit stuff" had passed away. The school set an appointment for me to speak with a fellow student. She had experienced a mental breakdown and blamed it on being filled with the Spirit. She might have experienced a spirit. However, it wasn't Holy if it caused her those problems. The dorm parents that cared for my children the night I was spirit filled were horrified. They couldn't believe I'd been with "THAT Dianna girl." All this prompted me to take my Bible and stay shut up in my apartment pouring over scriptures for a month.

I came out only for classes and work. I needed to know what I'd experienced was from God and not a counterfeit from the devil.

> Study to shew thyself approved unto God, a workman that needeth not to be ashamed, rightly dividing the word of truth. 2 Tim. 2:15

At the end of a full month in the Word, I was convinced. I believed that if it was good enough for the disciples, it was good for me. I could see throughout the New Testament that the Holy Spirit led and directed everything they did. I was like an explosion looking for a place to happen. More in love with God than ever.

I was extremely grateful that the traveling minister had shown me in the Bible how the disciples were filled with the Spirit. If not, I might have believed some of what I was being told. I was young in the Lord and didn't know how to study. It took me a while, but after my time studying God's Word, I was thoroughly convinced that what I had experienced was a gift from God.

During this time of searching, I asked God for the Spirit of Discernment. I didn't want to be deceived. I felt dishonest people had lied to me, pretending to be someone they weren't, and I never wanted to be fooled again. Once again, I didn't know what I was asking for, but I have learned to treasure it. It's a precious gift from The Father to me.

I was so in love with Jesus that I walked around like Dianna, with a glow. The guest speakers at the college occasionally pointed me out as being exuberant in my faith, and an example for other students. They usually got clued in later by college staff that I was a "divorced tongue talker" and not one to be praised.

None the less, God continued to give me favor at this college. I was given the position of the assistant registrar. It reminded me of the favor given to Joseph in Potiphar's house.

> And Joseph found grace in his sight, and he served him: and he made him overseer over his house, and all that he had he put into his hand. Gen. 39:4

I had access to every student's record, past and present, while in this position. Which meant entry into the safe as well. It was indeed the favor of God. Despite the naysayers, God touched the hearts of people that mattered, and opened doors for me that were impossible in the natural.

I was still a new Christian and now had been filled with the Holy Spirit just two months after surrendering my life to Jesus. Joe had searched for years for what I had received in such a short time. It simply fell on me. It didn't seem fair to him. He wanted what I had.

About that time, our home Church back in St. Louis, had two visiting ministers that taught on being filled with God's spirit. This was a church of about a thousand members. When the ministers asked people to act on the message, the response was overwhelming. Over three hundred people came to the front of the church to receive the Holy Spirit. The solution was to take them all to the basement and pray for them as a group. What was being offered was the infilling of the Spirit with no expectation of anyone speaking in tongues. Much to their surprise, many did. However, Joe wasn't one of them, and he remained disappointed.

Joe decided to follow the minister's instructions. He made a list of everyone he could think of that he had sinned against or offended in his lifetime. One by one he went to them and asked for their forgiveness. Each time he made things right with someone, he could feel The Spirit rising higher and higher within him.

One Sunday night after visiting with me at the college, he made the long trip home alone in the dark. In the car he began to worship the Lord and in a moments time, he began to speak in tongues. There was no striving, it just began to flow from deep within him. This was something he had desired for years. Now he was experiencing a closeness with God like he had never known before. He couldn't wait to get home to phone me, to share his exciting news. Joe loved Jesus, and now he had an even more intimate relationship than before. He was rejoicing!

I have to say, I have never met anyone else that went through this process of asking others for personal forgiveness as a steppingstone to be filled with God's Spirit. All I know.... is that it worked for Joe.

Chapter 7
The Threats Begin

Guess who wasn't thrilled with my new-found faith and the new "religious guy" I was engaged to? That's right, Wayne.

Over Spring Break that year the children went to visit him. Kelly had just turned five and Jeff was nine. When they returned, she laid down on the floor, and proudly said, "Look Mommy, this is how you make babies." She obviously had witnessed something that she was way too young to see. She was making movements that were way beyond her understanding.

I became incredibly angry! I decided that if this is what they're learning when they're with Wayne, then surely they don't need to go back! I was afraid it wasn't safe, and I wanted to protect them. I asked Kelly where she learned to do that, and she answered, "From the babysitter."

Their father left them with a teenage boy whenever he wasn't home. When I questioned Wayne about this, it opened a fire storm of accusations back and forth. His response was to threaten a lawsuit for the custody of the children.

This was the first time I became fearful of losing my kids, but it wouldn't be the last. I was a poor struggling college student. He knew that I couldn't afford attorney's fees. I didn't believe he really wanted the children; it would cramp his style too much. It was simply a way for him to maintain control over me long after the marriage had ended.

Wayne never kept regular visits. He often missed the holidays and special events, so I was fairly sure this was a manipulation tactic on his part. Occasionally he'd take the children for his visitation time. However, he was never regular about anything concerning then. He'd make promises all the time and never kept them.

Wayne's threats began to cause sleepless nights. Then one Friday night during prayer at the Bible study group, someone spoke a word of encouragement to me. They told me that The Lord said, "You'll always have your children." I treasured that Word, and I wrote it in the back of my Bible. I felt so blessed that God would love me so much. He had literally come through the universe to speak a personal word to me just to give me peace! I didn't always know how to hear God clearly for myself. I clung to that word many times as I struggled to keep my children. I certainly didn't 'know then how to let them go, nor was it time to. I felt like David when he said,

> "Deliver me from mine enemies, O my God: defend me from them that rise up against me." Ps. 59:1

Wayne was feeling more like an enemy all the time. However, I made every effort over the years to never speak ill of him to the children.

> A good man out of the good treasure of the heart bringeth forth good things: and an evil man out of the evil treasure bringeth forth evil things. Matt 12:35

I wanted so badly to protect my kids from evil things.

Establishing God's Ways

Joe and I had been counselled by our Pastor and we agreed to wait for marriage before becoming physically intimate. We felt keeping sex within the marriage covenant would be God honoring. Our engagement was six-months long and seemed like forever. It was harder than we thought it would be. We were so in love with one another and desired to give ourselves wholly to each other. God blessed this decision to be obedient to His Word. It paid off in an amazing loving relationship for all our married life.

> For this is the will of God, your sanctification: that you abstain from sexual immorality; that each one of you know how to control his own body in holiness and honor, not in the passion of lust...1 Thes. 4:3-5

Before I met Joe, I'd never heard anyone pray out loud, except for my Father at a meal, or the preacher at church. Even while we were still dating, Joe often knelt with me to pray. Every time he'd thank God for me and my children. I'd never heard someone just talk to God out loud like they spoke to anyone else. It was coming from deep within his heart. This was foreign to me. I felt it was extremely intimate. Just like with Dianna, it felt like I was ease dropping on a private conversation. It was difficult for me to grasp that someone would thank God for me and my children. It made me love him even more deeply. I'd never met a man that loved God like Joe did.

> I give thanks to God always for you all, making mention of you in our prayers; 1 Thes 1:2

Joe was thirty-one and I was twenty-six when we were married in our home church in St. Louis. It was a beautiful ceremony late in May. Everyone could see how in love we were. There wasn't a dry eye in the place. Many of Joe's friends knew how long he'd prayed and believed for a bride. I made my dress and the two bride's maid's as well. Joe arranged for the reception hall and cake. We didn't spend much money, and yet it was a God centered wonderful exchange of heart felt vows. It was perfect in every way. Dianna was my maid of honor and both Jeff and Kelly were attendants.

After the wedding we moved to the country. Joe wanted the children to enjoy all the experiences of country life. We weren't sure what God wanted for us next, so we moved into a property that used to be Joe's Mom's. This location put us two hours away from Joe's workplace. So, he was on the road four hours a day, going to and from work.

I made good use of this time alone with the Lord, learning His Word and His ways. I was discovering what it meant to be a prayer warrior. There were times Joe would say, "How am I ever going to catch up to you?" I was devouring The Word. The truth is if it weren't for Joe, I wouldn't be who I am today. He was a wonderful example and mentor.

It wasn't long before the drive just got to be too much, so Joe found work closer to home. That meant a huge pay cut and learning to live more frugally. But we felt the tradeoff was worth it. We purchased what was my very first home, a thirteen-acre farm in rural Missouri.

The Kidnapping

Joe owned a home of his own before we met, but now this was our home together. I had always lived in the city. So, living in the country, having animals, and watching things grow was an adventure for me. I loved it. We were only in our farmhouse just a short time when we were served with a subpoena.

Wayne and I had argued back and forth about the custody of the children and visiting rights. He decided to hire an attorney. The subpoena instructed me to drop my kids off in a nearby town at the Sherriff's office for Wayne to pick up on Sunday.

Joe and I took the papers to a local attorney. He assured us that he would be able to help us. In a few days I got a phone call from him. He directed me go ahead and drop the children off to their Dad. He promised that If I did, he would have them back to me by Friday, which was the court date. I hated doing this. Against my better judgement, I agreed. After all, we had hired the attorney to give us good advice. We met Wayne at the Sheriff's department Sunday after church. The kids jumped into the back of his pickup which was covered with a camper shell. I wondered if Wayne could even hear them through the back window. I hated to see the kids go. Crying, I felt defeated that they were even going to be staying with their irresponsible father for any time at all, but at least they would be home by Friday.

I had no way of knowing we had put our confidence in ungodly counsel.

> Blessed is the man that walketh not in the counsel of the ungodly, nor standeth in the way of sinners, nor sitteth in the seat of the scornful. Ps.1:1

Friday came, and we went to court as instructed. Neither Wayne nor my children were there. We sat impatiently through all the morning court proceedings without having our case called. At the lunch break, I approached my attorney, and asked "when will our case be heard?" He said, "I don't know who you are. I've never seen you before."

I couldn't believe what I was hearing! I became angry and even more fearful for my kids! The Court Clerk checked the docket for me. She said, "Well your case was on the docket, but it's been crossed out." I asked, "How can that happen?" She had no explanation. My children were gone with someone I didn't even trust! I didn't know when, or if I would ever see them again! Wayne was that vindictive.

The copy of the subpoena had been given to the attorney, so we didn't have papers to show the judge.

When the judge returned from lunch, he noticed that we were still there after the morning session. He asked if there was anyone whose case hadn't been heard. I rose and tearfully explained my situation. My anger and fear reflected in my words to the point that Joe tugged on my shirt. He said, "Sharon you're going to be found in contempt of court, sit down, before they throw you out!" I pleaded with the Judge, "These are my children we're talking about, and now they're in danger!" I was nearly beside myself. My children were gone, and I didn't know where they were or when they might return. No one had any answers for me. I came to court believing I would be going home with my kids. This was no longer a court battle between Wayne and I; it was a case of missing children!

We left the court room childless. We had been lied to, deceived. We couldn't figure out what had happened. Had Wayne paid off our attorney? Why would our attorney say he'd never seen us before?

We began to search for the children but couldn't find a trace. Wayne had quit his job, shut off his phone, and moved from his current address which was in another state. I had no way of contacting them or checking to see how they were doing. I cried for most that summer. Not knowing where my children were, was nearly unbearable. I kept thinking about what the Bible says that nothing happens to us that hasn't happened to someone else, and how God gives us a way of escape. I had to trust Him to do that for me and my children. The previous trip with their father had produced such disgusting results. This time I feared for what might happen to them in his care, or lack of it.

We were newlyweds, with little money. We didn't know where to turn for help but to God. I think back on those days and feel sorry for Joe. I was a "basket case" of a wife for that entire first summer.

Right after we were married, Joe's brother was going through a divorce and needed help caring for his two sons until he could get established again. We agreed to help. It was hinted that this might be a permanent situation, that the boys might stay with us long term. They had been in a troubled home and had major emotional issues. We all loved them dearly. We'd worked hard to help them transition into a loving family atmosphere. Everyone was just getting comfortable with one another when we learned they would be going home soon. The idea of losing then was hurtful. All of us had become quite attached. So, one day I was the mother of four and then there were none. It wasn't well with my soul. (2 Kings 4)

I read and re-read the promise in the back of my Bible. "You will always have your children." God knew ahead of time how often I would need to be comforted by those words. Week after week passed with no word from the children. Complete silence. When they'd been with their father in the past, they'd call and check in with me frequently, but not this time. Nothing! Remember that Jeff and Kelly were nine and five. I was still so young myself that worry and fretting were my constant companions. Somehow, I still knew God wouldn't fail me. That he would return my children to me safely. I had His promise.

Then one day, without warning, Wayne drove into our driveway in his pick-up truck, with the children in the back-camper shell. He had grown tired of them and decided to bring them home. He didn't even make a phone call to see if we were home.

By then I was pregnant with Rachel. When I saw Wayne's truck pull into the driveway, all those weeks of fear displayed themselves in rage, I just let loose!! I flew off the handle with Wayne. I knew he had used the kids to get to me once again. This is how he operated.

I never really believed that he wanted to spend time with them. I was completely distraught! I wanted to make sure Wayne knew how horrible he'd made my life by taking my kids away. Again, Joe had to calm me down and remind me that I was carrying Rachel. He didn't want our baby to be traumatized because of the unresolved issues with my ex-husband.

In time I would learn that my fears about this summer were warranted. Jeff was sexually molested that summer. However, I wouldn't learn the truth about what had happened until Jeff was in his forties, and still dealing with the fallout. At age nine, while with Wayne, he began smoking and it took decades for him to be fully delivered from the hold of cigarettes.

When he was finally ready to talk about the worst summer of his young life it was only because it had tormented him for so long. In his heart he blamed me because I wasn't there to protect him. I wondered if that was because he saw me as the parent and the one who defends. Wayne was just somebody he visited with from time to time.

Remember, the devil is a bully and will use every trick in the book to destroy one of God's kids. I wasn't able to protect my children that summer. I learned that I had an enemy. Even though it felt like it was Wayne, the truth was it was the devil!

> The thief cometh not, but for to steal, and to kill, and to destroy: I am come that they might have life, and that they might have it more abundantly. John 10:10 NIV

In a way, I am glad I didn't know everything. I don't know what I might have done. All I knew was that my kids were home. God had heard my cry.

> Hear my cry, O God; attend unto my prayer. From the ends of the earth will I cry after thee. Ps. 61:1

I felt like I had been crying to the Lord all that summer. I was certainly not a great woman of faith. The children's return wasn't because I handled everything so well, or because I knew how to touch the heart of God. They returned to me, because God heard my cries and because He loved them even more than I did. He'd made a promise to me. "I would always have my children."

This summer was the beginning of the refiner's fire. God was beginning to build character in me. I wasn't only learning to stand through adversity, but I was learning the integrity and faithfulness of God. I did long fasts and spent many hours in prayer. I didn't know it then, but I was building a firm foundation for a life of trusting God. I'd grow more and more intimately in love with Him. Knowing that there's no shadow of turning in Him. He's forever the same. Heb. 13:8

Wayne tried a few more times to take the children by sneaking them out of school, but he was never successful. One way or the other, God revealed his plans to us each time and we were able to intervene.

> But as for you, ye thought evil against me; but God meant it unto good, Gen 50:20

Along the Way

I was so grateful to have my children home again. It was a time of learning to settle in as a family. After a crazy summer of fear and uncertainty there were lots of adjustments and getting used to one another.

The children were happy to be home, but they held secrets about that summer that they told no one. There was a strong bond between Jeff and Kelly, because only they knew what happened. They had survived abuse and just wanted to put it behind them. They felt like it was the two of them against the world. They believed they would always have each other, but they weren't sure how they would fit into their Mom's new life with Joe.

When they left with Wayne their cousins were there. Now they were gone to another state and they didn't get to say goodbye. They had a new home, a new dad, and a new school.

The kids loved the freedom of the farm. There were lots of things to explore and room to run. Joe had grown up in a rural setting and looked forward to sharing lot of adventures with Jeff on our little mini farm. Jeff wasn't sure that collecting eggs or clearing brush were experiences he wanted. He had to learn that when Joe said something that he meant it. Joe could be taken at his word; Jeff could trust him. So even though he resisted helping with the work at first, he soon learned that Joe's approval was something he greatly desired.

A wise son heareth his father's instruction: Pr. 13:1 a

In a very short time Jeff and Kelly both saw Joe as "Dad." Since that wasn't a name Wayne cherished, he told the kids to call him "Pop." So, Joe became Dad; he loved the children like they were his own.

When winter arrived, a deep snowstorm hit the farm. The wind was noisy and blew hard against the old farmhouse. The snow piled up at the doors and windows in drifts. Of course, the children were out of school with nothing to do. All they wanted was to play in the snow. So, Joe pulled out the old tractor he had just acquired at the local auction. Then he hooked a huge piece of sheet metal to the back of it with a couple of chains. The children gathered up everything they could find to help them stay warm. They put one layer of clothes on after the other until it looked like they could hardly walk without falling over.

Joe was the third born of eight children, and his father died when he was only eight years old. He grew up extremely poor. So, he and his brothers were always finding ways to entertain themselves without spending money. He taught us all to take whatever we had available and make it work for whatever was needed. He told the kids to jump onto the old piece of metal roofing he had found lying around the farm. Jeff and Kelly sat down on the metal, not exactly sure what to expect next. As Joe put the tractor in gear and took off, the laughter and squeals of delight began. Joe pulled the children all over the 13 acres in the snow. What fun!

The Missouri Farm is where the kids had their first experience with owning horses and other animals. This was something they never dreamed of while living in the city. They got to see things grow, play in the creek, have a dog, raise chickens, and enjoy the pleasures of being able to eat from their own labors.

I'd never seen anything grow before and found it amazing to watch. I took early morning walks through the vegetable garden while the dew was still on the leaves. Sometimes I waited till nearly sundown when I could enjoy the lovely country sunsets at the same time. I was astounded at the force of a leaf coming through the soil. It had enough strength to push a rock out of it's way as it pushed through the soil to the light of day. Seeing things grow everyday made the Bible come alive to me, because it contained so many parables and stories about plants and how to learn from them.

> ....The kingdom of God is like a man who casts seed upon the soil; and he goes to bed at night and gets up by day and the seed sprouts and grows- how, he himself does not know. Mark 4:26-27 NAS

The Bible was written to an agricultural society, so the experience on the farm greatly enhanced my understanding.

For the first time since I became a Mom, I was given the privilege of being able to stay home with my children. I didn't have to get up and go to work every day. I viewed this opportunity as a huge gift from Joe and a blessing from God. I could be the kind of mom I wanted to be, and not have to be concerned with being the bread winner. What a joy. I had time to read The Word, work on arts and crafts with the kids, go to school functions, and even create and sew cute little dresses for Kelly.

While living in the country, Jeff continually bugged Joe about learning how to drive the tractor. He was still just too young. As spring approached Joe had been working on an old car of one of my sisters, but it wasn't running yet.

Jeff was always a jokester. He was funny and often played tricks on others. April Fools morning, he tricked the rest of the family pretty good with one of his jokes. To get even, that afternoon when Jeff came home from school, Joe said to him, "Jeff, do you still want to learn to drive?" Jeff was extremely excited, as Joe handed him the keys to the old car outside. He said, "Just go out there and see what you can do." Jeff grabbed the keys and took off. Once out-side he tried his best to turn the engine over, but it wouldn't start. He tried again, but nothing happened. He came running inside and said, "Dad, I can't get it to go." Joe just looked at him and bent over in laughter. He declared, "April Fools!" The whole family got a good laugh, even Jeff. If Joe got tickled, he would laugh till he got tears in his eyes. This was one of those moments.

Chapter 8
Jeff's Early Encounters with God

For as young as I was, I had already endured a number of tests, but like my Dad said, "Life is hard, you fall down and you get up, then you fall down and you get up." Each time I did this, I became stronger, bolder, braver, and closer to the LORD.

Letting go of my children and turning them over to God was always a hard lesson to learn. I would painfully come to realize that they belonged to God and not to me. I wanted to protect and rescue them, no matter how old they were.

Even though Joe and I'd received the Baptism of the Holy Spirit, we weren't ready to leave the Baptist Church. That was all either one of us had ever been exposed to. It was our spiritual home base.

One crisp fall Sunday morning, we entered the local Southern Baptist congregation and took our places in one of the pews. There was nothing unusual about this particular morning, it seemed pretty routine. But what happened next etched this day in my memory. I can still see in my mind, exactly where we were seated.

The organist and piano players both began to play. The music sounded kind of like a merry-go-round. Jeff and Kelly had taken their seats between Joe and me when they both became disruptive. They kept chattering as they pointed upward. Naturally, I looked up to see where they were pointing, but saw nothing unusual. I thought, "They know how to behave in church, something must be going on." They were trying to whisper, but all the pointing was drawing attention to them. Others were looking our way, wondering what was going on with our children.

Joe said to me, "Sharon, put one of the kids on the other side of you, so they will stay quiet." As I told them to move, Jeff said, "Mom, we see angels!"

Kelly who was still talking rather loud and excitedly, told Joe the same thing. Joe and I just looked at one another in bewilderment, and he whispered, "After the service we'll separate them and see if we can figure out what just happened." Once the music stopped the kids settled down.

After the service, I took Kelly one direction and Joe took Jeff another. After speaking with them, we realized that both children had seen some form of Spiritual Warfare going on in the sanctuary. To our amazement, their stories matched exactly! Jeff was old enough to write it down, so I ask him to do that for me. I had been journaling since I met Joe, and so putting things in writing was quite familiar to the children. We knew if we wrote things down, we'd remember longer. We'd learned, that writing also triggers the memory, helping to fill in blanks where we might have forgotten something.

This is what the children told us:

There was a total of eight low hanging lights in the sanctuary. They all dangled on long rope-like wires from the vaulted ceiling above. They looked like huge elongated Christmas tree ornaments, ivory colored with gold trim. When the organist began to play the very cheerful music, angles appeared. Both the children saw eight of them, in flowing sheer white robes. One angel swirling around each light. As they continually circled the lights as if they were dancing in beautiful praise and worship, keeping time with the music.

Then suddenly a huge black chariot with a black horse and a black rider came up from out of the baptistry. It galloped thunderously right down between the lights where the angels were worshipping. As soon as it appeared, the angels in white broke their worshipful movements and aggressively came together as one. They chased the evil entity out of the sanctuary, charging in after the dark chariot and ran it right out the back of the church! Jeff said, "The dark rider was afraid of the angels!"

There was a huge stained-glass window high in the rear of the church. That's where the evil chariot and its driver exited.

Because of this experience, Joe and I became much more sensitive, realizing how easily children see into the spirit realm. It taught me to be more alert. I often wonder what might be going on in a service that we aren't aware of? There's a whole other world moving about us all the time. Most of us don't stop to realize it exists.

> The chariots of God are twenty thousand, even thousands of angels: the Lord is among them, Ps 68:17

It must have been quite a sight!

Once home, Jeff sat down and drew a picture of what he'd witnessed. His drawing made it much easier for Joe and me to visualize.

Jeff had been born again and baptized after his first Vacation Bible School experience. He preached to Wayne every time he went to visit. Jeff had the heart of an evangelist. He would waiver in life from time to time, but he had a passion for the lost and he loved helping the underdog.

Joe established a daily Bible study with the children. We gathered in the living room every evening after dinner. Jeff was about ten when I shared with the family from a book I had been reading. It was about Oral Roberts and how he had been filled with the Holy Spirit. When I was finished, I asked the children if they had any questions. Jeff's reply was, "Can I have that too?"

So, we prayed and asked God to fill Jeff with His Spirit. I was sitting next to him on the sofa and praying softly in my heavenly language when he startled me with a loud noise! He slapped both hands on his legs, making a loud clapping sound. Then he sprung to his feet and exclaimed, "I've got it! I've got it!" He was obviously surprised, and more than excited! God had touched him; he began to speak in tongues. This experience would prove to be pivotal for Jeff in years to come. Regardless of the things Jeff had gone through, or what secrets he held, he knew God loved him.

Texas, Here We Come!

Joe had become unhappy with his job in our little farm community. He began to feel that we were supposed to move to Texas. I didn't share his feeling and I didn't want to go.

I thought God wanted to use me to share my newfound faith with my family. They were in Missouri, not Texas. This decision was difficult for me. God was always teaching me things about myself I didn't want to face. One of those things came to me while I was holding Rachel in the church nursery, during a church service. She was born the summer that Jeff turned eleven.

I had been memorizing 1 Peter 3:1-10 about the woman with the meek and quiet spirit. As I was pondering that in my heart. I said to God, "What exactly is a meek and quiet spirit?" His answer back to me, "Well, if you had one, Joe would have been in Texas a month ago." I guess I had my answer. It wasn't the one I was looking for, but I knew it was God.

On the way home from church that day, I shared with Joe what the Lord had spoken to me. Joe didn't want to move the family if I didn't want to go. It was a huge decision. It meant leaving our friends, church family, selling the farm and moving back into an apartment until we could get established again.

However, once Joe had the green light from me he was on his way. In a week's time, Joe had made a trip to Texas, got a job and we were planning a garage sale before a move to Texas.

Joe had to report to his job right away, so I was left with taking care of the move. I hooked a U-Haul trailer to our old station wagon and away I went. Rachel was an infant, and she cried the entire trip. Jeff and Kelly were both great to help, but it didn't stop the crying. By the time I met up with Joe I was exhausted, and very glad to see him. Joe's brother had a friend that lived in the area. He offered to keep all of us for a few days till we could find an apartment.

Fortunately, Wayne didn't seem to be too concerned about the distance we were putting between him and the kids. He had been distracted by a new woman in his life.

Surprise! God is Watching!

It didn't take long for us to settle into an apartment complex and get the kids enrolled in school. It was here that Jeff learned about the watchful eye of God.

> The eyes of the Lord are in every place, beholding the evil and the good. Pr. 5:21

Jeff was the big brother, even if he wasn't great at that role. He understood that Jesus was his savior and he had been baptized in the Holy Spirit back at the Farm. Rachel was beginning to walk; she was Joe's and my first child together, although to Joe, he was Daddy to all the kids. Kelly was only seven.

Every day I'd give money to Jeff to purchase milk at lunch time. Kelly wasn't old enough to handle money on her own, so Jeff did it for her. They always walked home together, but one day Kelly ran on ahead of Jeff to get to the house first. She burst through the door and proclaimed, "Mom, I didn't get any milk today. Jeff said he lost my money."

A few minutes later, Jeff came into the dining room. My back was turned toward him as I tended to Rachel, who was in the highchair. I ask, "Jeff, what happened to the milk money?" He answered, "I lost it."

As I turned around to look at him, there appeared a panoramic video playing before my eyes: a vision. I saw exactly what happened to the milk money. Without missing a beat or even thinking about it, I replied, "No you didn't. You bought cookies with it." He looked at me in total shock! He proclaimed in a high-pitched voice, " Where were you? Were you hiding behind the curtain? How do you know?"

God had shown me the volunteers from the PTA selling cookies, two for five cents. They were in the multipurpose room/cafeteria doing a fund raiser. I saw Jeff take Kelly's milk money and buy cookies with it. I didn't even think about what I was saying. I just knew beyond a shadow of a doubt that what I saw was from God.

Why would God do such a thing? Why would He care about something so small as milk money? Why would He care so much that my son would be caught in a lie at a young age? The answer to that is that God loves my son that much. He's His Heavenly Father, His creator. God cares about your child's destiny and purpose and He cares about yours as well.

I laugh as I remember this episode. There was nothing in the world I could've done to see this on my own. It was the love of God for my son.

> He that planted the ear, shall he not hear? he that formed the eye, shall he not see? Ps.94:9

When I told Jeff that I wasn't at school, but that God had shown me what happened, it made a lasting impression for sure. For years he believed that his Mom would know what ever he was doing. He just figured that even if he lied, I'd find out the truth somehow. As he grew older, he would test this theory from time to time, just to see if it still worked or not. I'm in awe of God, that he would love my son so much that he put an awareness of God's watchful eye on him at such a young age. Many believing adults have never even come to this reality.

God Answers Prayer

Before Joe and I married, Jeff struggled in school. As I look back, I realized he was dealing with the trauma of going through the divorce and being caught between Wayne and me. However, in time we'd learn that Jeff was really one smart kid.

He went away to Bible camp when he was twelve, and felt he'd been called to preach. He did his first sermon for Children's church. I still have that sermon, somewhere in storage on a cassette tape. He prayed often for his natural father to know God. I'm sure Jeff's constant sharing didn't set well with Wayne at the time.

Unfortunately, Jeff's interest began to change as he entered junior high. He was beginning to show some signs of rebellion.

He was smart enough that the teachers told us, "Jeff knows exactly what to do to get a passing grade. He doesn't do anything that's not absolutely required of him." I found that disappointing.

He'd been smoking since his terrible summer with Wayne when he was nine. I'm still not sure how he managed to hide that from us. Where in the world did he get the cigarettes? He'd learned to hide his deepest hurts and fears. So, by then he was quite sure that Mom didn't always know what he was up to.

We weren't in Houston very long before we moved out of the apartment and into our own home in the suburbs. Jeff attended middle school there, had his first paper route, and eventually his first business experience.

At thirteen, Jeff and Joe started a little business together. Joe and

I went to the open markets where the farmers brought the watermelons up from Brownsville, TX. We purchased hundreds of watermelons and then set up a spot on the side of the road for Jeff to sell them. Joe had a home base CB radio that stayed connected to Jeff on the road, just a mile from home. That way if anything went wrong, Joe could be there in a matter of minutes. It's obvious this kind of arrangement wouldn't work in the world we live in today. Life was much safer in the late seventies.

This business gave Jeff another opportunity to see God work in his life. It was a sunny Texas afternoon and Jeff was selling watermelons alongside of the road. He checked in hourly with us to let us know how he was doing. But this time we could tell by the sound of his voice that he was quite upset. He exclaimed, "Dad, somebody just stole four watermelons!" Jeff was really distraught. Joe said, "I'll be right there, son." Joe jumped in the car, not knowing exactly what was going on. He wanted to be sure Jeff was ok.

When Joe drove up, Jeff ran over to him. In a very incensed tone, he said, "While I was waiting on another customer, a lady took four watermelons! She put them in her car and just drove away!" Joe's response was, "Well, Jeff, what do you think we should do about that?"

Jeff answered, "I don't know Dad." Joe responded, "Let's just pray about it and call either the watermelons back, or the money." Joe was teaching Jeff to do as God does. To call things which be not, as though they were.

> ….God, who gives life to the dead and calls those things which are not as though they were. Rm. 4:17 KJV

Joe held hands with him to stand in agreement, and he let Jeff lead in prayer.

"Lord, whoever that person is that took my watermelons, I pray you speak to them to come back and pay me for them, in Jesus name."

Joe encouraged Jeff to just wait and trust God. The two of them hung out together for a while and talked about how Jeff might be more watchful. As they chatted, cars kept pulling over to Jeff's location to buy watermelons. Once Joe was confident that Jeff was safe, he went back to the house.

Within an hour or two we heard Jeff on the radio again. Very excitedly he proclaimed, "Dad, she came back and paid me for the watermelons! She even apologized. She said she spent so much time picking out the absolute best ones, that after she put them in her car she forgot to pay." Regardless, if that was true or not, Jeff's prayer had been answered very quickly.

Jeff was impressed with God's quick response. He had turned to Him with his need, and his prayers had been answered almost immediately. Oh, if I could've learned my lesson then. If I would've learned to let God answer their prayers instead of trying to be the answer for them, I could've saved myself and my children a lot of anguish.

Chapter 9

Ride 'Em Cowboy/Jeff's Teen years

Baby number four was born in Texas. We were only in the new house a short time when Samuel arrived. One evening, I walked into the bedroom where Joe was praying. He had been kneeling at the end of the bed, then he got up and stood facing the outside wall. That seemed strange, it wasn't something I'd seen him do before. I didn't say anything, I just knelt on my side of the bed to join him in prayer. In a little while he said, "Sharon, The Lord is speaking to me about something, but I can't tell you what it is. He'll have to tell you Himself." I thought that was odd, since we normally prayed about everything together.

I prayed in the Spirit for a while and then asked The Father what He wanted to say to me. He answered with one phrase, "Phoenix, Arizona."

I looked up at Joe in a questioning manner and exclaimed, "We're moving to Phoenix, Arizona?" That sounded bizarre to me, since it wasn't anything we'd ever discussed before. I thought we were settled into our new home in Texas and would be there for years.

Joe simply turned to me and said, "Yes."

Wow, I think that was the first time Joe and I had heard from God in this manner. Since we each received this Word individually, it was hard for either of us to dispute. So, we began to plan the move to Arizona. We didn't know anyone there and hadn't even ever visited the state before. We didn't have a clue what kind of employment opportunities we'd find. This was a faith move for sure. There was a lot of uncertainty, but there was also excitement. We could only imagine what Arizona held for us.

Someone asked why we would make a move like this with a family of six and no job or place to live? How could we move so far away and not know what we were going to do when we got there? The answer is we'd become people of faith. If God said it, we did it. He'd spoken clearly, and He'd caused Joe and I to be in agreement. We knew there must be something there that God wanted to reveal to us. It wasn't any different than how God had spoken many times in His Word to others. Sometimes He told them to just get up and go and He'd show them a land. At least we knew where we were going.

Our house sold almost immediately, and we packed up and began our long haul across the big state of Texas, on to New Mexico and into Arizona. It was an eleven hundred and seventy-four-mile journey. Joe drove the biggest U-Haul we could rent. Behind that he towed our van, followed by a trailer loaded with the kid's bikes and a swing set. I followed Joe driving a used thirty-five-foot motor home and towing another car. We looked like a caravan traipsing across the country. We stayed in contact with one another with our CB radios. His radio handle was "Father Abraham" and mine was "Rose of Sharon." We had four children by this time, Jeff, Kelly, Rachel, and our baby Samuel. He wasn't even walking yet. There were no GPS, cell phones or internet to guide us across the desert. At night, the long stretches between towns were in shear darkness.

When we finally arrived in Phoenix, we located an RV park and stayed there until Joe found employment. We held Church services in the recreation building at the park every Sunday. While we were there, we met people that we would remember for a lifetime.

Joe's first job as a teenager was a butcher. So, when all else failed he could usually find work in that field. At first, we rented a nice little bungalow and eventually we purchased a home on the west side of Phoenix. It had an in-ground pool and a huge room added on to the side of the house. It was simply perfect for a day care center. So, I began praying about a home day care business. In the beginning there were just a few, then another and another. Soon I was hiring people to help with the thirty children that were attending our Day Care and Pre-School.

From the very beginning I wanted to start teaching the children to read. I didn't want anyone to go through the struggles learning that I had. I latched onto a reading program with lots of music and crafts, and I began to teach little children to read. Jeff was good with the children; I always felt he'd make a great dad. He never minded changing a diaper or holding crying babies. He genuinely enjoyed being around the kids.

Eventually our Day Care area doubled for a home church. That's where I learned how hard it is to Shepard a flock. Consequently, I've had great compassion for pastor's wives. It's a balancing act that is nearly impossible to juggle.

Once Jeff became a teenager, he'd sneak the keys to the extra car. He thought he was cool, picking up his friends from school and cruising the streets of Phoenix, without his parent's knowledge. Years later, he confessed that he'd been taking one of our cars joy riding since we lived back in Texas. He wasn't of legal age to drive, so our insurance wouldn't have covered him if he'd had an accident. Kids live in the moment; they never think anything bad will ever happen to them. That's for someone else. Thank God for His protection.

> Foolishness brings joy to those with no sense; a sensible person stays on the right path. Proverbs 15:21 NLT

This was a smart kid, but common sense seemed to escape him at times. I loved Jeff with all my heart, but he nearly drove me nuts before he was grown and left home.

He started chewing tobacco. It was cool in this cowboy atmosphere of the west. He was a good-looking kid, handsome and charming in ways like Wayne. Physically he was his natural father's spitting image. Even his voice sounded the same. He can still do a perfect Wayne impression that's so realistic that it makes everyone laugh. He picked up the southwest cowboy persona easily. He and his cowboy buddies hung out together after church. Leaning up against the fence, they all looked alike. Each wore western boots, shirts, and of course, cowboy hats. It was the local teenage boy dress code.

Jeff was a talker. He could double talk to the point that when he stopped, a person would wonder what in the world were we talking about? He managed to talk his way into a job running a mechanical bull at an outside amusement park. The owner had never hired anyone under the age of eighteen, but Jeff represented himself well. He did an amazing job convincing people they needed to ride the bull. Jeff make a lot of money for the owner, so the age requirements were overlooked.

Even though we lived in a lovely home in a nice neighborhood, there were reports of violence coming from the local high school. Just blocks from our home the billboards were covered with spray painted graffiti from opposing gangs. The rivalry was being played out in the schools.

Troubled about what we were hearing. We began to look to the Word of God for answers. After searching the scriptures regarding the training of our children, we concluded that their education was our responsibility.

We began working with the education minister of our local church to establish a Christian school. We spent a full summer in meetings, planning, choosing curriculum, establishing policies and procedures and enrolling students. We were ready to open when the church became fearful over finances and shut the door of opportunity.

My heart sank. I was so disappointed. I was sure this was God's direction. I had become so passionate about establishing a school that I couldn't let go of the dream. If our church wasn't going to offer Christian education for our children, then we needed to establish one independently. We were compelled and zealous about fulfilling what we believed was God's mandate. We began with about six students plus my children in my living room, in a one room schoolhouse setting. It was just the beginning of many schools that we'd establish over the years.

There were so many people desiring Christian education for their children. However, there was no way I could handle any more than I already had. I was still running The Day Care Center.

Home schooling was virtually unheard of at the time. It was mostly reserved for the children of missionaries. I made an appointment to meet with the publishers that were supplying my reading materials for The Day Care Center. We'd never met anyone who had homeschooled. This was all new territory for us in 1979. We began working with parents to help them in educating their own children. We were criticized by family and acquaintances for our decision, but we were convicted that this was God's will.

(I removed an entire chapter from this book about our home school convictions. It's another book for another day.)

Jeff wasn't opposed to the idea of home school. He was entering the ninth grade and he'd be attending High School. We'd moved a lot and he knew what it was like to constantly make new friends. Facing new situations and always being the new kid, could be intimidating. He was delighted that we'd made the decision to homeschool.

Once I was directly involved in Jeff's learning process, I discovered that he had a photographic memory. He had been making C's in public school but at home he made a 100% on every test. I suspected that he'd gotten hold of the answer keys. So, I tested him orally, and he still got every answer correct. It seemed so unfair; he didn't even have to work at making good grades. No one had realized he had this gift. Remember, Jeff struggled in public school up till the fourth grade. So, it was amazing to find that he had this ability! This discovery proved to me that a child must want to learn, even if he is gifted. At home Jeff competed with himself. He was eager to see if he could master every single test, and he did that with ease.

The publishers we were working with were ecstatic to discover there was a whole new market for their materials among the home school community. It wasn't long before Joe and I were representing the publisher doing seminars and setting up Christian Schools in three different states.

One winter holiday we drudged through the snow in the RV to make a trip home to Missouri for Christmas. We stopped in the Springfield, MO. area along the way, and Joe fell in love with it. He couldn't get it off his mind. He prayed often for the area and began to feel we were being called there. He started looking for ways to make another move.

This was another time I wasn't thrilled about moving. We had a lovely home in Phoenix, friends, and a thriving business. I had built a relationship with all these little children and their parents. They counted on me and I'd miss them in my life.

Joe was a man of God, and I never questioned his direction for the family. I wasn't trained to see that he was also dealing with PTSD from his time in Viet Nam. It was a good thing that God used these moves for his glory, because it was just hard for Joe to stay in one place for very long.

He placed an ad in the Southern Missouri newspaper asking if anyone wanted to swap a lovely home with a pool in sunny Phoenix, Arizona for one in the Springfield area. We must have had twenty calls and we narrowed it down to about ten that we went to see. We found one family that was already packed and headed for Phoenix on a new job. Our realtor did the paperwork to swap houses for us, and we were headed back to Missouri.

Too Much Freedom

We were still house shopping in Springfield, when Jeff met his first girlfriend, Cammy. Shortly after meeting her he'd saved enough money to buy his first pick-up truck. This truck gave him a freedom he'd never experienced, and Cammy was all he could think about or talk about. He was "in love." She lived thirty miles south of us and Jeff was gone all the time. Joe was all for Jeff purchasing his first ride, but it brought out an independence in him that was on the verge of rebelliousness.

> For rebellion is like the sin of witchcraft, and stubbornness is as iniquity and idolatry…"1 Sam.15:23

I realize the prophet Samuel was speaking to King Saul in this scripture, but the truth of it still applies to all. It felt like Jeff knew how to press every button that I had. He knew how to stand on my very last nerve until I just wanted to throw him out of the house. We argued about everything, from keeping his room clean, to missing dinner and coming in late at night. I'm sure some of you can really relate.

Joe was always there to reason with me when I felt like I just couldn't take any more. Jeff and I butted heads about everything. By this time, I had grown enough in the Lord that I didn't lose my temper so much, but I still became extremely flustered when I didn't know what the answers were. This was my first child; I was still learning. I'm glad that I had more than one, because I needed the practice. Jeff was my experiment for parenting. I concluded that the rebellious teenage years are designed to help Moms to find a way to be more willing to *let* go when their children strike out on their own.

Jeff made it hard at times for me to keep my faith. He was book smart but not life smart. He couldn't wait to graduate and leave home.

The First Heart Break

We were still contending with the visits to see Wayne and the influence he had on the children's lives. In the early years it took Joe and me an entire year to get the kids back in line again. By then it was time for another visit. The visits had become fewer and fewer, with longer times in between. Despite the inconvenience and consequences of their time with their Pop, the children needed to know who their dad was, and where they came from. Both Jeff and Kelly struggled with feeling unwanted by Wayne.

Feeling this way is a hard pill to swallow and takes years of inner healing to recover fully. If that's even possible. One thing I know, God always wants us, even when we feel others may not.

> For you created my inmost being; you knit me together in my mother's womb. Ps. 139:13
>
> Before I formed you in the womb I knew you, And before you were born I consecrated you; Jer.1:5

Jeff wasn't an accident. He was planned by God. He was designed and given a destiny by the creator of the universe.

Jeff wanted to see Cammy every day. He was crazy about her and even began to talk about getting married. That was way too fast for her, by the end of the summer when Cammy went back to school, the romance was over. Jeff had been dealt his first official heart break by the opposite sex.

God continued to open doors of ministry for Joe and me, as we started establishing Christian Schools in more cities in other states. When we weren't setting up and training new schools, the children were home schooled. After a while Jeff learned to adapt with ease. As an adult he says all the moving trained him how to adjust to any circumstance or environment he found himself in. It has taught him to be very flexible. We usually stayed at each church school for a year, but at times it would only be for a semester before moving on to the next.

Even though much of Jeff's education was at home, he completed his senior year in a school we had established in Oklahoma. He was ready to graduate and wanted to be out on his own. This whole Christian life was all he had ever known, except for the times with Wayne. Now the world was calling.

Just before his eighteenth birthday, he really got mouthy and smart with me in an extremely disrespectful manner. As I mentioned, Jeff was always a very verbal person. If he got started on a topic, he could go on forever. Our conversation had turned into a battle. The arguing had escalated to the point that it just needed to stop. So, I told him to bend over and grab his ankles. Jeff knew what that meant. This was the swats position in the principal's office at school. It didn't happen often but was effective when it did. He looked at me with hatred in his eyes, but without hesitation he bent over, grabbed his ankles, and permitted me to give him swats with a paddle. I was almost surprised. He still had enough respect for me to comply and to do as I told him. I swatted him a couple of times and it was over.

> Foolishness is bound up in the heart of a child; The rod of discipline will remove it far from him. Pr.22:15 NASB

All the words had quit flying. Jeff knew he deserved to be corrected. I'd hear Jeff tell this story many times in the future. Like it was unbelievable that any parent would give a nearly eighteen-year-old swats. It's amusing that Jeff would find himself in this same position in years to come.

On his eighteenth birthday we bought him a used slide in camper for his pickup. It was fully self-contained, with a refrigerator and toilet. We knew Jeff wanted to strike out on his own. This gave us peace knowing that if he fell on hard times, he'd have the camper as a backup.

As planned, after graduation, Jeff left home at age eighteen. He'd held jobs in some of the other locations where we lived, so he returned to one of those jobs where they were happy to give him back his position. He'd always dazzled his employers with his willingness to work hard, but that was before he decided to see what the world had to offer.

He began to hang with people that were known in the community as pot heads, and soon Jeff was drinking and partaking of marijuana which was still illegal. His behavior would occasionally put Joe in a strained position.

As Principal of a Christian school, people expected more from our children. Jeff was not quite the model child for our success as parents. However, that wasn't my main concern. I was praying for Jeff to be caught doing something small, before he ended up doing something with greater consequences. Like it was with the cookies and the milk money. I knew God could do that, and He did. Within a year, Jeff was back home. He wasn't finished with the world, but he'd learned some truly valuable lessons, that would redirect his path.

While writing this last paragraph, I had to stop, and offer up praise and worship to My Father for increasing my understanding. Oh my God! I have always wondered why my kids didn't go the same way as some of the people they associated with. They didn't always make wise choices about friends.

I'm so grateful that I didn't rescue Jeff out of paying for his mistakes. Instead I prayed that if Jeff were ever headed in the wrong direction, that he'd be caught and corrected the very first time.

God answered my prayer. Late one evening we received a phone call. The voice said, "This is the Sheriff's office. Is Jeff your son?" My heart was pounding waiting for the next words. I first felt fear, then relief as they explained that Jeff was ok. They suspected him of tampering with someone's car. The atmosphere of the police station and being in custody, shook him up enough that it was the last time we ever got a call like that. He was given a warning and released.

We were in a small town and it didn't take long for most everyone to know about Jeff's little ordeal. My kids were far from perfect. If any of them did something unbecoming to "Christian" behavior, we could count on the usual question, "Are you sure The Cluck's are qualified to be leading our children?" Jeff didn't only put us on the spot but the pastor as well.

Because of our son's choices, our professional ability to lead was put in question. We lived through it. Jeff was wiser for it. The whole thing blew over and I doubt that all these years later if anyone even remembers this except our family.

So, here are the questions for this situation:

1. If your child makes a mistake, is it a reflection on you?
2. Does his failure, make you a failure?
3. Who are you really rescuing? You or him?

Jeff began to realize he needed to make some changes, so he sat down and discussed his future with us. He wanted to join the military. Joe wasn't excited about this decision. His military life was an experience he spent a lifetime recovering from. At least when Jeff wanted to join our country wasn't involved in a conflict. We didn't think he'd be going off to war.

None of us had any idea how many hoops we'd have to jump through to prove Jeff's home education. For over a month the phone calls went back and forth from the recruiting office in Oklahoma City to our home. They wanted to know what curriculum we used; did we do standardize testing to keep up with how Jeff compared to the national average. They wanted to see the test he had taken and wondered if we'd kept copies of them. The answer was yes, I'd done all that. The recruiting office decided to send an officer to our home to review our records. They kept saying Jeff hadn't graduated from an accredited high school. Finally, there was a decision: Homeschool couldn't be accredited, therefore it couldn't be a requirement. Jeff had tested so high on his MOS that they just agreed, he was good Army material. Jeff had set the precedent for Home School graduates to be inducted into US military service in the state of Oklahoma. He was the first home schooled recruit to join the military. He paved the way for thousands to come.

Jeff was sent to a duty station in New Jersey. Even though his presence could irritate me, I found that I missed him terribly. I couldn't even speak with him on the telephone. It reminded me of the awful summer of silence when he was kidnapped.

That year his birthday fell on Mother's Day. It was the first Birthday in his life that I wasn't with him. I wanted to be able to wish him Happy Birthday, and to hear his voice saying, "I love you Mom, Happy Mother's Day." I was learning to *Let go*. I had to trust that God would take care of Jeff.

As usual, that Sunday we attended church. Joe was teaching the Adult Sunday School class. Before we got started with the lesson, Joe ask if there were any prayer request? I was holding back tears already as I raised my hand and ask for prayer for Jeff and myself. Being away from home on Mother's Day and his birthdays seemed like a double whammy. Joe said, "Well, Sharon since that's on your heart, why don't you pray?" I was so distraught; I couldn't pray. I stumbled on every word as I cried all the way through my prayer. I later told Joe, "Next time someone asks for prayer, it's because they need someone else to pray for them. If they could do it themselves, they wouldn't be asking for prayer." I was just a little aggravated with him. I was wanting to be comforted. He was right. I wanted to be comforted by a human, when only God's comfort could satisfy. I wasn't worried about Jeff's safety. I was more concerned that he might feel alone. I just wanted to let him know he wasn't forgotten. He was loved and missed. I wasn't sure he knew that, and I had a need to reassure him.

I had to "*let go*". He was out in the big world, out of my reach to help or rescue him. I missed him so. I had spent seven years with Wayne. He was an Army Company Commander. So, I had a clear picture of what it looked like to be a new recruit. In addition, I'd heard Joe's stories from his training during the Vietnam era, and none of them were pleasant.

Chapter 10
The Trap

Jeff had completed basic and advanced military training and was stationed close enough to us to come home on the weekends. There wasn't much to do in our small town. Consequently, when he visited us, the skating rink was his choice for entertainment. After an evening of skating with his army buddies he came back to the house. On his arm was a sixteen-year-old girl who was literally hanging on him. She was pretty, with dark eyes and curly dark hair. Anne was rather voluptuous, chesty, and appeared quite seductive. She was constantly brushing herself up against Jeff.

The red flags went up right away. She certainly wasn't the girl of my dreams for my son. I asked her about school and how much longer she had until graduation. She said, "I don't really want to finish, but my Mother says I'm too young to get married, unless I get pregnant." I couldn't believe she just said that to me! I thought, "OH my! What are we in for now?" I desperately tried to warn Jeff that this wasn't the kind of girl that he wanted to have for a wife.

> For the lips of a strange woman drop as an honeycomb, and her mouth is smoother than oil: But her end is bitter as wormwood, sharp as a two-edged sword. Her feet go down to death: her steps take hold on hell. Pr. 5:3-5 KJV

Jeff was about to learn a very painful lesson. He was raised to believe that sex was for marriage, and this was his first real dating experience. Cammy and his relationship amounted to a few kisses and holding hands. This was about to go way beyond that. I didn't only want to rescue Jeff, I wanted to lock him up and throw away the key until this girl disappeared. However, who he dated wasn't up to me.

He made it clear to me that he was being tempted. He wouldn't listen to my warnings of a "trap" that was being set. His hormones were raging. Anne was very bold, not shy at all about what she had in mind. Even to the point of removing her clothing when they were out alone in the car. After knowing her just a matter of weeks, together they planned to get married. There was no waiting. It reminded me of that old June Carter song, "We got Married in a Fever." They drove to the Justice of the Peace and got married.

Kelly cried and pleaded with him to change his mind, but he couldn't hear her or anyone else. He was over eighteen and could legally make that decision on his own. The girl was only sixteen and her mother was happy to have someone else be responsible for her. She gladly signed the marriage consent form. After all, Jeff had a steady income and an education. He seemed like a decent catch. Jeff was always strong willed, and this was one of those times he couldn't be reasoned with.

They were married only two weeks, when Anne announced that she was pregnant. I knew she couldn't be sure of a pregnancy in such a short time. I suspected she was already pregnant before meeting Jeff. There wasn't any in-home pregnancy test available at the time. She'd have to be three months along to confirm a pregnancy, and they hadn't even known each other that long. However, Jeff was naive and ecstatic about becoming a father.

I had just learned a huge lesson from my first born. The people your child bring home with them can change every dynamic within the entire family. Your family will never be the same again.

I tried to reason with Jeff that this couldn't be his child, but he resented my interference. From the day he heard he was going to be a Dad until today, his daughter has always been treated as his very own. Even though she was born "early" it made no difference to Jeff. This was his daughter. He accepted her as a gift from God. For that I'm grateful.

This was one of many times I asked myself, "What in the world is he thinking?" I thought he was smarter than this! Did I want to rescue him? You Bet! I could see only disaster ahead, but I had no power to fix this. The truth was too painful for Jeff to even consider. He had felt unwanted by Wayne, and there was no way this baby would ever feel that way.

All we could do was to support Jeff's decisions. I was guarded where Anne was concerned because I knew she was a deceiver. I wondered what else she might be capable of? Our hope was that Jeff had been thoroughly grounded in The Word. We wanted to believe that would give him what he needed to endure whatever was ahead. There was always the possibility she'd find God. We prayed that this marriage would turn out to be successful.

It wouldn't be long before Jeff realized how very promiscuous Anne was. After the baby was born, she openly had one affair after the other. She made no attempt to hide it from Jeff. There were many one-night stands. His life became a living nightmare. He had a military career and a daughter to raise; both were in jeopardy.

He was given an overseas assignment and was able to take his family with him. Life there didn't improve, instead Anne stepped up her destructive behavior. When Jeff was in the field for training, she was out on the town. Her new trick was writing bad checks. There were so many that Jeff was called in for disciplinary action about his finances. Anne made the rounds with one man after another until it came to the attention of Jeff's supervisors. This was totally unacceptable behavior for a US citizen as a guest in a foreign country. Jeff wanted to make a career of the military. He had eight years in already, but with this wife, that wasn't going to happen. He was given some ultimatums. He decided to come back home.

It would be years before Joe and I understood how terrible this time in Jeff's life was. He was so emotionally distraught he could barely function. Anne was uncontrollable!

Another baby was born while Jeff and Anne were overseas. Her activities left the family wondering if this was Jeff's child or not. Jeff had been the child of divorce and he didn't want to repeat that history for his own children. When he returned from the military, he came home to Missouri with our two grandchildren. It was the first time I'd seen the youngest.

When Your Hands Are Tied

Often parents are hit with the realization that their children have children. They're now YOUR grandchildren, and your kids can't seem to take care of them the way you think they should. What do you do? Most want to rescue those sweet little babies. You feel responsible. This is where the sleepless nights begin. You imagine the worse. Maybe they're hungry, maybe they're cold. Maybe they don't have enough warm clothes. Now your peace has been disturbed.

We prayed about the situation. Most of those prayers were asking God what we could do to fix things. We weren't asking God if he had a plan. Most people don't really focus on how God wants to show himself strong. We're too busy wanting to swoop in and take care of things ourselves. Is it possible we have a secret wish to be a hero? Just something to consider.

When our child's finances or their marriage is in trouble, often the response is, "What can I do to help?" That seems to be the norm in this country. We don't want our children to go through the same struggles we did. So, we try to step in to FIX it for them. Sometimes we reason within ourselves now that there are grandchildren to consider we feel more obligated than ever.

How do we explain that most of us survived without too much help from our parents? For some reason in today's world, parents don't believe their kids can do the same thing.

Jeff's marriage was a disaster from the very beginning. It was built on lies, deception, and two people being unequally yoked.

> Be ye not unequally yoked together with unbelievers: for what fellowship hath righteousness with unrighteousness? and what communion hath light with darkness? II Cor. 6:14

Jeff had fallen into the same trap I had. He was losing his faith due to the choices he'd made. Choices determined by the flesh and not by the spirit.

> This I say then, Walk in the Spirit, and ye shall not fulfil the lust of the flesh. Gal. 5:16

After Jeff and Anne returned to the states, they had baby number three. Joe and I helped financially whenever we could. We still had Rachel and Sam at home, and I had gone back to school. They moved into one of our rental houses and Jeff took a job as an over the road truck driver. Anne rarely told him what was going on in his absence. We had bailed them out a few times, but it never seemed to last. When the next month rolled around, they needed help again.

The brisk cool days of fall set in, followed by those cold, snowy Missouri nights. The electric and gas were both shut off at their house for non-payment. There was no heat in the middle of winter! Anne and the grandkids were using candlelight to see their way around. We worried that one of the kids might turn over a candle and start a fire. Anne was a terrible housekeeper, and only left pathways to walk through the clutter. We were alerted to the situation when Ashley, our oldest granddaughter, said something about how she loved all the candles, causing us ask questions.

We spoke with Jeff about our concerns on the phone, but he took it as criticism. Anne had already put her slant on things, saying we were trying to control her. Jeff knew better, that we were just worried about the kid's safety. We were busy and had our own lives to live. We weren't looking for more responsibility. Anne let us know that if we didn't mind our own business, she'd cut us off from ever seeing the grandchildren.

I know many of you have faced similar situations. If you haven't, count your blessings.

> There hath no temptation taken you but such as is common to man: but God is faithful, who will not suffer you to be tempted above that ye are able; but will with the temptation also make a way to escape, that ye may be able to bear it. 2 Cor.10:5 KJV

The fear of being cut off is a pretty common problem for parents. This seems to be one of the "go-to" control maneuvers that is often used, prohibiting contact with the grandchildren. Even if not verbalized, it can be an implied threat. The enemy will make sure those fears are projected in your direction.

That's why the scriptures tell us:

> Casting down imaginations, and every high thing that exalted itself against the knowledge of God and bringing into captivity every thought to the obedience of Christ. 1 Cor. 10:5 KJV

It can be hard to think rationally when the enemy is bombarding you with threats and negative thoughts. Sometimes we feel like we're darned if we do, and darned if we don't. Fear is the root of confusion in these situations. I remind you:

> There is no fear in love; but perfect love casteth out fear: because fear hath torment. He that feareth is not made perfect in love. 1 John 4:18 KJV

Fear really does have torment. It makes the imagination project all kinds of scenarios. What can you possibly do? How can *you fix* it?

The big question is why do we think that fixing it is our job?

Jeff's solution to the problem was to get home as quickly as possible. He picked Anne and the kids up and took them in the truck with him. They acted as if we were the enemy and they needed to escape from our critical influence.

After years of this craziness, one evening Jeff drove by the house to have a talk with me. I was glad he still felt that he could confide in me. Anne had no relationship with her family and resented that Jeff had one with his. He began opening up to me. He said, "Mom, I'm going to get a divorce." I knew something had to have prompted this decision. It had to be greater than the fear of losing his kids. That threat was a powerful controlling tool Anne had wielded over him for years.

Jeff had befriended someone who had been in a similar situation. They found the courage to get out and start over. Their story and friendship empowered Jeff to think there might be life after this disastrous mess he found himself in. Anne wasn't only immoral; she had become physically violent with Jeff. He was beginning to better understand why I had left Wayne. He was now living his own nightmare.

Bypassing all the ugly details, Jeff's marriage ended in divorce. I never wanted Jeff to have to endure this kind of pain. It was a terrible ordeal for him. We could only watch as he struggled to hold onto his sanity. Anne played one mind game after another with him. She continued taunting him about losing his children. He had an out of control wife. Jeff loved his kids and loved being a Dad. Joe and I could do little except to help out financially and pray. Jeff would have to do some letting go of his own. He hated the idea of having a failed marriage. Jeff stayed until he could endure no more.

In the divorce Anne got custody of the children and moved back to Texas. Jeff didn't give up. He believed with all his heart that he would get his kids back. Anne was just mean! She tried to crush him, tormenting him that his first child wasn't even his. She insisted because of that Jeff would never get custody of her. That was a fact Jeff never wanted to face. It was a fear that haunted him in the back of his mind for years. Now it was being weaponized against him.

Jeff tried to move on with his life and that's when he met Les. She had two children of her own. Jeff saw this as a second chance at love. In addition, having Les in his life, gave him hope that he just might be able to regain custody of his children.

The Pennsylvania Road Experience

Jeff was still driving the semi-truck for a living. Occasionally Leslie road along with him. His life with Anne had pulled him further and further away from God. One wintery day on a snowy Pennsylvania Highway, Jeff began to sing a song he remembered from his youth. The words went like this: "The zeal of God has consumed me deep in my soul, A fire that keeps burning, A fire that cannot be quenched. Oh Hallelujah, Hallelujah, Oh Hallelujah, Halle, Halle, Hallelujah."

First, he started to hum. Then he began singing softly, as he remembered the words more clearly. As his heart welled up with the memories of a loving God, he kept singing the same words over and over. As the presence of God intensified his voice became louder, and louder. Then warm tears began streaming down his face. Without realizing it, Jeff had begun to worship God. He remembered the passion of his youth serving God. The zeal of God truly was consuming him. These were not just words to a song. It was really happening. The presence of an All Mighty God filled the cab of his truck that day. Finally, his vision was too blurry from crying to continue to drive. He was weeping so hard under the power of the Holy Spirit, he had to stop. It had become difficult for him to see the road in front of him. He pulled the truck over at a rest stop and got out in the snow. His crying had become wailing. He fell to his knees in worship, lying face down in the snow as he cried out in repentance. He began speaking loudly in his spiritual prayer language before the LORD.

Les had never seen anything like this before. She was fearful, not understanding what was going on with Jeff. She hurried to find a pay phone to call us. When I answered the phone she said, "Sharon, I'm with Jeff in the truck and I think he's having a nervous breakdown!" When she told me what he was doing and how it started, I simply said, "Les, leave him alone. He'll be fine. He's praying in tongues and repenting."

She was relieved to learn all this was a good thing. I hung up the phone and told Joe what was going on. We wept and thanked Jesus for restoring our son. His Word was true! "When he is old, he will not depart."

This event, which we call "The Pennsylvania Road Experience," turned Jeff around. Les was involved in a religion many consider to be a cult. As Jeff shared his faith with her, she began to embrace his God. He had returned to the God of his youth. Hallelujah!

Chapter 11

The Test

By the time Jeff married Les, we had helped him out financially several times. Joe decided to start a ledger for what he owed us. We felt this was a way to teach him responsibility. It allowed him to see in writing that we'd helped him. It was just too easy to forget. We still had two children at home ourselves and only Joe was working.

Jeff was looking for a way to be self-employed. He asked Joe and I about helping him establish a carpet cleaning business. Together we sat down and worked out the details, paid for equipment, ran ads. We obligated ourselves for a year on a yellow page add and telephone cost. Shortly after the launch of this new adventure, there was a misunderstanding about letting Jeff's little sister, Rachel, take a job for him. He wasn't able to work into the customer's time schedule, so Joe asked her to do it. Instead of working things out, Jeff just quit. We ended up with all the equipment, expenses and no one to do the carpet cleaning business. For a year, the phone rang with people wanting their carpets cleaned and we had to tell them the Yellow page ad was no longer in effect.

> He that is surety for a stranger shall smart for it:..... Ps. 11:15

We've learned, it doesn't matter if it's a stranger or not. Surety is not a sure thing. It is just not a smart thing to do. Even for your own children.

Jeff and Les didn't rush into marriage, like he did with Anne. They planned a simple wedding in a local park where they were married, and Joe performed the ceremony for them. Les had two children of her own. Their biological father wasn't in the picture. He'd moved to Canada to avoid child support. So, Jeff did as he'd learned from Joe. He took on two more kids. He'd be their Dad in every way.

Jeff was determined to get custody of his children but had no idea how it would ever happen. He heard reports of the children being neglected and abused. He was becoming desperate to find a way to get them back in his care, into a safe environment. He hadn't forgotten the roots of his upbringing and his faith in God. He prayed about this often. Then one day, for some unknown reason, Anne phoned Jeff and told him if he still wanted custody of the children, she was willing to give them up. To make it legal she'd be required to sever her parental rights and it would be necessary for Les to adopt all three.

Several days before Anne's call, Joe and I had been praying for Jeff. The Lord showed me how we'd been enabling our son. As I prayed, I had a vision. I saw Leslie and Jeff gripped securely in the hand of Almighty God. They were being held in His fist and it was facing downward. God slowly opened His hand and released them. They started to tumble downward, tossing and turning in mid-air. As they were falling, they were calling out, but they weren't calling out to God! They were calling out to Joe and me. In this vision Joe and I ran under them trying to catch them in our hands to take care of their circumstances. We always wanted to make life easier for them. We wanted to rescue them.

The Lord spoke strongly to me. He said, "*Sharon get out of MY way!* If you will get out of the way, when I let go of Jeff and Leslie, they'll see that you aren't going to catch them. When they realize that you aren't going to soften their landing, then they'll call out to me. **I** will swoop down, and **I** will catch them in the palms of my hands. I'll become forever their God. I'll become their provider. I will be their God and not the God of their Mother and Father, but *YOU* must first get out of the way!"

Wow! I had been spanked. I had become God in my children's life. I was promoting idolatry in my own son. I had become the answer to his prayers. Joe and I both knew I had heard from God. I couldn't disobey. We knew if God had spoken so clearly, that there would be a test. I had no idea how difficult this test would be.

This was a *big* correction from Yahweh. I knew what I heard was true. I was in God's way.

> For whom the Lord loveth he chasteneth, and scourgeth every son whom he receiveth. Heb. 12:6

Joe and I had become Jeff and Les' god in a sense. Why did they need God? They had us. This was a hard word for me to hear.

> Trust in the Lord with all thine heart; and lean not unto thine own understanding. Pr. 3:5

In one fleeting moment, in one picture, I had a complete understanding of what God was asking of me. Joe and I prayed together and agreed that we'd be obedient to the vision. We'd have to let Jeff and Les find their help in The One True God.

Just days after this vision, the telephone rang, it was Jeff. He said, "Mom, Anne called. She said she'd agree to let me and Leslie adopt the children. But I've got to act quick. She might change her mind. I need to have at least $500.00 before a lawyer will even talk to me. We're going to need to do three adoptions."

I had the money to give to Jeff, but I couldn't do it. I told Jeff what God had told me. He couldn't believe what he was hearing! This was his Mom and Dad that had been there all along. We'd been there to help with the rent or utilities, or to help set up a part time business. We'd borne the expense on other things that weren't nearly as important as this, and now we were saying, "No."

Jeff was desperate, he needed help with getting the kids, and I had to say "No." Jeff was really angry with me! His response was, "Mom, these are your grandkids we're talking about, how can you say no to me about this?" I answered, "Yes, Jeff, I know that, but I've heard from God and I have to be obedient to his voice. I'm sorry."

I knew this decision would cause me to experience rejection from my son. I desperately didn't want that to happen. More than that, I didn't want to be disobedient and a disappointment to my God.

I knew the grandchildren were in a bad place. Anne's phone call to Jeff was an answer to prayer for him. If he could get them back, it would end the evil influence of their mother once and for all. We all believed the grand children were in danger. However, we also knew this was *THE test* of obeying God or being deliberately disobedient to His instructions. I wanted so badly to say, "Yes," but I knew God must have a better plan, no matter what it looked like at that moment. I wanted to help, but I trusted that it was better to obey God. That His ways are higher than ours. It didn't make sense to me, but I would choose to obey. I'd better be sure that I'd heard from God. My grandchildren's futures were at stake.

> Ye shall walk in all the ways which the Lord your God hath commanded you, that ye may live, and that it may be well with you, ...Deut. 5:33

Well with me.... I knew if I were obedient, God would make sure it would be well for Jeff and for my grandchildren. God was so much smarter than me, but I had no clue how He was going to work this all out.

I told Jeff, "I've been instructed to get out of the way, and let you work this one out on your own." It would've been very easy to be persuaded by Jeff's anger and disappointment with me. No mother wants to feel like she has abandoned her child to the point he may never speak to her again. I'd never told him, "no" about money before, and to start saying no with such a monumental issue was very hard for him, and for me as well. I was *letting go*, I was relinquishing any and all influence in this situation. It was scary, but I had no choice. This is what The Lord had clearly spoken to me.

> Examine me, O Lord, and prove me; try my reins and my heart. Ps. 26:2

I hung up the phone and cried. Joe held me as I wept in his arms. I chose to obey God, but would it cost me my child and my grandchildren?

We were about to find out. Joe and I were praying for God to show up Big Time, but How? We couldn't even imagine. Together we began to thank God for taking care of our kids better than we could. This was an extremely hard place for all of us. It was all by faith.

Definitions:

One of the definitions of a test is: the means of determining the presence, quality, or truth of something; a trial.

God Answers Big Time

Jeff phoned Wayne to ask for help. He too said "No." In our estimation, Wayne had become a wealthy man. With Jeff's influence he had been born again. I don't know what made him say, "no," but I believe it was God's direction that he did. Leslie called her parents who also were financially able to assist. They owned a trucking company in another state. They said "No".

All their earthly sources had dried up. Jeff and Les had to turn to the only source they had left, and that was God. Together they sought Him for direction. Then it happened! Jeff felt impressed to start calling around and talking to attorneys, even though he had no money. Now he was moving in faith!

As he began to make calls, he was told by each lawyer that they required a retainer, but Jeff didn't give up. The next call produced some hope. This attorney spoke with him and asked, "Where are you from? Did you grow up in this area? Where did you go to high school?"

Jeff replied, "I was home schooled." That was it, that was the answer! Jeff's reply caught the attorney's attention. He stopped Jeff in the middle of his sentence, and said, "Wait a minute, you graduated from home school?" Jeff answered, "Yeh, why?" The attorney began questioning Jeff about his home school experience. He realized Jeff was quite knowledgeable about the subject,

Home schooling was still a new concept in those days. Not many people were familiar with the process. The attorney desired for his children to be taught at home but had no idea how to get started. They had been praying for direction, and now it appeared that was coming through Jeff. The lawyer realized this phone call was his answer to prayer as well as Jeff's. It was a doubly answered prayer!

He said to Jeff, "I'll tell you what we can do. Let's barter. You teach my wife how to get started home schooling our children and I'll handle all three adoptions for you, no charge." Here was a professional man willing to barter with Jeff for knowledge he came by just through experience. He could've never known that something that seemed so simple to him, would be so valuable to someone else. God had provided the answer for both of them!

As I reflect on this, I realize that Jeff's answer to prayer had been put in motion for him back in the ninth grade, when I decided to home school. Had I continued to rescue him then, I might still be doing it today.

God had heard Jeff's cries. He heard the heart of a man just wanting to be a father to his children, just like God wanted to be to my son.

The two men became friends, building a mutual respect. Jeff's attorney buddy handled all legal matters for Jeff for many years. My grandchildren were finally going to be with their Dad. There would be no more fear of the conditions or unknown situations that the kids were being exposed to with Anne.

Together Jeff and Les had five children. Over time they had eight more, all with Biblical names.

Years later, Anne had other children that ended up in foster care. When one of them became eligible for adoption, Jeff was contacted. His children were half sisters and brothers to her fostered child. They were this child's only relatives, so Jeff was given the opportunity to adopt her as well. She was already sixteen. To my surprise, he and Les agreed. I still shake my head in disbelief that there are people in this world that do these kinds of things. I have never known them to ever turn away anyone that needed a place to live. I'll say it again; my children are unique individuals. They aren't perfect, but both Jeff and Les have very big hearts.

Jeff stayed upset with me for a few months and did the same with Wayne. In time, after the fear had passed, he began to call again.

My Daddy used to have a saying. They get mad, and they can get glad. Just give them time.

Thoughts to Ponder

The definition of extortion: The practice of obtaining something, especially money, through force or threats.

I'm not implying in any way that my son attempted to extort anything from me in any way. He simply asked for a loan.

However, because I have been in health care for decades, I have seen family extortion repeatedly. When a person wants to freely give out of the goodness of their heart, things that are theirs to give to whomever they wish, *that* is a *gift.* When a person is manipulated, coerced, or controlled with threats, spoken or implied, it becomes *extortion.*

Ten Questions to ask yourself when it comes to helping someone financially:

1. Why am I doing this?
2. Do I have to do this?
3. Do I feel obligated?
4. Do I really want to do this out of the goodness of my heart?
5. Do I feel threatened in any way? (ie: isolation, rejection, loss of control)
6. Is this for the good of everyone involved?
7. What will happen if I don't do this?
8. Are the consequences real or imagined?
9. Am I stealing glory from God by being the answer when He is just waiting to deliver?
10. What happens when I'm no longer around to be the answer?

This isn't about being stingy. It's about being led by God to do what is best for your children and yourself even when it's uncomfortable. It's about walking in faith towards God. If He becomes the answer, He gets glory and we get freedom. Will it be you or God who walks through the valley with them? Money and what we do with it can be a good thermometer in gauging our trust in God.

Vindication

As the adoptions were completed Jeff could clearly see that God had answered his cry for help in a miraculous way. He began to relax as the fear of losing his kids passed. He realized that what Mom said was true. God really was his provider.

Remember, Jeff loved the underdog and the needy. He had started a ministry to the homeless in Kansas City, Mo. He touched many lives in this community.

One Christmas holiday, Joe and I drove to visit Jeff and his family and to meet some of the men he was helping on the streets. Most these men lived under the bridge by the railroad tracks. Jeff had befriended them and gained their confidence to the point that they readily accepted Joe and me into their camp. They were eager to meet Jeff's Mom and Dad.

During that week, one evening after visiting with the men, the four of us, Jeff and Les and Joe and I, stopped to have dinner at a near-by restaurant. We were doing some reminiscing and the subject of the children's adoption came up.

Jeff and Les got quiet for a second or two, and then the two of them looked across the table at Joe and me. Jeff said with all sincerity, "Mom, I need to thank you." I was surprised. I waited for him to continue. "I want to thank you for saying No to helping us with the adoption." I could hardly believe my ears. Jeff added, "Mom, that was the best thing you ever did for us. Les and I have learned that God is our source of supply, and that He isn't just the God of my mother and father. He's our personal Savior. He wants to meet our needs. He cares about every little detail in our lives and I can tell you that He's never failed us this far." Les nodded her head in agreement. Tears came to my eyes. I realized that I had *let Jeff go*. God directed me to do one of the hardest things in my life.

I didn't want to tell Jeff, "No." I wanted to tell him, "Yes." He never knew when I hung up the phone that day, that I bawled my eyes out. I had the financial means and I wanted to help. I felt like my heart was breaking because I couldn't help him when he needed it so badly. The reward of seeing Jeff learn to trust God was great! This was so much better than if Joe and I had been his answer. He had learned a priceless lesson. He had learned to make God his own personal savior and provider.

When it Looks like you are the only answer to your children's prayer/situation, it's just not true. God is on His Throne, and He wants to reign in your child's life.

If we, as parents, don't allow our children to fall into God's hands, because we are always there to catch/rescue them, they'll never know him as *Father*. They will not have a relationship with the Father as their personal provider. He'll always be the God of their Mother/Father, and they'll never know The King of the Universe as their source in every situation.

> ... for your heavenly Father knoweth that ye have need of all these things. But seek ye first the kingdom of God, and his righteousness; and all these things shall be added unto you. Matt. 6:33. KJV

> ….no good thing will he withhold from them that walk uprightly. Ps. 84:11 KJV

The year Jeff turned forty he and Les both decided to go back to school. They both graduated with highest honors, in the education field. They managed to do that with a house full of children and keeping the bills paid.

A year or so ago, Joe and I visited with Jeff and his family in Alaska.

We were blessed to be able to sit in on some of their classes and to witness firsthand what great teachers they are.

They'd been married nearly twenty-six years then. The first five children are all grown and have children of their own. While there, Les said, "I want to tell you again how grateful I am that you were obedient to God about the adoption of the kids. It was a test for all of us. We still live our lives by that vision. We learned such a great lesson. It's the way we deal with our grown children. They must learn to live this life without us holding them up. We want them to have their own personal relationship with God and to know He's their provider. They know we expect them to be productive, successful adults, and Thank God, they are."

God's word to me that day has stood the test of time. They've filtered down now to the second and the third generation. How grateful I am to my Creator for the "rhema." (the words He speaks directly to our hearts in the midst of a situation) He already knew what the outcome of my obedience would be. I was the one that didn't.

I believed I was really taking a chance by telling Jeff, "No," but God is faithful.

> Know therefore that the Lord thy God, he is God, the faithful God, which keepeth covenant and mercy with them that love him and keep his commandments to a thousand generations; Dt. 7:9

In my heart I knew it was better to obey God than to be controlled by what any man, including my son would think of me.

> Then Peter and the other apostles answered and said, We ought to obey God rather than man. Acts 5:29

This was a huge lesson for me to learn as a parent. I had to *let go,* and let God, for Jeff to become the man God had called him to be. It helped that I had a Godly partner that kept encouraging me to remain faithful to the vision. Thank you Joe.

Chapter 12
Then There Was Kelly

One sleepy afternoon, I laid down for a short nap, and I had a very vivid dream. As the dream unfolded, I could see there was a family that had a missing child. Some speculated that he might be a runaway. However, all the parents knew for sure was that he was missing, and they were worried sick. He was on the streets, who knew where? I was feeling the anguish of these parents as they worried. They wept and sought God fervently for his return. I was feeling their intense longing after him and all their fears. There was such pain as they wondered where he is sleeping tonight. What is he finding to eat? How is he existing? Who was he with, and yes..... was he even still alive? Had he left of his own free will? Had he chosen to completely reject them and their entire family? Maybe he was kidnapped. Was he coerced to leave? "Where God! Where is he?" I saw as they pleaded with God, "Please God, please, bring our son home safely." Their imaginations went wild as they were bombarded with thoughts from the enemy.

As I awoke, I was so troubled. This dream seemed so real. I felt like I was living it. All the fears and emotions were mine. Even though I was watching from afar, I could feel everything these parents were feeling. I began to realize how much I could relate to them. After all, I too had a missing child. She was not a runaway. She hadn't willfully rejected us, but she had been captured by someone that we trusted. She had been, in a sense, brain washed. She was just gone like the young man in the dream. I questioned God. Did she choose this path? Is she abused? Is she being held captive against her will? How could she willingly reject everything she ever knew, and choose to believe lies? How could someone so deceive her?

...who you yield your members to is your master. Rm. 6:16

Kelly's Story.

Kelly, Jeff's little sister, was born in the throes of the Viet Nam war in the late sixties. Wayne was going through military flight school when she was conceived. We had just survived another separation and were living through yet another reconciliation. This time was different I thought, because Wayne had agreed to counselling. With fresh hope I believed the major issues were behind us.

Flight school seemed to be fertile ground. Nearly every day we heard of another wife of a flight student announcing her pregnancy. I envied them because I wanted a second child. When I found out I was pregnant, I was delighted. I thought our marriage had stabilized, and this baby was the blessing that would expand our family.

I was only twenty years old, living in a little military town in southern Alabama. I was a long way from home, and I missed my family. Many mobile home parks speckled the landscape, filled with the temporary residents from the flight school. None of us were fortunate enough to afford a telephone. The cost of long distance was completely out of reach on a flight student's puny income. At least once a week I sat at my kitchen table, in my tiny ten by fifty-foot trailer, to write a letter home. In all the time I was gone, I never received one letter in return. My Mom never wrote back. My parents were working people and had a very active social life. Every few weeks, I'd head to a pay phone with a hand full of quarters and call Mom for just a few minutes. Getting to hear my mother's voice was a boost for me. Now and then I got a letter from my Mother-in-law or my sister Sandy.

Completing flight school was a major event for both Wayne and me. His graduation was the first of many formal events we'd attend now that Wayne was an officer. Wayne's mom and stepdad flew down to attend the festivities with us. We were all so proud of Wayne's accomplishments.

After flight school Wayne was stationed in Kansas, where the winds blow hard, winters are cold, and the summers are hot. We hadn't yet moved to base housing when Kelly was due to be born. Instead we found a cute little house off base. It was on a dirt road in a tiny country town of about 200 people. The old man across the street loved having Jeff around. He enjoyed taking him for buggy rides, drawn by his horse. Jeff was just four years old and I'll never forget the wonder and amazement he experienced as he witnessed One of Mr. Green's ponies being born. He was in awe that it "learned" to walk the very first day of life.

I was past my due date with Kelly, so we had a scheduled labor induction planned at the hospital in Abilene. Once labor started, Kelly was born within an hour. I learned later that when labor is induced, often the child will have a more aggressive personality. That certainly proved to be true of Kelly. I so wanted a little girl, and now I was happy to be holding her in my arms. Oh my! Those eyes! Huge, round blue eyes that could win your heart at a glance. She was cute as a button, constantly smiling and just a happy soul.

She was the only baby in the nursery, and the nurses drove me nuts with wanting to hold her. Kelly was beautiful, with her red hair, ivory skin, and happy nature. What a joy she was!

When I became pregnant with Kelly, I was forced to learn to sew. I didn't have much choice. I was expecting and there weren't any shops locally to purchase maternity clothes. Wayne and I went shopping for a sewing machine and fabric. Neither of us had any idea what I should buy or what we were doing. Eventually, I learned by trial and error. One mistake at a time. I ripped out stitches and tried until I got it right. Over time, I became exceptionally skilled, and used this talent to bless others with many unique creations. The memories are plentiful.

Kelly was only about four months old when her father was deployed to Viet Nam. I went back home to St. Louis, where I had been raised. Conditions for military families were extremely different than they are today. There were no cell phones, computers, or skype connections. I managed to speak to Wayne one time over a delayed ham radio the whole time he was overseas. It was more like the TV series "MASH." It reminded me of watching Radar trying to crank up the radio for Colonel Potter to contact headquarters.

Our marriage was on the rocks again when he left. He had completed only three months of his tour of duty, when he was summoned home because his mother was dying. It's highly questionable that our marriage would have continued under any other circumstances.

I'd learned to love my Mother-in-law and the notion of losing her was painful for me. She'd taught me lots of little things I hadn't learned from my own Mom. Like how to make a great gravy and to stew a chicken. Oh, most importantly, she taught me to say yes or ok to her when I was with her, then go do as I pleased when I left. She actually told me, "When we're together, just act like you're listening, and nod your head ok, then when you leave do what suits you, and we'll get along just fine." She was a strong woman. She had been through a lot being married to Wayne's dad. She fought so hard those last few months of life. I'm sure she knew God.

I think she was teaching me to know how to choose my battles. Not everything is worth a discussion or worth fighting over.

After her funeral, Wayne was reassigned state side again. The war was winding down, so instead of requiring him to return to Viet Nam he was given new orders. The constant moving was one of the things that drove me crazy about the military. We had to be ready to move at any time, without much notice. We never knew where or when that might be. There seemed to be no stability for military families.

Wayne was transferred to Kentucky. This is where he fell back into his old patterns of cheating again. It was worse than ever, one woman after the other. I was so finished.

The kids and I piled everything into my new little VW bug that I had purchased with money from my part time job. We headed home to be near family. I never looked back. I knew I had finally made the right decision for me and for my children.

After a time at Mom and Dad's and then with my sister, I settled in a place of my own. That's where my Dad came to see me and got me to break enough to finally cry again.

He taught me that I couldn't be afraid of being hurt. I had to allow myself to be vulnerable to truly live. I learned to live my life by that lesson. The rest of my life I would look at every disappointment as an opportunity to get up again. Thank you, Daddy. My Dad had been abandoned by his own father and placed in an orphanage. He had no example of what a Dad is supposed to be. Looking back, he did an incredible job with the hand he'd been dealt.

With this lesson learned, I got through my first semester at the University. I found a new job and moved back to my parent's neighborhood in the city. This is where I met Diane and recommitted my life to the Lord.

Kelly didn't respond to pain like other children do. We finally realized she was born without a sense of pain. Consequently, she had to be watched carefully, because she couldn't let me know when she was hurting. Before I left Wayne, she'd already broken a leg sliding down a playground slide. We couldn't tell there was anything wrong, she never cried or showed any signs of pain. The only clue was that her body shook when she stood up.

Around two years old she burnt her forearm badly on the oven door, and we didn't realize it till the next day when her skin was stuck to her pajamas. Another time her eardrum broke, and it wasn't detectable until it began to drain. From all this, Kelly learned that she might get hurt and not know it. Her response was to overreact, carrying on like she was dying when it was just a little scratch. This irritated her teachers in kindergarten and first grade. I explained to them that if they reassured her that she was ok, then she'd stop crying. She just had no way of knowing if she was hurt or not.

By the time Kelly was seven the sense of pain was beginning to develop, and I could relax a little. I didn't have to be so vigilant in checking every little booboo to see if it might be something more sinister. The doctors told us she had a slow maturing nerve connection. That in time it would resolve itself. Until it did, it was scary for us both.

Kelly has no memory of ever living with Wayne, the breakup, the broken leg, or any of those events mentioned. That's probably why she took to Joe so readily; she was four when I met him. Kelly was a happy, active little girl that never knew a stranger. Her red hair had faded to blond and it was beautiful. I always said Kelly had enough hair for two people, it was so full and thick. She laughed and smiled all the time. She was a delightful child.

Jesus Loves Me

Kelly loved Joe from the first time she laid eyes on him. He was her Daddy. Joe was her "real" Daddy. Over the years Kelly would try to connect with Wayne, but she kept coming away disappointed.

Kelly loved sitting in church with Joe and me. Each week when the alter call was given, she'd ask to go to the front of the church. She kept asking if she could go to be saved. She'd say to us, "I want to go up and give my heart to Jesus." Joe and I both felt that at four and a half years old, she was too young to make that decision. This continued each week until one Sunday morning Kelly said, "Please can I go? If I don't go now, I'll never get a chance to go again." She was always saying stuff like that. She'd make remarks that sounded like she knew something we didn't. Joe and I looked at each other a little confused, but then we agreed to let her go to the front of the church and make a commitment to Jesus. We figured the Pastor would know best how to handle it. He spoke with Kelly for a while, and when he was finished, he announced to the congregation, "I know this child is small, but I believe she knows exactly what she's doing. She wants to give her heart to Jesus." He didn't want to hinder her in any way, so he scheduled her baptism.

As I helped Kelly into her little white baptismal gown, it was apparent that she was seeing something that I wasn't. According to Kelly, it was a very active day, back behind the baptistery curtains. She said, "Mommy there's angels here. They came to see me baptized." This is how it would be with Kelly. She knew God and could see into another realm. She was never quiet about her encounters. She knew what she was seeing and found it hard to believe that others didn't see the same things she did.

> Take heed that ye despise not one of these little ones; for I say unto you, That in heaven their angels do always behold the face of my Father which is in heaven. Matt. 18:10

Chapter 13
Simple Faith

Following our wedding Joe and I moved the family to the country. Farm life was so different for the children and me. I had lived in the city all my life, but Joe was a country boy. He was raised very different than me, in many ways. His heritage was more wholesome, less about things. The kids and I had never even had a pet, and now there was a dog and a cat, chickens and eventually a couple of horses. As you might expect, Kelly really connected with nature. She was an animal lover extraordinaire. To hear it from her, you could never have enough animals, and even at five, she fancied herself an expert.

I don't know how this started but she had a connection with rocks. They just fascinated her. (As a grown woman, she has vases of rocks all over her house like other women have vases of flowers.)

She had just turned five, when she decided to take a walk by herself on the backside of our thirteen acres. This was a beautiful piece of property, with large trees blowing gently in the wind. The grass was high in the back field as it swayed in the breeze. It was probably up to her waist in places. On this warm summer afternoon, the sounds of the water could be heard flowing in the nearby creek that ran through the property. The bottom of the creek was covered in large slate rocks that stood up just over the water level in spots. It formed little bridges across it here and there.

Kelly had been gone for a little while when I looked out the window and saw her running toward the house. She burst through the door panting breathlessly, and exclaimed, "Mommy, Mommy, I can speak in tongues!" I knelt down in front of her where I could see her eye to eye. I said, "Kelly, tell me what happened." She answered, "I was walking through the field singing to Jesus and telling Him I love Him. Then this great big wind came and knocked me backward. I fell on the ground. When I got up and started to sing again it came out different. Not English, but a different language!" One she hadn't known.

Wow! Joe had struggled to be filled with the Spirit of God for years, and all Kelly had to do is take a walk. For sure God is sovereign. Kelly had received her heavenly language, and no one even prayed for her. It was just dropped on her by the Holy Spirit.

> .....And Jesus saith unto them, Yea; have ye never read, Out of the mouth of babes and sucklings thou hast perfected praise? Matt. 21:16

> He that believeth on me, as the scripture hath said, out of his belly shall flow rivers of living water. Jn.7:38

Kelly wanted to tell everyone about her Jesus and her experience in the back field. We were always active in church and did devotions twice a day. Consequently, she and Jeff had knowledge of the scriptures from an early age.

She's Not Yours

I was still new in my faith and sometimes my exuberance overwhelmed Joe. I thought if there was a church in town with their doors open, we should be there. It didn't matter if it was a work night or not. I didn't want to miss out on one thing. Joe was much more mature than I, but he was also kind and patient with me. It goes without saying, we didn't make every service. However, from time to time we'd attend a local revival.

One night we visited a revival service near us. Without a word, Kelly headed up to the front of the church. She raised her hands in the air and started to worship the Lord. Before I knew it, she was laying down on the floor under the power of God. Again no one touched her or prayed for her. She laid on the floor with her arms straight up in the air, praying in tongues and weeping for over an hour. I looked at Joe and said, "How can anyone do that? How can

126

someone hold their arms in the air that long?" I began to pray and asked The Lord, "What on earth does this all mean?" I wondered, is she some kind of super spiritual child? In my heart I heard him say, "She's not yours; she's Mine. She's only on loan to you." That was a sobering reality check! All this time I thought she was my little girl, and now God was telling me I had only borrowed her from Him. She wasn't mine; she was His. Wow!

If we could only grasp the reality of that! The truth is that our children were in existence and in the presence of God before they were conceived. The Word of God says that.

> Before I formed thee in the belly I knew thee; and before thou camest forth out of the womb I sanctified thee,..Jer. 1:5

God chooses when and where you show up on this earth. He chooses who your parents are, what sex you will be, and what family you'll be born into. He chooses your race, and your culture. He chooses if you're born into a Christian home or not. These are His choices for your life. He knows what will mold you into the person He desires you to be. He is the God of the Universe. We see in moments, He sees eternity.

We only get one set of parents. It's our responsibility to learn to love them unconditionally. We may as well learn to accept that this is God's choice for our life. Like it or not, He chooses your brothers and your sisters. He chooses the era you are born in. Your life is in His hands. Then he gives you a will to choose to follow Him or not.

We are eternal beings. We are created by Him. We started with Him and will return to Him. Hopefully, the choices we make while on earth, will be ones that bring us closer to Him and make us more like Him.

> Beloved, now are we the sons of God, and it doth not yet
> appear what we shall be: but we know that, when he shall
> appear, we shall be like him; for we shall see him as he is.
> 1 John 3:2

I realized Kelly was simply getting blessed and worshiping the Lord. When she got up, she went around praying for everyone at the altar, and people were being healed. I asked God, "What am I supposed to do with her?" She seemed to be much more spiritual than me. I confess, when He said, " She's not yours; she's Mine; she's only on loan to you," it frightened me. Maybe she was going to die or something. I wasn't sure what that meant. I would think about that often in the years to come.

That wouldn't be the only time God spoke to me and I didn't understand for sure what it meant. I had to learn to only hear His words. Exactly what He said and not what I thought He said. To assume that I understood was dangerous and could lead to wrong conclusions. It was easy to read things into what was spoken. I'd have to weigh what I heard in my spirit with what I saw in His Word.

> The law of the Lord is perfect, converting the soul: the
> testimony of the Lord is sure, making wise the simple. The
> statutes of the Lord are right, rejoicing the heart: the
> commandment of the Lord is pure, enlightening the eyes.
> The fear of the Lord is clean, enduring forever: the
> judgments of the Lord are true and righteous altogether.
> More to be desired are they than gold, yea, than much fine
> gold: sweeter also than honey and the honeycomb.
> Moreover, by them is thy servant warned: and in keeping of
> them there is great reward. Ps.19:7-11

Around Kelly's seventh birthday, she fell down the basement steps headfirst. We had an entrance to the basement that opened in the floor. I never opened it for any reason without warning everyone in the house. "Don't come into the utility room while the floor door is opened!" It hadn't been three or four minutes since I told Kelly, when she came flying around the corner and flew right down the concrete steps, making a huge gash in her forehead.

Head wounds bleed profusely, and the possibility of a concussion sent us heading to the ER. When we arrived, Kelly talked non-stop to the nurse about Jesus and how he was going to heal her. Fortunately, she was just too cute for the nurse to be annoyed with her. Kelly was full of life all the time. She was just exploding with what was in her little heart.

> ......for of the abundance of the heart his mouth speaketh. Luke 6:45

I loved having a little girl. I made nearly all of Kelly's clothes from the time she was a toddler, right up through her teenage years. She was always excited about the next unique creation. She never had the attitude that it wasn't as good as store bought. She felt her clothes were specially designed just for her, and they were. Even when we were struggling financially, she got new clothes.

Because we were in ministry there were a lot of clothes given to us that we might never wear. These were the ones I'd rip apart, and repurpose the fabric that was still good. We have some very fun "Cinderella stories" in our family about how we remade old things into something lovely and beautiful for a special occasion. No one ever had anything like Kelly.

Rachel, Kelly's little sister, was born just after Kelly's seventh birthday. Ultrasound technology hadn't been invented yet so there wasn't any way of knowing a child's sex beforehand. I'd made up my mind that we were having a boy. Consequently, in preparation for her birth, I just bought neutral colored baby items, and nothing girly. When Rachel arrived, I had to reassure a very worried Kelly, that her little sister wouldn't be dressed in boy clothes.

As my due date got closer with Rachel, Kelly came to the kitchen sink where I was doing the dishes, and asked, "Mom, will this baby be black?" I didn't understand where she was coming from, so I explained that when two white people have a child, that the child will also be white. I questioned, "Kelly, why are you asking that?" She replied, "Because we don't have any black babies in our family yet, and I just think it's time to have one." There were black children attending our church, and she didn't understand why there weren't any in our family.

I remember going to pick Kelly up after Sunday School one morning and I said, "Hi, I'm here to get Kelly." Well, they didn't have a Kelly in that class. I was a little bewildered since I had dropped her off there before church. After pointing her out to the teacher, she said, "Oh, you mean Elizabeth." Kelly had changed names on her teacher and had been going by the name of Elizabeth for weeks. When we asked her why she did that, she replied, "I just thought it was pretty so I changed my name!" This went on for about six months before she decided it was ok to call her Kelly again.

She loved to help with the younger children. She was eager to assist in the Day Care Center that we had established in Arizona even when she was ten and eleven years old. Those were years when we were blessed financially.

However, there were times that wasn't the case. I was forced to get creative. Kelly loved being involved in my projects like making rag dolls or puppets. These weren't hand puppets; they were more like Bert and Ernie. There were years when we were so poor, that if I didn't make gifts for everyone at Christmas, there wouldn't be any. She and I went to the stores to see what was selling, drew pictures of them and went home and duplicate them from scratch. Like the Strawberry Short Cake doll that was so popular in the 1980's.

Kelly was liked by everyone. She was social, talented, creative, and fun. She was a character, uniquely different, just full of life all the time.

Chapter 14

Kelly's Teen Years

Although Kelly was cute as a little girl, as she grew into a teenager, she became a guy magnet. Her thick, flowing, shiny blond hair hung to her waist. She became shapely and was a real head turner. Not only was she pleasant to look at she had a beautiful voice. We'd have to get used to the attention she drew. It was never ending.

As a family, we traveled and established Christian Schools. Several of these were in Oklahoma. Some of them are still in operation decades later, and for that we are thrilled to know our labors weren't in vain. At one church, Kelly helped with the worship services, in the sanctuary. She was only fourteen. Her God-given talent, and strong voice, caught the attention of a music teacher in the congregation.

She was impressed to offer Kelly piano and voice lessons for free. She felt strongly that it would be a great loss if Kelly never received any formal musical training. This was such a huge blessing. We were on a faith mission with the church and there wasn't enough money to cover lessons for Kelly or any of the other children. We were so grateful that God had put it in this teacher's heart to bless her.

Kelly not only assisted in the worship on the platform, but she oversaw the nursery and taught the preschool classes on Sunday. She took on adult responsibilities when she was still a kid.

As Kelly matured, she and I became extremely close. She was my intercessory prayer partner. We built an incredible bond through our times together with the Lord. It was a relationship that few mothers ever have with a child. She was my sister in Messiah, not only connected genetically, but by the Spirit as well. We had so much to pray about since we were both teaching Bible classes, and leading worship. Together we tore down strongholds in The Kingdom of Darkness and built up the waste places. She was turned like me; and we never lacked for something to talk to each other about. I cherished this relationship.

....they that shall be of thee shall build the old waste places: thou shalt raise up the foundations of many generations; and thou shalt be called, The repairer of the breach, The restorer of paths to dwell in. Is. 58:12

That's what we were doing as we joined forces in prayer, we were a powerful team together. Joe and I had regular prayer times together and saw many answers as well. However, Kelly was a warrior, she knew how to do battle in the Spirit realm. When I think back, she must have made Hell tremble with what God had in store for her. I didn't know when I named her that her name meant warrior. Her middle name, Jeanette meant the grace of God. She was a warrior for the grace of God.

At the end of each school year there were awards given, and it was no surprise that Kelly had won "The Abigail Award" that year. It was for Spiritual Leadership. The awards ceremony was a formal event and had us fretting over what Kelly would wear to accept her award. That's when we pulled off the biggest "Cinderella" dress of our lives. We still talk about that amazing Southern Bell formal that we made from an old lime green, Mexican Fiesta-dress. One of the other teachers had donated it to my pile of fabric. We tore that thing apart and began designing one of the most beautiful formals either of us had ever seen. It was trimmed in white lace and she wore a hoop skirt under it. Think "Gone with the Wind." It was most definitely one of a kind. God is sure good!

Kelly proved herself to be a good organizer. She was always proud of Joe's and my wedding anniversaries. She took credit for us getting together at the altar the day I got saved. That wasn't exactly accurate, but she liked to believe it. She decided to throw a ten-year anniversary party for us, and she managed to pull off a surprise, without either of us suspecting what she was up to. She scheduled a hayride, invited all the guests, planned the meal, and delivered a wonderfully fun day for everyone. Of course, she employed the help of some of our good friends from church, and her brothers and sister, but it was her idea and organization that made it happen. Pretty impressive for a fourteen-year-old. It was nice to have the kids appreciate the love that Joe and I had for one another and want to help us to celebrate it. Their Mom had enjoyed ten years of love and faithfulness with her soul mate. With God's guidance I had made a great choice in choosing Joe.

Around this time a young, highly anointed, and gifted minister came to visit our church. He moved prophetically in the Word of Knowledge. It was like he knew every secret in the congregation and his visit brought life changing moments to everyone.

Somehow, he missed the fact that Kelly was so young. He was later embarrassed by all the attention he'd given her. He was single and thought he'd found a bride. They spent all day together at the church picnic before someone told him that she was just fourteen years old.

There were a couple of young men in the community that snuck out of their houses at night. On separate occasions they showed up and pecked on Kelly's bedroom window just to get a chance to talk to her. Her little sister shared a bedroom with her and together they never let on that Kelly had after dark visitors we knew nothing about. It was her and Rachel's secret.

While in Oklahoma Kelly renewed her love for horses. We had enough acreage at this house to board a couple of horses for a friend. Kelly and all the other children soon learned to ride very well. Our friend Burt thought Kelly might enjoy participating in the local rodeo, so we signed her up for two of the events. Joe and I sat in the stands watching and cheering her on. She did fine in the first event, but we laughed till we cried when she came out for the barrel races. She waited at the gate for the signal to go. Then she yelled, Yah! Real loud like she was in a John Wayne movie. She was so loud that she startled the horse. She lost several minutes just getting her horse back under control. That was Kelly for you, theatrical and dramatic.

Once when one of her guy friends visited, she wanted to show how well she could ride. She took off out of our gravel driveway in that same "John Wayne cowboy" fashion and turned sharply down the gravel road in front of our house. As she did, her saddle slid sideways on the horse and she took out our mailbox as she flew by. It was good for another laugh. Joe loved to tease Kelly and she never took it badly. She was good at laughing at herself.

When the school year ended in Oklahoma, Joe felt lead to return to Missouri, where he pastored a small congregation in a little store front building in St. Louis. Kelly was our pianist, and she amazed us all on a regular basis. When she sat down to the piano, she'd break into these incredibly anointed melodies during the worship service. The lyrics were amazing truths of God's Word. They were original, straight from the throne of glory, none of us had ever heard anything like them. The words and the music would just carry us away into the presence of the Lord. It seemed like the Holy Spirit just filled the room, much like I would imagine it did when David played the harp for Saul, so anointed. She was truly gifted.

After the service I asked her, "Where did you learn that beautiful song? I never heard it before." Her reply was, " The Lord gave it to me." Right on the spot, she'd open her mouth and God filled it with praise and thanksgiving. They were unbelievably beautiful. I always felt the world was being robbed of these God given melodies. I felt they were so anointed that others needed to hear them. I believed someday Kelly would be a much sought-after song writer. She had an amazing and rare gift. She didn't just keep repeating phrases as she sang, these were structured psalms coming right from heaven.

> By him therefore let us offer the sacrifice of praise to God continually, that is, the fruit of our lips giving thanks to his name. Heb.13:15

Once again, at this new location, Kelly led the children's classes.

Chapter 15
My Missionary Daughter

We really struggled financially as we pastored this little congregation. Joe began to feel as though he was beating his head against a wall, not accomplishing anything spiritually. He became greatly discouraged and started looking for ways to better support the family. After many sleepless nights and agonizing over his decision for weeks, he decided to take a job helping my sister's husband with his company in Texas. It's painful when a person realizes that what they felt called to do, hasn't produced the fruit that they had so hoped it would. We were on the move again.

Kelly completed her last two years of high school at home. She graduated early, as many home-schooled children still do today. Joe and I agreed to permit her to join a missionary couple in Ecuador. They were one of the missionary families supported by the church we attended in Texas. We were excited for Kelly to have this opportunity. It was something I'd have loved to have done when I was her age. God was opening doors for her to experience the mission field in a supervised manner, under this experienced couple. However, this didn't turn out be the wonderful experience we had envisioned for Kelly.

While on furlough and home in Texas, the Missionary couple spent time getting to know Kelly. They were so excited to have a new disciple to break into the Mission field. They needed an extra pair of hands to help and this was a great arrangement for them all. The Mission couple flew to Ecuador before her, and then prepared for her arrival. Kelly had to take the flight from Texas by herself. She was only seventeen at the time and had never flown internationally. There was all the uncertainty of getting through customs and not being able to speak the language.

On the flight, Kelly sat next to a friendly sort of fellow by the name of Abaer. They talked, laughed, and visited the whole trip. He told Kelly that he was involved in the oil industry in Ecuador. She would later learn that he had great political connections with the current government. He was impressed with Kelly as she shared that she had come to the country to help teach English. She told him all about the great reading materials her Mother had used for years to teach hundreds of children to read. She shared how exciting it was to open the minds of little children. He was quite taken with her youthful enthusiasm, and her heart to help others. She recently had a birthday, so to help her celebrate he paid a Mariachi band on board the plane. They played Happy Birthday to her in five different languages. She had a delightful flight with Abaer attending to all her needs and telling her all about the country. She was grateful to have made such a lovely friend even while still in flight.

Kelly couldn't tell Abaer that she had come to do mission work. As far as the government knew, Birdie and her husband were in the country only to do business with the oil companies. Their mission work had to be done secretly, since the government had banned all missionaries.

Once the plane landed, Kelly could see this country was extremely different than America. It was a busy crazy atmosphere. Abaer told her to keep her head down and to stay close to him as they ventured through customs. Every time her luggage came through a place where it should have been inspected, it was slid through to the next station. The atmosphere at the airport was alarming to Kelly. There were many soldiers standing guard with large automatic weapons. She'd never seen anything like this before. She was perplexed because Birdie, her Missionary host was nowhere to be seen. Kelly was in a strange airport in a strange land and feeling quite uncomfortable. It seemed she was missing her connection with the only person in the country that she knew.

It was a tiny airport with a six-foot fence all around the perimeters, and armed guards at every door. When Kelly didn't see Birdie inside, she decided to wait outside the gate. Abaer drove by in his limo and saw Kelly waiting. He stopped to offer her a ride to wherever she needed to go. She didn't have any idea where that might be. She surely couldn't leave this location, what if Birdie came and couldn't find her. Abaer gave Kelly his business card and told her to phone him if she needed anything at all. She was grateful and relieved to have a name and phone number of someone in case something had happened to Birdie, and she found herself alone in a strange country. Kelly was in a very intimidating situation.

Birdie and her husband were there all along. They'd been holding back from entering the airport because things had become unsettled in the country and there was talk of a coup. It just seemed safer to wait for Kelly outside. However, this left her not knowing how to get through customs or what to expect from everything she was seeing. They finally made connections and then spent the next few days showing Kelly all around the local countryside. She went to the markets and up in the mountains and she talked to everyone she encountered. Kelly had never been shy, and it didn't seem like it was time to start now.

Because of Abaer's political connections, he was able to find where Kelly was staying and began to send her welcome gifts. First there was an ocelot, (huge cat) and then a very verbal talking parrot. Even though Birdie was happy that Kelly was going to be training under them, she could have done without the cat and singing parrot that just happened to know lots of vulgar songs.

On Kelly's eighth day in Ecuador, a loud pounding on the door alarmed her and Birdie. It was the police. They came to take Kelly and Birdie into the Police Station for questioning. They were both terrified. They weren't told why. They both kept wondering what was going on. Why were they in trouble?

The coup had taken place overnight, and there was a new

government in power. Kelly's new-found friendship, and connections with Abaer, had made her a suspicious person to the new government. It turned out that Abaer was deeply involved with the former leader who had just been overthrown.

Birdie was quite fearful and tried frantically to explain to the police that Kelly was just a kid. She had simply spoken to a stranger on the flight. She didn't really know this person well. Then Kelly and Birdie were separated, adding to the fear and intimidation, and placed in different rooms for interrogation. The questioning seemed endless, agonizing, going on the entire day, from early morning till the late evening hours. Their story never changed. There was nothing to tell.

At the end of the day, Kelly was given an ultimatum, leave Ecuador immediately or go to jail. The authorities did everything they could to frighten her. She was an inexperienced, naïve teenager. They told her stories of other Americans who had been imprisoned in their country and forgotten by everyone, left to rot in their jails. She wouldn't be able to count on the American government to rescue her. There was no real choice. When she was permitted to return home with Birdie, she quickly gathered all her belongings and was placed on the next flight home. They knew they were being watched and had to act quickly. Her foreign mission trip had ended abruptly, leaving everyone asking, "What in the world just happened? Did we all just miss God on this, or what?"

What an ordeal for a young woman. As she flew home, she rehearsed all that had happened leading up to this trip. All the hopes and desires to serve just dashed to the ground. She began to wonder what next? The plan had changed. Kelly never spoke to Birdie again. She never knew the outcome of the coup, or if Birdie and her husband were also forced to leave the country.

As a family, we began to re-evaluate what direction Kelly was to take. She still had a heart for missions and wanted to pursue that.

After discussing options, she decided to take some extra courses at the Vo-Tech school. But her desires to serve hadn't changed, she was still determined to do missions. So, the entire family took a trip down to "Youth with A Mission" (YWAM) in Tyler, Texas. After some research and touring the facilities, we agreed this was a good place for Kelly to grow. Joe and I felt her time with YWAM would help her to know better if this was going to be her life's work or not. She'd be staying in the United States for her training and we'd feel easier knowing that we could get to her if she needed us.

She completed the basic missions training and loved every minute of it. She felt lead to stay on with YWAM for Advanced Leadership Training. This turned out to be a great spiritual experience for Kelly.

She had the honor of being chosen to play the lead part in "Toy Maker and Son." It was a stage production about the Messiah and His Eternal Father. The YWAM team performed this musical play in churches and on the streets of large cities, and college campuses all over the country. She loved the fulfilment of using her talents to perform and witness. She saw many people make commitments to follow Jesus. She felt she found her heart's desire and planned to stay with YWAM indefinitely. This is where she belonged. Not only was Kelly feeling fulfilled in her calling, but she became very close friends with her co-star David. They were nearly inseparable. She and David pretty much assumed they would marry and win the world for Jesus together.

While on the road, Kelly's mission team was scheduled to come through our hometown. This gave us a chance to visit with others that had served with Kelly on the field. One of the elderly missionaries traveling with the team told me, " You know, Kelly has no fear. She goes where angels fear to tread." He told stories of the team doing street ministry and how Kelly would approach anyone, anywhere, to tell them about Jesus. He said, "She thinks nothing of going up under the bridges with the homeless, no matter how scary some of those people can be." After her Ecuador experience, she could have been intimidated to be less bold, but not Kelly. She was a powerful, fearless, talented, gifted instrument in the hands of the Lord. By now we had just assumed Kelly would spend her life in the ministry.

> Fear not, for I am with you. Do not be dismayed. I am your God. I will strengthen you; I will help you; I will uphold you with my victorious right hand. Is. 41:10

As I look back over Kelly's years in missions, I can see the covering protection of the Father all over every situation. So many things could have gone wrong. We had entrusted her to faithful people, and yet she still needed protection that only God could have provided. Kelly's travels gave us no choice except to *let go* and trust her to God's care.

All this happened in the 1980's. It was long before our current turbulent terrorist situations. Our society has had to adjust to a whole new world. What Kelly encountered in Ecuador was out of the box for us to even imagine. I thank the Father for His angels that surrounded Kelly on every turn and returned her home to us safely. Unfortunately, there would be a time when I would wait for her return, and it wouldn't come for years.

Chapter 16

A Wrong Turn

Kelly had learned so much while at YWAM. Joe and I were blessed to see how she had developed so much understanding about the love of the Father. One of the courses taught there was "The Father Heart of God," and Kelly seemed to really be taken with that knowledge. She had grown to be a woman. We were both quite proud of her, as were her brothers and sister.

She was nineteen now and made a trip home on furlough from her missionary journeys. She was her bubbly, energetic, excited self as she arrived home to spend time with family. Her intentions were to return to YWAM in just a few weeks. She was fairly confident that she would eventually marry David, (her Toy Maker leading man). Because YWAM didn't permit team members to date one another, this relationship had not gone past holding hands. Yet Kelly and David had experienced many tender moments together sharing their mutual dreams and desires to serve God.

Then, what seemed like a very harmless request from an old friend, would completely change the entire course of Kelly's life.

Enter Ken: He was ten years older than Kelly. His parents had been friends of ours for over a decade. We went to church together. When we first met them, they owned the local Bible bookstore in a little town near-by. They were loved and respected in the community.

I remembered Ken from when he was a teenager. He was interested in my little sister. She came to help me when Rachel was born. We knew him from hanging around our little farm trying to get a date. Joe and I had witnessed Ken's enthusiasm as a youth when he returned from Bible Camp proclaiming that God had called him to the ministry. We had fond memories of him in church as a teenager, excited about God.

When Kelly came home from YWAM, Ken was pastoring a little church in North Carolina. He was still single and was coming home to see his family as well. At his mother's request, Kelly agreed to a friendly dinner with her son. Kelly thought she was in love with David and she was just being nice to another believer in the ministry.

After their dinner date that night, she said, "Boy, I didn't like him." I responded, "Well, maybe you should give him another chance."

There would be many times I would want to pull those words back, as if they had never been spoken.

> Thou art snared with the words of thy mouth, thou art taken with the words of thy mouth. Pr.6:2

Kelly agreed to see him again, and before we knew it, he proposed marriage. Kelly accepted, leaving David completely heart broken.

Kelly and Ken dated just a couple of weeks before he had to return to his congregation in North Carolina. During these two short weeks, Joe and I were picking up clues that weren't adding up. The picture that had been painted of this spiritually sound young man was seeming a little distorted. However, Ken was very charming, funny, and handsome. Kelly thought what we were feeling was Ken's desire to protect her. She thought she was getting the man of her dreams. He told her his heart was always toward God and that he would stay in the ministry for the rest of his life. This is just what Kelly needed to hear. She wanted to serve God and now they would be able to do it together.

Ken returned to North Carolina, and Kelly began preparing for a wedding. There wasn't enough time to really get to know one another. It was a whirlwind courtship. Joe had proposed to me ten days after meeting, but we took our Pastor's advice and made the engagement last six months. I was twenty-six at that time, but Kelly was only nineteen. During our engagement time, we learned many valuable lessons about one another that prepared us for a lifetime together. Ken didn't want to wait any longer than he had to.

> ...It is not good for a person to be without knowledge, and he who hurries his footsteps errs. Pr. 19:2

Everything went on fast forward. Kelly, Rachel, and I spent hours every day preparing for the wedding. It seemed to consume all our thoughts. It was like the event was more important than the relationship, and it most definitely got more attention. Joe and I were stressed, trying to figure out how to pay for a wedding that we hadn't planned for. We had so little notice and time to get ready. We wondered, how we would afford the kind of wedding expected of Kelly's future family? They had become quite wealthy.

Kelly and I enjoyed shopping together, and we had fun as we began the search for a dress that would make the grade. After visiting every affordable shop, she and I agreed on a simple basic gown that we were blessed to find on sale. After all, this wouldn't be our first *ball*. We had done this before. Together, we knew how to make something out of nothing. At least this time we had a dress to start with. We always seemed to have more creativity than money. Kelly and I loved doing this kind of thing together. We began the process of sewing on sequins and beads to embellish this simple but lovely dress. It seemed we were all caught up in the details when we should have been insisting on a longer courtship. However, Kelly and Ken were both of age and he wasn't appreciating our input at any level. His mother had assured us of his great spirituality and dedication to the Lord. Because of that we ignored the red flags. We should have paid more attention to them. We should have listened to our spirit. Joe and I discussed some concerns, but then quickly dismissed them. We thought that maybe our apprehensions were just because it was hard to give away our little girl.

Ken returned for a few short visits during the engagement, and his behavior was troubling to us. He refused to honor our house rules on curfew. Joe spoke with Ken about getting Kelly home at a decent time, but his answer was, "She's engaged to me. Your house rules don't apply anymore!" He seemed arrogant and unwilling to bend or respect our wishes as Kelly's parents.

He repeatedly brought her home hours after the established curfew. Then he stayed even later, till the wee hours of the morning, sitting in our foyer smooching with Kelly.

It was on one of these short visits that Ken began to quiz me about Kelly's past. She had confided in him about some things I had no knowledge of. When he asked me, I answered, "Ken, I don't know what you're talking about." I felt like I was being interrogated, like he wanted to see if I had a different story than Kelly's. I felt as if he was trying to catch Kelly in a lie. He seemed confused that I wasn't aware of the situation, and I was feeling uncomfortable with his suggestions and tactics. The subject was dropped but this wasn't the end of it. It would come up again and it wouldn't be pleasant.

When I had the opportunity, I asked Kelly to explain what Ken was talking about. She began to share a story of a date rape that happened when she was sixteen. It wasn't exactly a date, but it was someone she knew.

Joe and I had agreed for her to stay overnight in our RV alone while she was working at a near-by restaurant. The RV was parked on Joe's work lot just a block away from Kelly's job. It was safer for her to stay there than to drive home alone late at night. That night she was closing the restaurant but had to be back early the next morning to open it up again. She had just gotten back to the RV and locked the front door, when she heard someone knocking. As she looked outside, she saw her manager from work and his manager with him. She thought, I must have done something wrong, or they need something for work. So, she opened the door to them and allowed them to come in. At first, they were funny and friendly and then became forceful. Her words were, "Mom, before I knew it, he was on top of me."

She had her reasons for not telling us before now. She thought we would tell her how stupid she was to have opened the door in the first place. She blamed herself for allowing this to happen. She also reasoned that we would probably feel we were to blame for allowing her to stay alone. She was also afraid of what her dad would do to the young man if he knew. She feared we wouldn't rest until he went to jail for this. That would involve the police, and endless court appearances, reliving the whole thing. It made sense to her to keep quiet about the whole thing until now. Kelly's reasoning sounded much like other victims who are too afraid to come forward to report these kinds of violations.

But Kelly didn't stop there. While she was baring her soul, she told us about a family member that had molested her as a little girl. So now, in the middle of planning a wedding, we had these emotional bombshells dropped on us! Plus, our daughter had borne the pain of these circumstances in her heart alone for years. All this was being brought to light right before she was to marry.

We just felt a sense of disbelief. How could we have not known? We should have been in tune with God enough to pick up on these. Why didn't we? Where did we miss it? We had a lot to process. We laid awake nights in bed running all this through our memories trying to make sense of it all. How could we not know? What were we supposed to do now?

What about the family member being accused of molestation? How should we address that? It happened when she was very young and so was the other person. We needed the mind of Christ, and instead we were caught up in the wedding preparations.

I knew she had been wounded and now there wasn't any time to help her in dealing with these hurts. She was entering into a life-long commitment without working through the pains of the past. She wasn't designed to carry this alone. That's what Jesus did for us.

> Surely he hath borne our griefs, and carried our sorrows: yet we did esteem him stricken, smitten of God, and afflicted. Is.53:4

Jesus had already paid for ALL of this. But how could we help Kelly to let go of the pain, and give it to Jesus now? She would soon be married. Our time of influence was coming to an abrupt halt and we didn't realize how abrupt it would be.

Originally, we thought this was going to be a marriage made in heaven, now we were having second, and even third thoughts. Both Kelly and Ken appeared to love the Lord.

From the outward look of things, it was easy to reason; they both had beautiful voices, it seemed they would make a great team, and would make beautiful music together for the Lord. I imagined they'd do wonderful things together in the Kingdom, but that never materialized.

As we got to know Ken better, we began to see things more clearly. Shortly after they were married, we discovered than he had a great deal of debt. We had questioned him about being able to support a wife and he assured us he was debt free. He said he wouldn't have trouble caring for Kelly or children. He had chosen to mislead, in fact he out and out lied. (not real good character for a Pastor)

We also learned that he had literally been left at the altar twice before, and I was beginning to understand why. I can only imagine what an ego buster that must have been to be abandoned twice in a public forum. Both Kelly and Ken were carrying their own baggage of the past into this marriage together.

On the morning of the wedding Ken came to our house. He and Kelly began to have an argument over a dog that his sister had given Kelly for a wedding gift. It was a beautiful Alaskan Husky, and Kelly just adored it. He didn't want the responsibility of a pet, but this was a huge part of who Kelly was. She had always loved animals, so much so that she had often dreamed of becoming a veterinarian. I could hear loud voices and crying coming from Kelly's bedroom, so I headed down the hall to see what was going on. I didn't want to get into the middle of their business, but it seemed this could have been settled without the tears, especially on their wedding day. I said "If you're going to argue like this now, what'll happen when you're married? It's not too late to call this thing off. Ken, maybe it's your turn to leave someone at the altar."

Ouch! I didn't choose my words well. I had hit a huge nerve! Ken would never forgive me for suggesting such a thing. To call off a wedding the third time would have been just too much humiliation to bear. Joe and I could see already that our ability to have input into Kelly's life was dwindling fast, and I had just squelched that opportunity for good, as far as Ken was concerned.

Chapter 17

I'm *Losing My Daughter*

Kelly's little sister, Rachel, was twelve years old now. She and her little brother, Sam, adored Kelly. She was their terrific big sister and they were all remarkably close. Jeff was already out of the house and stationed in Germany. Rachel was eager to help with the wedding in any way she could.

Even though we didn't have the money for the perfect dress, we three gals had the heart to work, and lots of talent between us. Rachel worked tirelessly sewing on hundreds of sequence and beads. I made all the bride's maid dresses for four attendants, the silk floral arrangements, bouquets, and church decorations. Together we managed to pull off a beautiful wedding.

After the ceremony Kelly and Ken spent one night in town at a near-by Hotel Honeymoon Suite. They dropped by the house the next day, before heading out on their honeymoon to Niagara Falls. They both seemed to be really happy. Joe and I prayed that our concerns were just unfounded and that everything would be fine.

After the honeymoon Kelly was swept off to North Carolina where Ken was still serving as a pastor. That didn't last long. His church consisted of a hand full of women, and once he was married, many of them disappeared. Soon the church closed, and because of his delinquent student loans and tax debt Ken needed to find work right away. The stress was on. This was the last of Ken's ministry. He never pastored again. In fact, he rarely attended church again. Kelly has said that was one of the greatest disappointments of her marriage; she never knew what it was like to sit in church with a partner. If Ken couldn't be in the pulpit, he didn't want to be in church at all.

> Am I now trying to win the approval of human beings, or of God? Or am I trying to please people? If I were still trying to please people, I would not be a servant of Christ. Gal. 1:10 NIV

This pretty much says it all.

Early in the marriage Ken told Kelly, now that they were married, the singing and dancing she had so enjoyed with YWAM wouldn't fit into their lifestyle. There wouldn't be any more stage productions. That was Kelly's passion, and she was being robbed of fulfilling her calling or enjoying the great talents she had been blessed with. That was only the beginning. Eventually Kelly, who had always been an extremely social individual found herself completely isolated from everybody and everything.

Ken didn't like Kelly calling home. He stubbornly insisted that Joe and I had known all along about the childhood molestation and the teenage rape. He accused us of not caring that it had happened. His position was that we didn't protected Kelly. He continually insisted that we were aware of everything and willfully did nothing about it, we'd permitted her pain to occur. These were the lies he used to convince Kelly that her parents didn't truly love her. Kelly was made to feel like she was used material and unworthy of Ken's love, as if she were tattered merchandise. He acted like he'd gotten stuck with used goods, less than he deserved.

He made it clear to her; stop all contact with your family! So, after the first few months of marriage, the phone calls home ended. During those early calls, she was usually crying. She couldn't understand why he was withholding himself from her. He refused to respond to her touch. He would roll over in bed with his back to her, shutting her out. She felt rejected and alone. She was a nineteen-year-old girl married to a man ten years her senior, being made to feel that she was just not good enough.

Of course, I wanted to fix all this. I suggested she might think about an annulment. I have no idea why Kelly told Ken what I said, but it made things even worse. It proved to him that I was a danger to his marriage, supporting his decision to forbid Kelly to speak to me.

This was unbelievable! She wasn't only my daughter, she was also my prayer partner, and sister in the Lord! She had been completely removed from my life. I began to agonize over her.

After Ken found work, he moved Kelly into a ten by fifty-foot trailer, in the country, with no one around and no telephone. When I was in a tiny trailer, I was surrounded by lots of flight students. She was completely isolated.

Ken was selling insurance and she was left alone for long hours with no car or phone. For a very out-going person like Kelly, it didn't take long for depression to set in. She hated the isolation.

Kelly was out of reach. I didn't know where she was or how to contact her. All I had was "silence!" Where was she and why wasn't she calling? I wondered, had she chosen this or was it being forced upon her? Was she a prisoner in her own home? When I asked her mother-in-law to help, her response was, "I can't go against Ken's wishes."

She was no longer a friend. The betrayal was overwhelming! Ken wasn't what she had portrayed him to be. Now she wouldn't even tell me where my daughter was. Only Ken's Dad acknowledged that what he was doing with Kelly was wrong.

I cried out to God to return my daughter. I didn't want her marriage to end, I just wanted Ken to realize we weren't the enemy. I knew she was in trouble and my hands were tied. I hoped if we could just speak with Ken, we could clear up some of his issues with us. That wasn't happening.

What helped me keep my sanity and get through these early days without Kelly, was my decision to attend nursing school. I'd taught and preached in different venues for years, but now I was having a desire to heal in any capacity. Nursing was the direction I felt I was being led.

It was a profession that allowed me to minister to people in so many ways. I could pour my love and energy into others. Looking back, I'm so grateful for this huge distraction. I had deadlines and exams to prepare for, and other children and a husband to consider. All these things helped to keep my mind occupied and off the constant thought of my daughter and her situation. She was missing! In my mind, she was just like one of those faces on the side of a milk carton. I needed the distractions.

> Idle hands are the devil's workshop; idle lips are his mouthpiece. Pr. 16:27 TLB

Ken and Kelly's financial problems continued to mount and eventually the IRS caught up to them. They were in a mess. Ken's Dad stepped in and drove to North Carolina to bring them back to Missouri. His parents gave Ken a job with their family business. Now, at least, Kelly was in the same town as we were again. I hoped I would be able to make contact with her, even though her husband was opposed. I knew all the scriptures about a wife obeying her husband, and how he should be the head of the household. However, this had become a very oppressive situation for my daughter. I wanted to fix it.

Kelly was expecting her first child. I'm sure she was excited about the prospects of becoming a mom. I wasn't permitted to be part of that. I never got to help her plan or shop for the new baby. I wasn't invited to a baby shower, and I don't even know if she even had one. We both missed out on so much!

Kelly lived with the tremendous disappointment of so little affection in her marriage. We were a huggy, lovey family, and she was missing that greatly. She was suffering from *affection deprivation. Ken had no interest in intimacy.

Occasionally Kelly would sneak by the house, and even park in the back. She could only stay for a few minutes. She feared he would drive by and see her car. It was apparent that she wanted to see us and knew that we loved her. However, she was willing to do just about anything to keep her marriage intact. I recognized this kind of control. I had experienced it in my relationship with Wayne, but not to this degree.

Ken's family owned several businesses that cared for the elderly and mentally disabled. Ken hated this business, but it was a paycheck. So, contact with the residents was something that fell to Kelly. No one knew how valuable this experience would be to her in the years to come. In one way or another, Ken's mother was always his financial source of supply until her death.

Kelly felt that if Betty, Ken's mother, had left them alone, they would have had a chance to make things work. Instead, Betty constantly interfered in their lives trying to control and manipulate Ken's time and attention, especially after his father's death. She had money and she controlled her children with her resources. She looked for one venture after another to keep Ken active in her affairs.

At times Ken worked hard when he helped his mother build new subdivisions. Other times he received a hefty allowance as he worked on projects of his own that always promised a big payoff but never delivered.

One crisp morning in October I received a phone call from Kelly's father-n-law. He said, " Sharon, I want you to know Kelly had a baby boy last night. She had some trouble and she had to have a C-section. They're both fine now, but the nurses have been instructed to keep you from seeing Kelly. You can't go to the hospital to see them." I appreciated his call, but I was incredibly angry. I hung up the phone crying. I felt so rejected, totally left out of one of the most important days of my daughter's life. I should've been there to support her, instead I was being forbidden to see her, or my new grandson. Even though she had complications and needed a major surgery, I still wasn't notified. Joe just held me in his arms trying to console me. When the tears stopped, and we had time to gather our thoughts, we agreed we'd go to the hospital anyway, regardless of Ken's wishes.

> Oh my God, I trust in thee: let me not be ashamed, let not mine enemies' triumph over me. Ps.25:2

I was trusting the Lord that I'd get in to see my daughter and new grandson, regardless of Ken's edicts.

None of this made any sense. My daughter lived five blocks from me. She gave birth to her first child and I wasn't even called. I couldn't believe that my daughter could be so brain washed to allow this to happen! Where was the gutsy, brave daughter that used to go where angels feared to tread? How could this happen? At this point I felt like it would've been easier if Kelly had died. At least this wouldn't have been her choice. The pain and rejection might have been easier, at least that's how I felt at that moment. I'd find out years later this wasn't true, there were greater pains than this.

I'd been taking my nursing clinicals at the same hospital where Kelly was, and knew my way around well. I thought, there's no way I'm being kept from seeing my own grandson! I'd been there for Jeff's son's home delivery, but not even allowed to come to the hospital to see my daughter and her newborn son.

We took the elevator to the second floor of the hospital and walked right into the nursery. No one even tried to stop us. We just stood and stared at our amazing red headed grandson. He looked just like his mama when she was born. He was so beautiful. Then it was time to head to Kelly's room.

We were sure Ken would be standing guard. I wanted so badly to hold Kelly but didn't dare get close. I anticipated Ken pressing the button, calling the nurse to throw us out. Joe and I stood at the door and simply said, "You have a beautiful son." We congratulated them both. I'm sure at this point Ken was seeing me as very defiant to his authority over Kelly. He said nothing. He just stared at us. Kelly responded with, "Thanks Mom."

I only saw Kelly a few times in the next few years. I'd miss out on all the wonderful things that happened in my grandson Noble's first few years.

Jeff was now married to Les and Kelly had become friends with her. Kelly was away from the family for so long that she didn't realize at first that the lady she'd met at the park was her brother's wife. Les decided to keep her family relationship to Kelly quiet for a while until she could get to know her better. So, at least I'd get periodic updates on Kelly through Leslie. I knew Kelly and Ken were still having marital problems. They were more like roommates than husband and wife, but she wouldn't ever consider leaving. She was in this for life. I'd taught her well. Marriage is for life.

I was in such emotional pain without my daughter, that those beliefs were sorely shaken. All I wanted was my daughter back.

There were times that I spent hours on the floor crying and pleading with God to bring Kelly home, to release her from the prison she was in.

I did this so often, that my younger children wondered when I'd ever stop crying and praying. They hadn't only lost Kelly, but in a way, they were losing me as well. The grief of missing Kelly was making me less effective in every area of my life. There seemed no way to hide it. There'd be times of laughter and light heartedness, but then the heartache would set in again.

> Laughter cannot mask a heavy heart. When the laughter ends, the grief remains. Pr. 14:13

Chapter 18
My Awakening

Finally, one night in the same tearful prayer mode, the Holy Spirit began to speak to me. He broke through my tears and said, "Sharon, why are you crying?" I answered, "Because my heart is breaking. I want my daughter back." He responded, "But why all the crying?" I said again, " My heart is breaking." He spoke very clearly to me. "You have asked Me to return your daughter over and over again, and yet you continue to cry. The truth is, you're really crying because you think if you cry long enough and hard enough, that I'll do this *your* way instead of Mine."

What? Those words shook me to my very core! Where'd that come from? I knew when I heard it this was true. It's not like I knew it before, but I realized immediately that God was speaking. What came to my mind was *manipulation*. I knew manipulation was a form of witchcraft. Surely that wasn't what I was doing!

> Now the works of the flesh are manifest, which are these; Adultery, fornication, uncleanness, lasciviousness, Idolatry, witchcraft, hatred, variance, emulations, wrath, strife, seditions, heresies, envying's, murders, drunkenness, reveling, and such like: of the which I tell you before, as I have also told you in time past, that they which do such things shall not inherit the kingdom of God. But the fruit of the Spirit is love, joy, peace, longsuffering, gentleness, goodness, faith, meekness, temperance: against such there is no law. And they that are Christ's have crucified the flesh with the affections and lusts. If we live in the Spirit, let us also walk in the Spirit. Gal.5:19-25

Oh! My! I didn't believe that I had a *manipulative* bone in my body. Was this true? Is that what I was doing?

> ...for the Lord searcheth all hearts, and understandeth all the imaginations of the thoughts: if thou seek him, he will be found of thee; but if thou forsake him, he will cast thee off forever.1 Chron. 28:7b

My Heavenly Father obviously knew me better than I knew myself. He understood the imaginations of my thoughts. I began to realize that if I'd just trust Him to resolve this issue in His timing, according to His will, that I'd see the hand of God. I had to trust Him. I had to know that God loved my daughter more than I did, and that He'd work it out in His own time. I quit crying. I began to thank Him. I repented for any form of manipulation and asked Him to show me anywhere else I might be trying to control. What a lesson! A wake-up call for sure. He simply wanted me to trust Him with one of my most valued possessions, my daughter. Trusting Him, and letting go of my rights as a Mom, was the *only* way I was going to recover.

I don't believe it is wrong to ask in prayer more than once, but there's a time we must move in faith. No more vain repetitions, but in all things, begin to thank him. He has a plan and it's to do us good. It is just not the plan we have for ourselves.

> Rejoice evermore. Pray without ceasing. In everything give thanks: for this is the will of God in Christ Jesus concerning you. 1 Thes. 5:16-18

> For I know the plans I have for you, declares the Lord, plans to prosper you and not to harm you plans to give you a hope and a future. Jer. 29:11 NIV

I'd been corrected! I had to quit striving and start trusting. Every day, I'd thank God for Kelly's return. Whatever God's plan I was on board. I was now able to focus more on the tasks that were at hand. Getting through nursing school, being a wife and partner, and raising the children I still had at home.

A truth I learned while in nursing school was that everyone is in pain, for one reason or another. I used to think, if the instructors or other students realized what I was going through, not knowing where my daughter was, they'd wonder how I even made it through. In time I learned that everyone had their very own set of trials; and we were all struggling. We get so focused on our own pain, that we can't see what others are going through.

I completed nursing school and graduated at the top of my class. I give God glory for that. I was the kid who struggled to learn to read, and now I had excelled, completing my science degree. I might not be able save my daughter from the pain she was suffering, but at least now, I had the skills to help so many others.

I graduated from nursing school in 1991. Kelly was still in town. It was a huge accomplishment in my life! I'd returned to school and successfully completed the task at nearly forty-four years of age. Yet Kelly wasn't permitted to attend my graduation ceremony, although she wanted to. I'd gone through this whole nursing school process without being able to share any of it with Kelly, not even graduation. My whole extended family showed up from out of town, but my daughter who lived just blocks from me didn't come. She managed to sneak away long enough to pop in for 5 minutes at the reception after the ceremony ended. She had to leave quickly. She was always living in fear that Ken would find out where she was. Seeing her was bittersweet. I loved to see her, but hated what she was going home to, and the control I knew she was under. I couldn't fix it. I had to *let go.* I had to trust God.

Eventually, Ken moved Kelly out of town again, completely away from any influence of her family. He told his mother, "If you tell Kelly's family where we are, we'll cut you off as well." In his mind, he owned Kelly. He controlled her, and apparently controlled his Mother as well. Somehow, Ken had convinced himself he was protecting Kelly from parents that didn't really love her. He felt he was the only one capable of doing so. Ken's father had died, and so I no longer had anyone willing to keep me informed about Kelly's well-being.

Several years passed without hearing from Kelly. Ken's Mom slipped with some information. It gave me an idea where Kelly might be. I had no phone number for her, so I decided to drive to that little town where I thought she was living.

I knocked on the door; she was inside alone with her son who was about three years old. She barely opened the door, slipped out onto the porch and guardedly spoke to me for a few minutes. She had to go back inside to make sure her son hadn't seen me. She was concerned that he'd tell his dad that I was there, even though he had no idea I was his grandmother. I could have been the fuller brush salesman, but Kelly was too afraid to think of that.

She came back out on the front porch for a short while. She confided in me that she was so depressed that she'd started drinking. I was so concerned because Wayne's Dad had been a hopeless alcoholic. I was afraid there might be a genetic predisposition to alcoholism, and she might not be able to stop. I just wanted to hold her and say, "Get in the car and come home with me." She wouldn't even let me get near her; she was so distant. Eventually, Kelly would tell people that *her parents were dead* to avoid any questions about us.

This would be the last time I that I saw her for nine long years. I continued to pray for her safety and that one day she'd be free from her prison. I had let go and was trusting God to do this His way in His time.

I'd been cut off from her, to some extent, from the day she was married. There'd be times when I wondered if she was still alive. I'm not sure anyone would have told me. I simply had to trust God.

> I will be glad and rejoice in Your mercy *and* steadfast love, because You have seen my affliction, You have taken note of my life's distresses. Ps.31:7

I'd have to rest in this, knowing that God has seen. I had to keep trusting and thanking him for the answer that was on the way, although there were no signs of it ever coming.

Chapter 19

Waiting for Gods Timing

Joe and I purchased a Residential Care Facility in a little town about two hours away. I often wondered how Kelly would ever find me if she needed to come home.

I contacted Kelly's mother-in-law occasionally over the years to see if I could learn anything about Kelly. The only thing she'd say was, "She is fine." She wouldn't even hint about where they were, what they were doing, or provide any details. There was no information about my grandson. How was he doing, were they all well? Were there other children? So many questions and no answers.

So much for being my long time "Christian" friend! Once or twice I couldn't hold back tears during our conversations. She was never moved. She'd simply said flatly, "If I tell you anything, Ken will cut me off too." It was ok with her that I'd been banned from Kelly's life, as long as it wasn't her. I expected her to understand and to have compassion. I hoped she would throw me a bread crumb of information, so my concerns could be eased. I came to realize she wasn't the friend she had presented herself to be. Just as her son wasn't the man which he had presented himself to be.

I felt she stole my daughter from me. She had years with her and my grandchildren, that I was deprived of. She didn't care how difficult this was for me or our family. It was all about keeping peace with her son, and not about doing what was right.

It was never quite clear who was manipulating who. Ken and his mother were two peas in a pod.

Ken was a controller and he had managed to control his Mom as well as Kelly. His Mom's financial status lent itself to recognition within her church and community. They viewed her as a great intercessor, someone who spent hours in the prayer rooms ministering to others. As for me and my family, there was no compassion. How twisted!

> Put on therefore, as the elect of God, holy and beloved, bowels of mercies, kindness, humbleness of mind meekness, longsuffering. Col.3:12

A little mercy would've been greatly appreciated. But then, God was gaining me. Did I trust Him with my daughter or not?

Time Marches On

I kept remembering the words spoken by the Holy Spirit that night in prayer while I was still in nursing school. He said, "Kelly *will* return, but we'll do this *My* way and not yours." I'd learned to lean on the Words from God for years. Every time Kelly came to mind, (which was often) I simply thanked The Father for her return in His timing. I'd become so sure of His Word to me that I just stopped fretting over it. I'd become confident of His plan for my daughter.

In moments of weakness, I'd sit down and write her a letter, telling her how I loved her, even though I knew I'd never send it. I did the same for Ken, trying to figure out why he hated us so. I wouldn't even have known where to send it. Putting my feelings on paper seemed to release the sadness that would come on Kelly's birthday nearly every year.

Nine years came and went with no word from Kelly or about her. These were busy years raising my other children, beginning a new career, and starting a new business. I remembered how hard this was when the children were kidnapped, to go just a few months without hearing from them. Again, I'd remember the words in the back of my Bible. "You will always have your children." I was holding on to those words by faith. Believing what I couldn't see.

> But without faith it is impossible to please HIM: for he that cometh to God must believe that he is, and that he is a rewarder of them that diligently seek him. Heb. 11:6

After three years we closed our Residential care facility in the little town where we moved after my graduation. We ended up converting it to a Bed and Breakfast. It was the largest house in town, in a highly recreational area of Missouri. As I busied myself with the many chores of preparing for guests to arrive, the phone rang. It was an old friend of mine I'd known from before Joe and I were married. You remember Diane who shared her faith with me. She said, "Are you sitting down?" I told her not to be so dramatic, just tell me what you have to say. She continued, "I went to the beauty shop today, and guess who was in the chair next to me?" I replied, "I have no idea." She said, "Debbie Blue, Kelly's ex-sister-n-law." Diane began to tell me where Kelly was and that she had given birth to another child, a girl. She even knew Kelly's exact location. She was only about an hour and a half drive from our house.

I was told that Kelly and Ken had been team driving a semi-truck when Kelly became pregnant. They had been living in the truck. Ken's Mom decided to buy them a motel. It gave them a home and an income once the baby was born. My first thoughts were, if they had another child, they must be getting along and are at least being intimate. So, this was good. I wasn't surprised that Ken's Mom had once again provided an income for him. She'd never stopped trying to be his God.

I hung up the phone and began to cry. I thought I had cried every last tear for Kelly already, but obviously I was wrong.

Another grandchild born that I'd never know. It didn't make sense to me that I could be serving The Lord and trusting Him for her return, and still be deprived of getting to be there for yet another grandchild. She was so near, and yet still so far away! I knew the Word of God and knew many righteous men and women in the Bible had children that didn't follow in their footsteps. I only cried a short while. I brought myself back to truth and began to thank Him for her return. I knew His word to me was true.

> Thou art near, O LORD; and all thy commandments are truth. Ps. 119:151

He had told me He would do this His way, not mine. Waiting was His commandment to me, and I knew it was truth.

I told the rest of the family what I had heard, Kelly was living close by. Sam, Kelly's baby brother immediately responded, "Well, I'm going to call her." Because we heard she was managing a motel, he figured she would be the one to answer the phone. He just knew that she would want to talk to him.

Kelly answered the phone. It was the first time any of us had heard her voice in years. The realization that she was alive and well enough to answer a phone, or run a business, left us in confusion. How could she be so close and not find a way to let us know she was ok? Why wouldn't she? Had she believed all of Ken's lies about her family? Until that moment, none of us had any assurance that she was even alive.

We were all taken back at her response to Sam. When he told Kelly, it was her baby brother calling, she said, "It's inappropriate to speak with you." Then hung up.

He was so hurt. He had a new-found anger related to her abandonment. The loss of his sister just went deeper into his soul. He was a young man by now and he couldn't believe she refused to speak with him. He felt completely rejected! He thought if she had a problem with Mom and Dad, that was one thing. But he expected her to be excited to speak to him. I'm not sure he has ever recovered from her disappearance from his life. At that point, he didn't care if he ever saw her again.

I didn't try to contact Kelly. The Lord had said He would do it His way. I continued to pray and trust for her return, thanking God every day.

In these years of silence, there was one time that I felt an urgency to initiate a contact with Kelly. The circumstances warranted it. In 2001, when The World Trade Center was attacked in New York City, a sense of alarm came over the entire nation. There was a possibility of war on American soil. I was concerned about Kelly living in a populated area. We were living in a remote country area of Missouri and had plenty of room to help others if needed. I decided to phone Ken.

My grandson answered the phone. I simply told him who I was and requested to speak to his father. I felt I would anger them if I had a conversation with my grandson, so I didn't try. When Ken came to the phone, I made an offer of a safe place for all of them if there was ever need for it. He politely thanked me, and that was the end of any contact. Now he knew, I knew where they were living. That was something that had been kept a secret from me for years.

As I continued to thank The Lord daily for Kelly's return, two more years passed. At least now I knew she was alive. I hoped their marriage was on better footing by now. I asked the Father if there was anything that I needed to do. I didn't want to take things into my own hands. He had instructed me to do this His way. So, I would wait until I had instructions from Him before doing anything.

I had trusted Him this long and I didn't want to fail now. He spoke clearly to me, "Send her a simple note. Say nothing except, I will ALWAYS love you, Mom." This was the first time in years I felt I had His direction and prompting to make a contact.

I took out the prettiest greeting card I could find, and in my fanciest handwriting, I wrote only what I had been instructed to. Under that I added our toll-free business number. If she wanted to call, I knew that number wouldn't show up on her phone bill. Ken wouldn't know she'd called. I knew if she contacted me it would have to be done without his knowing.

Do I think this is how a marriage is supposed to work? Absolutely Not!!

Husbands love your wives, even as Christ also loved the church, and gave himself for it. Eph.5:25

>...where the Spirit of the Lord is, there is liberty. 2 Cor. 3:17

Kelly hadn't been loved with the love of Christ, nor did she have liberty.

Chapter 20
His Time had Come

I had mastered the art of calligraphy in college. I knew if I used it on the envelope, Kelly would recognize that it was from me even before she opened it. I hoped it would trigger some fond memories from her childhood. She and I used to make all kinds of signs together for church and school events with *Mom's fancy handwriting*.

I completed the card with the love note to Kelly and dropped it in the mailbox.

Weeks passed with no response. Then one day as I rushed around the house getting ready for guests at the B&B, the phone rang. I expected it to be a guest calling for reservations, but the voice on the other end said, "Hello, is this Sharon?" I responded, "Yes." The voice said, "This is Kelly, (she included her last name) your daughter." Like I wouldn't recognize her voice or know who Kelly was.

She said, "I've been holding onto the card you sent me for weeks." She told me that she'd hold it in her hands, just looking at it. She'd wonder what if I dial the phone number on this card, how much will it change my life?

She told me that she opened the card, saw that it was very pretty and signed, Mom. She figured it was from Betty (Ken's mother). She was the person Kelly now considered as Mom.

I felt hurt. She and I both knew Betty couldn't write like that. I figured her remarks were intended to hurt my feelings. I ignored it. Any contact was good, and I wouldn't let a little offense stop what might be my miracle. We talked for just a short time. She chose not to call me Mom but addressed me by my first name. I felt insulted. However, I was sure she had gone through a mind-altering state and that she wasn't the daughter I once knew.

When I hung up the phone, I didn't jump up and down or shout Hallelujah! I simply looked up to The Father, and said very quiet and peacefully, "Thank you. You told me You'd do this in Your way and in Your time. Thank you." He'd done what He said He would. I had a heart of gratefulness and Thanksgiving. My lost daughter was on her way home. I knew the phone call was the first step in her long journey to rediscovering herself.

> God is faithful, reliable, trustworthy, and therefore ever true to His promise, and He can be depended on. 1 Cor. 1:9a

Kelly began to phone several times a week. She said the calls could only continue if she could lay down rules for our conversations. I wasn't to speak anything negative about Ken. I could only talk about pleasant things. We couldn't discuss any pain related to her disappearance or talk about how the other children felt. We couldn't talk about the rape or molestation. I agreed to her ground rules. The lines of communication had opened for the first time in a decade and I was careful to only speak what the Father was saying.

She continued to call me by my first name, instead of Mom. That was hard to hear. About the third week of phone calls she let down her guard, and I was once more, Mom. Music to my ears! Just typing this brings tears to my eyes.

I needed to be patient with her. She was frail and wounded, so I agreed to whatever terms she set down. At least we were talking and that was a start. I had to be careful, I didn't want to let her know how guarded her little sister and brother were about this new connection. They were fearful that I'd be hurt again. They felt so rejected by her that it would take them a long time to ever trust her again. They were both very verbal about their feelings. They didn't trust her in any way. They were the faithful kids as they saw it, and they intended to protect me. They were watching carefully how this was unfolding.

As I expected, Kelly was afraid to let Ken know she was speaking to me. All calls were done in secret. That was scary for her. We talked about her new baby girl. She told me how badly she had wanted me to be present at the time of her daughter Audrey's birth.

I had prayed that having a little girl would bring back great memories of her and I together. That she would begin to reconnect to that exceptional closeness that we once had enjoyed. Those were powerful moments buried deep in her soul. If she could reach down and touch them again, she'd desire those feelings once more.

It wasn't long before all her conversation rules started to fall apart. The walls came down as she wept and expressed how much she had missed me and how she needed me in her life. Soon we were spending hours on the phone each time, with buckets of tears flowing from both ends of the phone. Kelly's son was twelve years old now, and he had a very negative view of who his grandparents were. I'd missed all these years with him, and they didn't seem to be redeemable.

Cell phones had become more widely used and affordable. That made it easier for Kelly to call without being detected. Together, we worked through many of the lies that we both had been told, clearing up the ones that started this great deception in the first place. In time Kelly's courage began to mount. With great apprehension, she decided to tell Ken that she had been talking with me.

She told him, "I don't know what you think my Mom has done, or why she is so bad, but surely her punishment has been great enough. It's time to end this craziness. I want to see my Mom again!"

His response was, "If your parents will agree to sit down with me privately first, I'll allow you to see them." Kelly delivered Ken's ultimatum to me. It didn't matter what it was. I had determined I would agree to any conditions, even though I dreaded speaking with him. He'd been so judgmental and accusatory toward our family. He had power to interfere with all the work Kelly and I had accomplished over the past few months.

I didn't want to argue with him, or feel I had to defend myself. I didn't think I'd done anything wrong, but I purposed to not express that. I'd just sit and listen. Occasionally, I'd nod my head in agreement. Kind of like Wayne's Mom had taught me to do. Choose your battles wisely.

He never wanted to share Kelly with anyone. I thought of him as the man the devil used to destroy our family, and to rob my daughter of her destiny.

Chapter 21

The Dreaded Confrontation

A date was set for Joe and me to meet with Ken. However, Ken's target was me. He didn't seem to care if he spoke with Joe at all, only me. As the day approached, I laid awake several nights in bed going over in my mind what this meeting might be like. None of those thoughts were pleasant. I imagined being grilled under bright, hot interrogation lights, until I was exhausted. I knew I had to trust God and just cast down imaginations to be able to get through this. The devil loves to bombard our thought life and to bring fear.

> Casting down imaginations, and every high thing that exalteth itself against the knowledge of God, and bringing into captivity every thought to the obedience of Christ. 2 Cor. 10:5

I thought about Jacob in the Bible when he was meeting back up with Esau (Gen. 33-34). Esau had vowed to kill his brother Jacob who was returning from Laban with Rachel and Leah. Jacob feared his brother Esau, so he sent gifts ahead to help soften Esau's heart. They ended up hugging instead of trying to kill one another. I could only hope for such a miraculous outcome. I prayed and decided to follow Jacob's wisdom. I really needed The Father's help on this. I didn't know my grandson or my granddaughter who was going to be three years-old soon. I listened to what The Lord was saying would be acceptable gifts for everyone, including Ken. I gathered them together, and Joe and I loaded them in the car. Together we started our dreaded journey to meet with our son-n-law, whom we hadn't seen in over a decade.

With so much apprehension, we prayed all the way there. We parked in the lot at the entrance of the motel and made our way to the front door, not knowing what to expect. As we walked in the door of the motel lobby, I locked eyes with my son-n-law. Immediately, the Holy Spirit took over. Instinctively, I just went right to him weeping, hugging his neck, and said, "I'm sorry, I'm so sorry."

I didn't know what I was sorry for. Those were just the words that came out of my mouth. I humbled myself because I felt it was what was required to mend this relationship. He told me I was forgiven. After that Ken didn't feel the *need* to have his private conversation with me. He just backed off and let Kelly and I visit, allowing me to get to know the children. Amazing! The lesson: Most everything we imagine, or dread rarely happens.

> Humble yourselves in the sight of the Lord, and he shall lift you up. James 4:10

> Therefore if thou bring thy gift to the altar, and there rememberest that thy brother hath ought against thee; Leave there thy gift before the altar, and go thy way; first be reconciled to thy brother, and then come and offer thy gift. Agree with thine adversary quickly, whiles thou art in the way with him; lest at any time the adversary deliver thee to the judge, and the judge deliver thee to the officer, and thou be cast into prison.... Matt. 5:23-26

I had learned a great truth. You don't have to be wrong to say, "I'm sorry." What was important was my daughter and her children. I wanted to make her life easier. If that meant being the one to ask for forgiveness, I was willing to do that. I didn't plan it that way. I just yielded to what the Holy Spirit was leading, and He knew exactly what Ken would respond to. Just like Jacob and Esau. Jacob humbled himself before Esau, and they both wept. So, did we. We embraced and we wept. I had rushed to hug the man that I had resented for so long.

> ......and he passed over before them and bowed himself to the ground seven times, until he came near to his brother. And Esau ran to meet him and embraced him and fell on his neck, and kissed him and they wept. Gen.33:3-4

This is how I felt that day. I had dreaded meeting with Ken. I prayed about what gifts to bring, and I felt as though I'd wrestled with my own angel. I had to stay humble and follow the leading of The Holy Spirit.

I couldn't have scripted this meeting any better. God already had! We spent the day with Kelly's family and time with the children. I even got an invitation to my granddaughter's third birthday party, which was to be a tea party. I didn't know either of the children and even after much time those lost years still matter.

Chapter 22
The Outcome

Things seemed ok for a while, and Kelly's family even joined ours for Thanksgiving one year. However, their relationship continued to deteriorate. She was under stress of running the motel, and also a bakery. Ken seemed to have no interest in being involved with these endeavors. At times he helped with large construction projects but the day to day maintenance and workings of both businesses fell to Kelly. Every dispute or customer difficulty was left for her to resolve. She enabled Ken, just like his mother had done all his life.

Joe became Kelly's maintenance man for the motel, even though he had to drive over an hour to get there. Ken had found a new project. There was a divorced woman and her children in the community. He was passionate about wanting to help them. He even spoke of adopting the children and co-raising them with their mother. We knew this lady. She was related by marriage. It started out with him helping her with the children by building bunk beds. Eventually he moved the other family into his and Kelly's home with them.

Because Ken had little interest in sex, Kelly didn't feel threatened. However, Kelly was the old family, and now there was a new one. To Kelly and her son Ken seemed obsessed with them.

Kelly and Ken had slept in separate rooms for years and even though she honestly believed Ken was the love of her life. She had lived a celibate life for over thirteen years of marriage. Her daughter's birth had been the result of a onetime encounter after years of no physical contact. Now she was sharing what little attention she could get from Ken with another woman and her children. The feelings of rejection had become overwhelming. Kelly was feeling suicidal.

I was so grateful that she thought to phone me the night she was seriously contemplating taking her life. As she stood in the garage with a loaded gun, she allowed me to share the love of Jesus and the price He had paid for her to live. As she listened, she realized that killing herself was a permanent solution to a temporary problem. She caught just a small glimmer of hope and felt her life might still have some value to someone. The next day, she phoned her Daddy and asked him to pick her up and bring her home. She was finally leaving.

Kelly came home with both of her children but within days she returned. Ken was in trouble, and she went home to rescue him. His *charity project*, the other family that had moved in with him, got him in some hot water. He'd shown too much attention to one of the teenage girls and Family Services showed up to check it out.

Back and forth, back and forth Kelly went. She'd come home for weeks at a time to stay with us with no real intention of ending her marriage. She just needed space that she hadn't had for nearly twenty years. She'd say, "If I can't make it with Ken, I can't make it with anyone."

She asked Joe and me if she could manage a total revision of our gardens at the B&B, and we agreed. As the bulldozer arrived to tear up our already landscaped yard, we wondered what in the world had we agreed to! This was way more than we had planned on! There were times Joe and I had no idea what she was doing. Even though Kelly had every inch of the property diagramed, we just couldn't get the big picture, or even imagine the final outcome. The yard looked like a destroyed, torn up mess for months. But in the end, she'd created the hard scape and garden of our dreams. In the years to follow the gardens were used to host up to thirty-five weddings a year. It brought great memories and joy to many couples. We were glad we'd allowed her to get creative.

This project was therapeutic for Kelly and it gave her purpose. We could begin to see a small glimpse of the person that used to be our daughter resurfacing.

Ken's mom decided to sell the motel and bakery after the fiasco with Ken's *other family*. So, he and Kelly moved into one of his mother's houses in a near-by town. Ken received an allowance from his Mom until her death. He spent his time at the computer trying to learn the online trading business. He never quite got it right!

The final Ah-ha moment came for Kelly on their twentieth anniversary. She didn't even get a kiss good night! Kelly had spent twenty years of her life trying to save *a sinking ship!* No matter how much she tried to make things work, there hadn't been any change of Ken's heart in twenty years.

Kelly and her little girl came home to live with Joe and me. Her son stayed with his dad who initiated the divorce. Still, the failure was devastating. She'd put in so much time and effort only to have it end this way. The deciding factor for Ken was that Kelly had given up celebrating holidays that she didn't see in the scriptures. Ken refused to consider the new-found convictions of her faith, and for him, that gave him a way out. He taunted and made fun of her beliefs!

Calling on God is what had saved Kelly' life from suicide. She recommitted her life to live more fully for God, but in the end, that would be the final blow to Ken's religious ego.

Curious Minds Want to Know

Some may be wondering what happened that Kelly ended up having a second child. There were so many years of no physical contact between her and Ken. Kelly had been spending some time in the presence of the Lord when she had a vision of a little redheaded child. She was singing songs as she played in crystal rain drops.

Not understanding what she was seeing, Kelly asked, "Father, who is this little girl."

He answered, "That's your daughter."

She answered back, "I'm not Sarah, if you tell me I am going to have a daughter, I'll tell everyone I meet."

He spoke again, "This is your child Audrey, and she's singing because she has a beautiful voice."

Kelly went right away and told Ken what God had spoken. He laughed, and said, "I guess it'll be by Immaculate Conception."

For nearly three years Kelly told everyone she was going to have a little girl. Betty especially thought she was crazy. She knew what kind of relationship Ken and Kelly had. Then one night with no explanation, there was a moment of intimacy and Kelly conceived my granddaughter Audrey. Kelly's vision took on flesh.

It was when Kelly was in the delivery room having Audrey that she realized how much she missed her Mom and wished that I were there to be part of the birth experience. God was working.

To show how amazing our God is, and how completely He does what He says He'll do; Audrey was awarded "Composer of the Year" and "Voice of the Year" in a recent competition at the University of Missouri.

According to Romans 4:17, Kelly called those things which be not as though they were. God gave her the desires of her heart. Against all odds, she had a daughter

Chapter 23

Healing Takes Time

Kelly struggled for the first few years of being single, looking for acceptance in many places. She'd lost herself somewhere and just couldn't figure where she fit into life. She went to college which was a financial struggle. She was raising Audrey on her own. There weren't any provisions for her or her daughter in the divorce. That was Kelly's idea. She never wanted Ken to have a say in what she did with Audrey. I'm not sure that was healthy for her daughter. Children need to know their parents. They can make up their own minds as they mature, who that person really is.

Even with the tragic things that happened to Kelly and Jeff the summer they were with Wayne, Jeff especially has continued to need his Pop's approval in his life. Unfortunately, no one in Wayne's life even knows Jeff exists or that Wayne has twenty grandchildren. Even though Wayne flies for free he never once went to see Jeff for the ten years he taught school in Alaska.

When Kelly moved home, she didn't want to live with Joe and me. She insisted on having one of our cottages we used for our business. We gave in to that. She'd been so controlled we reasoned she needed the independence. This arrangement gave her freedom to come and go as she pleased. She could invite anyone she chose into her home. Eventually, she and Joe had frequent disagreements. This wasn't an easy transition for any of us.

Kelly and I began to take walks together like we did when she was young. We worked at rebuilding our relationship. This wasn't what I'd envisioned for my daughter's life. I felt the enemy had robbed her of her God given destiny, but I was glad she was free.

I had to learn to *let go*. I was still learning to trust God even though Kelly was back home. Since she lived next door to us, it was hard for Joe. We had some tough spots, major bumps in the road. Some of this required extremely difficult decisions for all of us, but God was faithful to His Word to me. He did it in His time. I prayed, I repented, but the real answer was to simply trust The Father. God wouldn't permit me to be the *fixer.*

Joe was a righteous man and he expected that of our children as well. Kelly had spent twenty years in Ken's family and Joe felt she'd retained their value system rather than ours. There were times they'd become so upset with each other that Kelly and I didn't speak for months. However, we both had learned valuable lessons. We needed family. We always found a way to make it right. We'd already lost so much time.

She's not walking in the anointing of her youth but carries an amazing passion for the hurting. God's not finished with her yet.

> Being confident of this very thing, that he which hath begun a good work in you will perform it until the day of Jesus Christ. Phil. 1:6

She's an accomplished woman. She walks with God to her own tune and she seems to be blessing everything she puts her hands to.

She established a business caring for disabled veterans with some of the most difficult cases of PTSD I've ever seen. She's the go-to person for The Veteran's Administration in our area to help veterans that can't be stabilized anywhere else. She has a heart of compassion and a determination to never give up on anyone. She freely offers unconditional love to each one of these men in a way they have never experienced before. She works to rebuild their self-esteem and offers an opportunity for them to find their place in life as they become part of a family with the other veterans.

Kelly is once again strong, confident, and successful. She took an idea and began an unique business using our B & B property which she eventually purchased from us. She acquired her brown belt in karate and the veterans know not to mess with her. Caring for so many emotionally stressed men occasionally puts her in a vulnerable position.

Those years working with the handicapped for Betty's business, gave her the experience she needed to get started. However, there's no doubt that the anointing that breaks every yoke of bondage comes from Jesus Himself.

> ....and the yoke shall be destroyed because of the anointing. Is. 10:27

Kelly has found love and acceptance in a very unlikely partner, vastly different from Ken. Occasionally, I remind her how she swore there could never be another man in her life but Ken. She thought that love had just been too painful to ever try again. I love seeing Kelly happy even though I don't get to spend a lot of time with her. She is so occupied with caring for her veterans.

Recently we managed some time to have coffee together. As we both left the coffee shoppe, we hugged each other goodbye. I was crossing the street when I heard her call from behind me in a loud voice, "*I love you Mama. You're my very best friend.*" I responded, "I love you too Kelly."

This clearly isn't a book about walking in victory all the time, or having my prayers answered immediately. It's about how Yahweh sustained me through the battle and brought peace and grace in the midst of my storms. In the process, He continued to build character into my life. He is teaching me to run this race to win. He may not do things my way. However, I know that He always has my best interest, and that of my children, in His heart.

> If thou hast run with the footmen, and they have wearied thee, then how canst thou contend with horses? Jer. 12:5a

We can't give up. We can't grow weary. We must keep running, hoping that tomorrow will be the day that we see the result of our trusting and prayers.

> And we know that all things work together for good to them that love God, to them who are the called according to His purpose. Rm. 8:28

The note in the back of my Bible was true. "I'd always have my children." Kelly isn't the great song writer I imagined she would be. However, she has resumed voice and piano lessons again and is as always, extremely gifted. Her daughter, Audrey seems to have the same gift. May God's will be done. Life is not a sprint; it is a marathon.

History Repeats Itself:

Kelly's son has grown to be a man and is now married. Noble's wife became offended with Kelly about something that seemed very minor to Kelly.

She went to the Lord to be sure her heart was clear. She checked to see that she had thoroughly repented for her part in our separation. Then she asked to get the mind of Christ on the situation with her son. She decided to do what her Mom had done. She relaxed and trusted God. She didn't have to go through the tears and agonizing that I did. She simply surrendered to God and his purpose for her son. The whole issued resolved itself in a short time. Kelly didn't have to live through years waiting for answers. She already knew that her tears didn't change anything. God is good, He's got this.

She has a loving and close relationship with her son. It has been rewarding to see both my older children learn from their parents in this way. It's a joy to see reconciliation happen so rapidly.

I wanted to fix things for my daughter, and I wanted it done my way and in my time frame. God had other plans. His ways are not our ways. I pray you learn faster than I did that God's plan is always the best plan. Don't forget to ask him what that is.

Questions to ponder:

1. Are there preconceived notions how God should answer?
2. What are they?
3. Why can't I let go?
4. Do I trust God with my child's future?
5. Am I willing to wait for HIS answer?
6. Will God to get all of us through this storm? Including me?
7. How do I respond when things are totally out of my control?
8. What does God say about that?
9. Am I able to say I am sorry, even if I'm not in the wrong?
10. Is there a way to find peace while you wait on God?

Chapter 24
The Old Soul

Have you heard of *The Old Soul*? You know, the person that's wise beyond their years. They rarely have friends their own age, and even as children they are more comfortable hanging with the adults. They're the kind of person who can hold their own in an adult conversation when they're only twelve. They're the responsible one. They seem to care about the big picture, what's important in life and in the world. They're usually deep thinkers, but loners, often feeling lonely and isolated. They want to be part of things but aren't fond of engaging in foolishness or what they see as frivolous. They are seekers of truth, wisdom, and knowledge. They're usually peace makers, benevolent in their service, desiring to make a difference in the world, determined, purposeful.

> ….aspire to live quietly, and to mind your own affairs, and to work with your hands, as we instructed you, so that you may walk properly before outsiders and be dependent on no one. 1 Thes. 4:11-12

That's who she was.

Enter Rachel

Joe and I were married in May of 1975. We were crazy in love and both exuberant about our faith. Joe was quite satisfied being Daddy to my two children which he inherited when he chose to marry me. He showed no interest in having more children, but God had other plans. Even after trying every kind of birth control available at the time, it wasn't long before Rachel was conceived. Even though this pregnancy wasn't planned, we were thrilled to be expecting. The whole family was excited.

> Lo, children are an heritage of the Lord: and the fruit of the womb is his reward. Ps. 127:3

We were being rewarded.

We were living on our little 13-acre farm and even though we were financially strapped, we were very happy. I felt blessed to be having a child with a believing partner, *a man of God*. I'd never known this kind of love before. I just felt there was something very spiritual about two people in love with Jesus, and with each other, being able to create another human being. It seemed supernatural to me.

One day I was on the telephone with my girlfriend. I told her how happy and grateful I felt, to be sharing the birth of a child with such a loving man. My son Jeff, who was ten, overheard my conversation. Jeff completely misunderstood what he'd heard. He proceeded to tell Kelly, "Mom thinks that we're cursed children from a cursed marriage, and the new baby will be a blessed child, from a blessed marriage." He never understood how wonderful it was to me to be truly loved for the first time in my life. It had nothing to do with how I felt about the other children. My conversation was about Joe, God and feeling extremely blessed.

However, that's not what Jeff's ten-year old mind understood. Eventually, this conversation was used as a set up by the devil. What started as a misunderstanding of a ten-year-old boy, would set in motion envy among the children all their lives. Even in later years, when we learned of these feelings and tried to correct them, the mind set was still there. Rachel would always be pegged as Mom and Dad's favorite even before she was born. This lie set up the spirit of competition in our family.

> You are of your father the devil, and your will is to do your father's desires. He was a murderer from the beginning. And has nothing to do with the truth because there is no truth in him. When he lies, he speaks out of his own character, for he is a liar and the father of lies. John 8:44

This is a perfect example of how the devil works. He picks on little kids; feeds them a lie. They receive it as truth, because they aren't mature enough to ask questions or understand what is truly being conveyed. Over time he continually reinforces it in their minds for the rest of their lives. So, the person they become, and who God intended them to be, is distorted by the lies of Satan.

His soul purpose is to destroy anything that is in the image of God or that will bring God glory. That includes our children. Once the enemy convinces a child of a lie, the only way to reverse it is with the truth from God. You can tell your children everyday of their lives that what they believe isn't true. But, until they hear that in their hearts from God Himself, the lie will continue to have power in their lives.

Because Kelly was away from home for so long, she wasn't around to see how this principal played out in all their adult lives. She still remembered all the special times she and Rachel had sharing a room together as children.

The Scare

During my pregnancy with Rachel, Joe and I lead a Sunday worship service every week in one of the local nursing homes. I learned to play four or five songs on the piano, to lead worship and to get the attention of the elderly residents.

The sound of the piano playing in the lobby alerted them that the service was starting soon. Every week, there was an old Pentecostal lady in her nineties who was the first to be in place. She always sat up close to the front. The assistant wheeled her out in her chair. As soon as she heard the music, she began to speak exuberantly in tongues. She had a very distinctive language. Some of it sounded like, "Shhhu-bah bah bah, Shhhu-bah, bah bah." She was a delightful lady, always upbeat and excited to worship Jesus. I'll explain later, why this is significant.

I loved being on the farm, learning so many new things and spending so much time just being Mom. Finally, the long-awaited day arrived. My first due date was in May, then moved to June and now, July second had arrived. When labor began, I phoned the doctor. He said, "Go on to the hospital and I'll see you in the morning." I thought, "Yeh, right!" Labor with Kelly was only about an hour long, and I knew I wouldn't make it till morning. By the time we arrived at the hospital Rachel was entering this world if the doctor was there or not. The nurses were frantic because they couldn't locate the doctor. Finally, he rushed in, dressed in a tuxedo with a light blue ruffled shirt. Apparently, Rachel had interrupted a big event. They quickly rolled me into the delivery room and in a few minutes, the doctor was gone, as abruptly as he had arrived. This turned out to be the most unpleasant delivery experience I had. I made up my mind if I ever had another child, I wouldn't deliver in a hospital again.

I was hoping for a boy, desiring for Joe to have an heir to carry on his name. I planned for a son throughout the pregnancy. However, when we were surprised with a girl it didn't matter one bit. She was lovely.

Rachel was born July second. It was the United States Bicentennial year in 1976. She had fiery red hair and big bright blue eyes. She had an alert look about her. At times, she almost looked surprised. Rachel had such a peaceful demeanor that my older sister, Sandy called her, "The Bible Baby." She said, "You know those Big old-time, coffee table Bibles? Well, Rachel looks like she was lifted right off one of those pages with the beautiful artwork on them."

On the night of Rachel's arrival, as I held her in my arms, we could hear the firecrackers popping loudly outside the hospital window. It turned out that Rachel never enjoyed the loud noises and crowds associated with our National Fourth of July Celebration.

She'd never be an extravert, like her older sister, Kelly. This was a quite different child. She was what my family called, an *Old Soul*. Kelly was turned like me, but Rachel was always more like her dad.

Joe had never experienced the joy of having a newborn. This was his first, and he couldn't get enough of her. The miracle of life was astounding to him.

At the time of her birth, Joe was teaching at the Vo-tech school. Every evening when he arrived home, he'd hug me and the children, then head in to see Rachel. He frequently held her on his lap all evening as he spent hours grading student's papers.

On these hot July nights, he'd take off his shirt to cool down and just hold Rachel against his bare chest. He loved holding her close, and smelling her sweet baby breath, feeling her soft, and extremely pale white skin. She was a delight to him and the entire family. Her presence seemed to make us all one. It seemed she was the element needed to make all of us feel we belonged to one another, like we were really family now.

When she was six weeks old, we went for Rachel's routine wellness check-up. The Doctor voiced some concern because baby Rachel kept sticking her tongue out. He said this was a symptom of a serious thyroid disorder. If he were right, it would prevent Rachel from growing properly and even affect her ability to speak. So, he ran several tests to confirm his suspicions. When they came back, he delivered the bad news that Rachel had tested positive for the feared disorder.

Joe and I flatly refused to believe anything was wrong with our perfect gift. We began to seek God for a miracle. We were attending an Assembly of God church that believed in healing. So, we took Rachel before the church and had her anointed with oil. The elders prayed the prayer of faith and we believed she was healed.

> Is anyone among you sick? Let him call for the elders of the church; and let them pray over him anointing him with oil in the name of the Lord: and the prayer of faith shall save the sick, and the Lord shall raise him up; James 5:14-15a

I so believed that Rachel was healed that I didn't want her retested. I dreaded the call back from the doctor because I knew he would argue with me. When his call came, I told him, "The Elders prayed for Rachel and now she's healed." He wasn't buying it. He pushed me to retest her. He said, "If she's really healed, then what's the problem with further tests? They'll only show that she's healed if she really is." Reluctantly, I agreed. I hated hearing her cry so hard while they tried finding veins to draw blood. I just wanted to trust God.

This time the blood was sent off to St. Louis for further testing, instead of using a local lab.

We waited to hear from the doctor. When the call finally came, he said, "Sharon, you're right. Rachel's been healed. They couldn't find one thing wrong with her blood test. I can't explain that. I guess God really did heal her."

> Heal me, O Lord, and I shall be healed; save me, and I shall be saved; for you are my praise. Jer. 17:14

How blessed we were to have God on our side. He healed our little girl. Every time Rachel reached a growing milestone, I'd think back of what might have been and how God had made her whole. I'd just quietly thank him again.

What is She Saying??

Rachel began walking at about a year. When she mastered running, she'd dart through the halls of our Houston home yelling, "Shhhu-bah bah bah, Shhhu-bah bah bah." How did she know that? Where did she learn that? She was speaking in the same language, or stammering lips as the old woman in the nursing home. It was unmistakable. How could that be since Rachel had never heard this woman speak?

Joe and I prayed for our daughter to be filled with God's Spirit while she was in the womb, but we both found this surprising. How could Rachel know this language? We moved to Texas right after Rachel was born. Was this Rachel's own prayer language, or had she heard it while she was in the womb? She wasn't even speaking English well yet. Either way, we found it remarkable. I guess it's not any stranger than when the baby, John the Baptist, leaped in his mother's womb, when Mary the Mother of Jesus came to visit his Mom.

> When Elizabeth heard Mary's greeting, her baby leaped in her womb; and Elizabeth was filled with the Holy Spirit *and* empowered by Him. Luke 1:4

I'm not comparing Rachel with John the Baptist; I'm just saying from this story in the Bible it's obvious that an unborn child can hear and be sensitive to God's Spirit even before it is born.

Rachel was easy to train, took little discipline, and she could be guided with your eye. As a toddler, if she ever misbehaved, I'd set her up on the kitchen table. Then I'd sit in a chair right in front of her. That way we were eye to eye.

Instead of using the word spank, we called a swat on the fanny a "pow-pow." I'd point to my lips and say to her, "Watch my mouth." She'd look intently at my face as I spoke, never moving her eyes one way or the other. Then I'd say, "If you do that again, Mama will pow-pow you." I'd clap my hands together each time I said pow-pow for a greater effect. When I finished talking to her, I always said, "What did Mama say?" She repeated my words, "If I do that again, you will pow-pow." This was the only correction Rachel ever needed. Once I took her down off the table, I never needed to correct her about the same thing again. It only took that one time for her to comply from then on.

Rachel was quite different than Jeff or Kelly. They were energetic and out-going. Rachel was quiet and reserved, extremely independent, but seemed to carry an unusual peace about her. She didn't need to be cuddled or held. At times she irritated me, because the only time she came to me or snuggled was when she was nursing.

After she started to walk, she loved being with Kelly and Jeff. Every day when they left for school, she followed them to the door. Then she just sat at the door and waited, hoping they'd return soon. I was beginning to feel that if we were going to have any more children, it should be sooner than later.

Joe had so enjoyed being a Dad and his opinion about having more children had changed drastically. Now he wanted a dozen. We were both in our thirties and didn't want to wait too much longer to have more children. We felt two children closer in age, would allow them to have companionship and to be best friends.

Joe was one of eight children and I was the middle of five girls, so we were used to large families. I still wanted another opportunity to have a son. Just before Rachel's second birthday, her little brother Samuel was born. I had my little boy and Rachel had a little brother. She adored him; they would become great friends. That is, when she wasn't trying to be his second mother.

The Escape Artist

One of Rachel's many talents was her unusual ability to escape. She hated being confined. We often joked about her being a little Houdini. When I put her into her highchair, she filled her little tummy with air. As soon as I wasn't looking, she would suck in her belly and just simply slide down, out from under the buckled strap, and onto the floor. When we got wise to her, and she couldn't get free in the same manner, she scooted the highchair across the room. She shook it back and forth to get where she wanted to go. She jerked it so hard that the vibration broke the pedestal free from the seat. We had to purchase a second highchair that could restrain her better. The first one was rendered useless. There was little that could hold Rachel down. She could get out of a highchair, a crib, or a play pen. It didn't matter what safety measures we used to protect her; she could find a way out.

One beautiful sunny afternoon I decided it would be nice for her and me to sit outside and get some sun. I put up the playpen in the backyard and placed her in it. The yard was surrounded by a chain link fence, so I felt sure there was no way she could get out or anyone else could get in. I ran inside to get a drink and when I came back outside, which was just a few short minutes, Rachel was gone.

My heart started pounding with fear as I tried figuring out where she could be. How could she have gotten out of the yard? Where was she? I looked all around and then I noticed my neighbor's sliding glass patio door was open. It was the only place I thought she might have gone. I hurriedly ran around to their front door and rang the bell, just hoping I would find Rachel inside. My neighbor answered the door and said, "She's in Nancy's room playing with the Barbie Dolls." Rachel wasn't even two and Nancy was five.

I went down the hall to find Rachel, who had climbed out of the play pen and over the chain-link fence in her bare feet. She went through the open patio door and wandered into Nancy's bedroom, where she was playing Barbie dolls. Just like the two of them were the same age. My neighbor said, "Rachel can come back again sometime. Nancy loves having her here."

Well, it might have been fun for Nancy but having a missing child was no picnic for me.

God's Gentle Reminder

Rachel was very intuitive. Often, she said things that seemed to come right from God himself.

Joe and I had been shopping for a motor home to use in the ministry, but after several disappointments, we lost interest and the search grew cold. We began to focus on other seemingly more important things.

One evening, as Rachel sat in her highchair with spaghetti smeared all over her face, she looked up at Joe and said, "Daddy, when are you going to get that motor home?" We both looked at each other in surprise. Joe said to me, "Have you been talking about the motor home again?" It'd been months since we'd even discussed it. When Rachel said it, Joe's heart was pricked.

After dinner Joe took some time in prayer as he often did. He felt God had reminded him through a toddler, to start looking again for the right motor home. Rachel's words put a fire under Joe, in a pursuit that had grown cold. He began his search that same week and finally made a decision to purchase a motor home. Within weeks of that purchase, the Lord gave us both clear directions as to when and where we were to go next. Joe never forgot how the words of a toddler in a highchair with spaghetti all over her face affected him that night.

> Out of the mouths of babes and sucklings hast thou ordained strength……Ps. 8:2a

Often people say things and you don't even pay attention. Then there are times it seems like their words pierce you heart and just grab you. That's how it was that night with Rachel.

We didn't know it then, but we'd need the motor home for the move to Phoenix. Rachel was about two and a half years old at the time. We had no idea that we'd end up living in that motor home for nearly a year before we'd find adequate housing. Sam learned to walk in the aisles of the motor home.

Fear of Abandonment

In Arizona we attended a large church where we were part of the ministry staff. Usually we drove our personal van and picked up people on the way that needed a ride. We'd done this nearly every place we lived.

On Sundays after service it was Jeff's job to get Rachel from the nursery. Joe and I gathered the rest of the children and all our passengers. One Sunday, after retrieving Rachel from the nursery Jeff strapped her into her car seat. Then he turned to visit with his buddies, just outside the van.

When it was time to go, everyone else piled into the vehicle. I was in the front passenger seat and couldn't see through all the people for a head count. So, I asked if we had everyone before we drove away. I was assured everyone was on board. We drove the first family to their home. As the woman got out of the van, she said, "Well, let me kiss little Rachel goodbye." We looked and little Rachel wasn't with us. She had performed one of her escape acts again! She managed to get out of her car seat and go back into the nursery. When the nursery worker asked her, "Who is your Mommy and Daddy?" she answered, "Mommy and Daddy." She couldn't tell them her last name. The church was so huge that the volunteer staff didn't realize whose child she was, and so the police were called. They were told that someone had dropped their child off to the church nursery and abandoned her. That seemed crazy to me, but I guess this kind of thing actually happens in some larger cities, even back in the seventies.

It was several hours before we had Rachel back in our care. Of course, I was panicky, not knowing for sure where she was or who she was with. We phoned the church but by then no one was there to answer. My apprehension made for an exceptionally long ride back to the church. Joe and I prayed all the way. Even though she was just a toddler when this happened, Rachel dealt with the fear of being abandoned from time to time. It made me ache for her. God knows she was loved, and we would never leave her intentionally.

As she grew, she was such an independent personality that most didn't realize she dealt with these fears. I'm sure her brothers and sisters never understood this about her.

Once Joe drove to another town to pick up some supplies from a friend. Rachel was about eight years old. She road along with him. When they arrived at the friend's home, Rachel took out her box of Barbie dolls and clothes and began playing with our friend's daughter. Joe went to back up the truck to load materials and Rachel was afraid he was leaving her. She screamed, "Daddy, Daddy, don't leave me!" She ran and jumped in the passenger's side of the pickup and wouldn't get back out. She was so fearful of being left, that she never went back to retrieve her toys.

We guard and care for our children to the best of our ability, but the devil will do his utmost to lie to them. When those lies are believed, they set up a pattern of how they see themselves. The devil is so slick, we probably don't even realize that our kids have been fed a lie until the fruit of it shows up later in life. I'd assumed that once Rachel was back with us that she would feel safe. I was wrong.

> But while men slept, his enemy came and sowed tares among the wheat and went his way. Matt. 13:25

We're doing everything we know to grow a good crop of Godly things in our children's hearts. While the enemy is secretly coming to sow tares and tries to plant as many weeds as he can. God help me not to be found sleeping. Teach us to be vigilant and not ignorant of Satan's devices.

> Be sober, be vigilant; because your adversary the devil, as a roaring lion, walketh about, seeking whom he may devour.
> 1 Peter 5:8

He uses every opportunity to destroy our precious possessions.

Chapter 25
The Little Seer

We were living in the Arizona house when Rachel turned four. To celebrate her birthday, the family traveled to Prescott, Arizona with friends for a camping trip. It was Fourth of July weekend and there was a huge rodeo in town. We couldn't afford for all of us to attend the rodeo, so we purchased tickets for the children and allowed Jeff who was fifteen by now to take the other children in to watch. Rachel didn't want to go. Remember she hated the fireworks and the noise of the crowds. She wanted to stay with Mom and Dad. So, we drove the other children to the rodeo, and made sure they got in safely.

Joe and I headed back to our camp site. Rachel was still small enough she could sit in the front seat between us. The firecrackers had been making loud noises all day and the town was overrun with bikers everywhere. As we drove down one of the main drags, Rachel said, "Daddy don't go that way, a man got shot up there." She pointed straight ahead. Joe and I kind of chuckled and figured she'd heard firecrackers and thought it was the sound of a gun. When she told us, we were blocks away from the town square and had a perfect place to turn off out of the traffic.

We paid no attention to her words. As the traffic worsened, we began to wonder what the problem was. We were at a standstill in the bumper to bumper traffic in this little town. Our car slowly inched up to the corner, and there off to the right was the ambulance, and a man being carried on a stretcher. He'd been shot while in a bar on the town square. Rachel was right. She'd seen in the spirit and warned by God, but we didn't listen to her.

I remember trying to get Rachel to take a nap one afternoon just before her birthday. I laid down beside her, and as we fell off to sleep, I said to her, "Rachel, your birthday is right around the corner. She thought for just a minute and then she said, "If you drive me, we'll get there faster." She was a thinker, a problem solver even at four.

A couple of years later, we were traveling in the motor home back to Missouri to see family. We'd hoped to be in St. Louis for their big Fourth of July Celebration on the Mississippi River. It was always spectacular, and the kids had fond memories of past years when we were fortunate enough to attend. This was a St. Louis tradition which had been celebrated for decades. There was always lots of entertainment and a huge fireworks grand finale, all displayed under the big St. Louis Arch.

We'd been in Oklahoma setting up another Christian School. As we headed out of state toward Missouri, the RV had a mechanical problem. Joe was feeling overwhelmed in the miserable July heat and not knowing what to do to fix the motor home. He didn't want his family stranded on the road and to miss the big event in St. Louis. He and I began to pray together about what to do. There was no place around to find help.

Joe sat down on the couch and put his face in his hands as he spoke to God. Rachel, who was almost six years old, came and stood in front of him. She gently pulled his hands down from his eyes. She stood in front of him and looked him square in the eyes and said, "Don't worry Daddy, you'll get it fixed and we won't be late for the fireworks either." Joe answered her, "Rachel, we're already too late to make it on time." She said, "No Daddy, it is going to rain all day on the Fourth of July, and they'll have to do it the next day instead."

There wasn't any rain in the forecast at the time, but we remembered the year before, so we just pondered her words. Joe went to work on the RV and was able to get it running again. The next day we'd see. It happened just as our six-year-old child had spoken. It rained *all* day on the fourth, and the celebration was postponed to the next day on the fifth. We made it to the celebration on time. We wondered, does God do this kind of thing just out of love for us. How does a little child just know things? We didn't have answers.

The older children had encounters with God as well, but they never knew what was going to happen before it did.

> ....I will pour out my Spirit on all people. Your sons and daughters will prophesy, your old men will dream dreams, your young men will see visions. Joel 2:28 NIV

This was also the year that Rachel got her one and only spanking. As I said before, you could guide her with your eyes and she was so intent on pleasing us, she just didn't take much discipline.

By age six Rachel understood that Jesus was the son of God and had died for her sins. She was baptized by her dad in a ceremony that took place in a local swimming pool. It was a special day.

The Awkward Years.

I was so blessed to be able to home school my children and once I started teaching Rachel to read, her little brother Sam caught on right along with her. It was a delight for me. After having so many learning difficulties in my childhood, I loved seeing my children learn with ease.

One morning after Rachel turned eight, she was moving a chair in the kitchen. She picked it up and when she put it back down, it bounced. It came back up and hit her front tooth, which broke off at the gum line. It was a permanent tooth that had just finished coming through after having lost her baby tooth. This caused years of problems, as we tried one solution after the other to get it corrected. Rachel's whole face would swell from the tooth becoming infected. It greatly influenced how she saw herself. It was so embarrassing for her.

At times, it affected her confidence. We finally had to have the tooth removed because it was the source of the infection. It was replaced with a temporary front tooth. Then there were ongoing problems with the replacement tooth. It troubled her often until she was an adult and could have a permanent implant.

Rachel was a great secret keeper. She and Kelly shared a room, and she spent nights scratching Kelly's back as she fell off to sleep. Rachel never let on that Kelly had a boyfriend that would come and peck on the window at night, as they flirted through the window. She never broke a confidence.

She and Kelly traded stories for back scratches. Kelly says she still owes Rachel two million quarters for scratching her back every night.

The same year as the tooth disaster she was taking a gymnastics class when her grandpa stopped by. This was a highly unusual thing for Grandpa to take any interest in what the kids were doing. So, they were excited when they saw him come in. As he watched Rachel practice, she hoped for his approval. Instead as she ran over to greet him, he said to her, "Rachel, you got a little tummy going on there." I couldn't believe it. Rachel wasn't even pudgy. She was always kind of wiry. All she heard grandpa say was "I think you're fat." So, in her mind she was FAT, even when she wasn't.

This had been part of my heritage all my life. My dad was super critical of overweight people and my Mother was right there with him. Now it had been perpetrated on my daughter.

> Do not let any unwholesome talk come out of your mouths, but only what is helpful for building others up according to their needs that it may benefit those who listen. Eph 4:29 NIV

Unfortunately, this can be a generational problem. If it's not stopped, it'll repeat over and over again.

Rachel desired to be out going like her big sister Kelly. Instead, she usually had one friend at a time. She did very well in school and after Kelly left the home, Rachel stepped up to help me in every way possible. I started nursing school when she was in the 8th grade.

I had home schooled the two younger children from kindergarten and now we decided to enroll them both in public school. I couldn't continue to manage home school while going to college. Rachel took care of everything. She cleaned house, did dishes, cooked meals, kept an eye on Sam, her little brother, and even helped me with my studies. She and Joe really rose to the challenge, and together they filled in everywhere I was missing.

I made flash cards to study with, and Rachel would hold the cards and ask me questions. She studied with me in the car, taking walks, in the living room, anytime I had a test coming up she was there quizzing me. She even helped me learn how to start an IV.

I had made a dummy arm and brought equipment from school to practice starting IVs. Using my flash cards, Rachel watched carefully to be sure I didn't miss a step. Then she'd say, "Ok Mom, what did you forget?"

She and Sam hurt badly for me during the first few years when Kelly went missing. Rachel's motherly instincts wanted to rescue me, and she was determined to never let me feel abandoned by her. When you're in the middle of that kind of pain, you can't see what it's doing to those around you.

> There hath no temptation taken you but such as is common to man: God is faithful, who will not suffer you be tempted above that ye are able; but will with the temptation also make a way to escape, that you may be able to bear it. 1 Cor. 10:13

Thank God I finally listened to what He was saying, and we were able to return to some normalcy, while we waited for Kelly's return. God was faithful and I was able to endure. I'm so grateful for my younger children that loved me so deeply and did whatever they could to help me get through my pain. Rachel and Sam both felt abandoned by Kelly when she disappeared. They adored her, and now she was just gone.

Rachel was in the middle of eighth grade when she was enrolled. This was her first time ever in school. The principal wasn't friendly to home schoolers. He told me she probably wouldn't go on to high school next year, because she wouldn't ever meet their standards. He soon had to eat his words.

Rachel only attended school two weeks when she gave up her study hall to work in the front office with the adult staff. The *Old Soul* just did better with adults than with students and the staff recognized her strengths right away. She was so far ahead of the other students in every way that there wasn't any need for her to have a study hall.

When her first semester ended, she asked Joe and me to come to the Parent/Teacher conference. We wondered why she was so intent on our going. In her mind, meeting her teachers was having us meet her friends. She wasn't especially good at making friends, but in this learning atmosphere that was different. All her teachers had become her friends.

As we were introduced to her teachers, they all told us the same thing. "We have to remind ourselves that Rachel's a student." One teacher said, "Often we teachers are in a circle talking, and Rachel just walks up and joins in. It's like she's one of us. We often forget that she's a student." That was Rachel. We'd raised her to be an adult, not a child, and we must have done a pretty good job of it. Not to mention, she just had an *Old Soul spirit*.

She had a favorite teacher, Mrs. Zufuto, who taught History. Mrs. Zufuto told Rachel that in her lifetime she'd see our country collapse. Rachel took that to heart. She was an extreme patriot, she loved America like no one I'd ever met. She prayed often for the strength of our nation, as if she had been here from it 's inception. This continued to be an ongoing passion of hers. As I see some of the governmental controls that have been set in place during the recent Covid 19 pandemic, I've wondered if Rachel once more had seen into the future.

Rachel was always a very determined person, and she decided when she was old enough that she and one of her girlfriends were going to go to YWAM (Youth with a mission). She wanted to follow in her older sister Kelly's steps. She felt strongly that Kelly really missed it by not going back to YWAM and marrying David, her co-star in the theatrical production. Rachel wanted a mission experience of her own. So, she figured a way to raise her own money to make this adventure happen. She never once asked Joe and I to contribute. She was going to do this on her own.

She and her friend Elizabeth began raising funds, but as time got closer Elizabeth backed out. That didn't discourage Rachel for more than one night. She was disappointed that Elizabeth wasn't going to go with her, but she wouldn't let her dream go. She determined to just go alone. It was nothing for Rachel to go somewhere alone. She was after all, a loner. She continued to raise money for the trip, and by summer she was in Mexico with the YWAM team.

When Rachel returned home, she had missionary stories of her own to tell. One of those was with an angel she encountered while in Mexico.

She and the mission team stopped for lunch in a little restaurant. After leaving, she realized she didn't have her wallet. She immediately began retracing her steps. She feared it would be impossible to find it with so many people around. As she looked intently, a man that seemed to come from nowhere spoke to her.

He asked, "Are you looking for something?" She answered, "I've lost my wallet." He said, "Look in the windowsill at the restaurant. Everything is still in it." She turned for just a second to look down the street toward the restaurant. Immediately she turned back to speak to the man again, but he was gone! She looked for him but saw no trace of him at all. He had vanished! Oh my, what a Savior we have! He cares about every little detail of our lives.

Stunned and confused by his rapid disappearance, Rachel hurried back to the restaurant as fast as she could. When she entered the restaurant, there in the windowsill sat her wallet. She checked it and found everything was still there. Not one thing was missing. Just as the stranger had said.

> Be not forgetful to entertain strangers: for thereby some have entertained angels unawares. Heb. 13:2

Chapter 26
High School & College

When I graduated from nursing school, we moved to a little town of three-hundred people in the hills of Missouri. We purchased a Residential Care Facility. It was a home where we cared for the mentally handicapped. Rachel and Sam were required to switch schools yet again. She was a junior by then and her brother a freshman.

The friendships in this small school had been established since kindergarten, so it was nearly impossible for Rachel to break into the midst of the cliques. Once again, the teachers became Rachel's friends. This little school had a Spanish teacher that didn't really know the language well. So, Rachel worked with all the other students to learn to speak Spanish. She planned and established a Cinco de Mayo day at the school as part of their curriculum. That turned out to be such a huge success that it is one of the school's biggest events of the year even today.

In her senior year she already had all her necessary credits to graduate. She decided she wanted to take some electives that weren't offered at the school. Her solution was to put together her own curriculum. It had to meet the standards and approval of the administration. Once they were reviewed and approved, she did a spelunking course (cave exploring) and a law course. She was creative and innovative in many ways. She was never stopped by the status quo. She'd simply work to change the rules. Rachel could be stubborn in some ways. She wasn't easily deterred when she believed she was right about something.

With her credits completed early, she began taking college courses before graduating from high school. That's common these days, but not so much then.

Rachel never dated in high school, not even once. She went to prom her senior year, but it was with a couple other single girls. She and I worked for days on her dress. She had become so chesty that it was hard to find clothes that were flattering on her or that fit well. Even though I was working, we made time together to design a dress for the special night. I'd done this for Kelly through the years. However, since I'd completed nursing school, it was a major effort to find time to do the same with Rachel. I was very happy we had the experience of working together on this.

During her Freshman year of college, Rachel met a young man named Sy. He was also home schooled, but he hadn't received an adequate education. It was more like being self-taught (unschooled). He was attentive to Rachel, and a truly kind young man. His family and ours often met for Bible studies together. The two of them never went anywhere as a couple without a guardian.

Sy and Rachel were from two different worlds. He lived in a home with no running water. They had an outside toilet and bathed in the creek, even in the cold of winter. Rachel lived in the local Mansion which was a Bed and Breakfast. They were worlds apart, except for their faith. That's what drew them together. However, their goals in life and expectations for the future had little in common.

In the summer that year, she took a trip with Sy's family to an Indian Reservation in North Dakota to do some missionary work. The trip ended in disaster after Sy's Dad spoke disrespectfully to her. She purchased a bus ticket and came home alone. Sy's dad had a reputation for being rude. We were relieved that Rachel made it home safely.

She was a true beauty. She was shapely and had beautiful features, but she'd always seen herself as fat. As independent as she was, she had low self-esteem when it came to her appearance. That's exactly where the arrows of his mean words hit. Sy's dad told him, "You don't want to marry that girl, she may be a beauty now, but what happens when she gets fat?" They argued loudly and Rachel heard every word.

Sy wanted to marry Rachel, but she wasn't ready for that. She felt she was called to be a nurse. Sy's idea of a wife was being bare foot and pregnant. She became passionate about helping others as she quizzed me while I was going through nursing school. The desire of her heart was to help others, and to save lives.

One evening in the middle of a semester, Sy told Rachel, "it's either now or never." He'd be coming to get her in the morning to go get a marriage license. Of course, his parents had to drive him because he didn't own a car.

Joe and I knew we'd both be working when Sy planned to arrive. Rachel didn't know how she was going to handle telling Sy, "No." So, Joe told her, "Just tell him your Daddy said No."

Sy drove up with his parents the next day, he came into the house expecting to take Rachel to get a marriage license. When she refused, he backed her up against the kitchen sink and insisted on her going with him. Perhaps he felt he'd lose face with his Dad if he weren't able to persuade Rachel. She said, "I'm sorry Sy, my Dad said no. I'll never marry anyone without my Father's approval." The thing is, she meant it with all her heart.

Joe wondered for years if he had given her the right advice. Rachel didn't date again until she was twenty-seven.

After completing her first two years at the local college she transferred to the University in her junior year. The cost was much more expensive. To help with that Joe and I cashed in what we had in our retirement accounts. She'd still have student loans, but this would help some. I'd come out of school with student loan debt and we didn't want Rachel to have to face the same thing. We realized we could never pay her back for all the hours she'd spent helping us to establish the B&B. We didn't know then how much this decision to help Rachel would affect Sam.

Rachel attended nursing school her last two years in St. Louis. It was a two-hour drive from home. Every Friday as soon as her classes were over, she headed home. She worked all weekend at the B&B. She had no social life and she was ok with that. There were many times after working the weekend with us, that she'd pull an all-nighter, completing class assignments or term papers. It drove me nuts because I planned everything ahead of time and finished early. She seemed to excel under stress. I never understood how she could go to the basement computer at 10:30 PM and emerge with a completed term paper by morning. I planned mine for months. Her fellow students asked her to go to celebrate with them after finals or a big project was completed. She always chose not to go. We were concerned that we were her only sphere of influence, she needed more than just us in her life.

Rachel stayed with her Grandparents during the week while attending class. Her grandmother told her, " Rachel, you'll never get a date. You have a sign posted on your forehead, *Not in this Lifetime*."

She'd resigned herself to being alone. She spent some of her evenings during the week taking my Mom shopping which wasn't an easy job. Mom loved going from store to store to seek the best deal.

Rachel managed to graduate with a BSN on The Dean's list. However, no one showed up for her graduation except me and Joe and my longtime faithful friend Diane. She was the first and only grandchild that had completed college and yet there wasn't any recognition. There weren't any brothers or sister, aunts, uncles, or even grandparents. Nor did she have plans to celebrate with other students.

After graduation she returned home and began working in the same little hospital where I worked part time. She was a *by the book* nurse. She demanded excellence in every way and there was no room for nonsense. She always spoke up for the underdog and often got herself in trouble for doing so.

In that respect, she was like the Proverbs 31 woman:

> Speak up for those who cannot speak for themselves, for the right of all who are destitute. Pr.1:18

Once Rachel had a year of nursing experience, she qualified to go on the road as a travel nurse. She loved moving around and seeing new places. She'd always had Joe and I or my Mom and Dad to sit down to meals with. Now she was totally alone. She hated eating by herself and going home to an empty apartment every evening. She prayed nightly for a partner.

Always being alone like this prompted her to want to purchase one of our houses next to our B&B. That way when she was between assignments, she'd have her own place near us. We were thrilled that one of our kids wanted to settle that close to us.

Rachel was always close to her little brother Sam. He ended up joining her on one of her nursing assignments in San Francisco. She enjoyed having his company. At first, he had a hard time finding a good paying job and it became a strain for Rachel to continue to support them both. Once he found work, she moved on to her next assignment in Sacramento. Sam decided to stay in San Francisco. He loved it and never wanted to leave.

They remained close while they were in the same area, but they drifted further and further apart as time went on. Rachel became more conservative and Sam's views became more liberal. They found it hard to have any common ground in their conversations. Over the years they tried to visit by phone, only to hang up frustrated at who the other had become.

I know by now you can see there was no reason to have to *Let Go* with Rachel. She was always connected to Joe and me. She always wanted us in her life. She was obedient, independent, educated, and financially better off than we were. The big deal here, was her *letting go* of us.

The Match

In 2003 Joe and I began a crazy new adventure. We decided to open a restaurant to enhance the dining experience of our B&B guest. There were no restaurants in our tiny town, so we had no other choice but to provide evening meals for our guests. This made for exceedingly long days.

We worked for months designing the restaurant inside and out. We structured a castle like facade on an older building across the street from the B&B. We gave it a rock finish with a draw bridge and turrets. The decor was influenced by Rachel. She always had a sense that she'd been born in the wrong century and on the wrong continent. She had an unusual fascination with Ireland and medieval art. Over time she collected a variety of items and portraits that worked well with the restaurant decor. She'd acquired an amazing sword collection that we decided to display on the walls. Which helped to create a lovely, unique dining atmosphere.

We thought we were blessed to find a trained Dallas Country Club Chef in our area. What are the chances of that? We expected him to handle the day to day operations, like hiring staff, ordering food and the planning of the menu.

Like many Chefs, he was very temperamental. Consequently, I found myself in the kitchen cooking when he decided to quit after just a few short months. That meant I was running a B&B and a restaurant as well. We had a small fortune invested in this venture. Now it was all up to us to sink or swim.

Rachel was still on the road, making great money as a travel nurse, but her heart was with Joe and me. She was determined to finish her last assignment and head home to help us with the restaurant. We knew we couldn't afford to pay her anywhere near what she was making on the road. None of that seemed to matter to her. Somehow, she thought she could rescue us. Just like I had tried to rescue my other kids in the past. I think women are worse with the rescue trait than men. We don't want anyone to fail.

Rachel was extremely comfortable working with us. Together we'd built the B&B business as a team. It'd become known Nationally. To have established this great romance and wedding location seemed next to impossible in this little remote, out of the way place. I learned to do all the photography, and floral arranging, as well as the catering. Joe tended to our extravagant gardens (which Kelly had established) and performed all the ceremonies. Throughout Rachel's college years she was with us building the family business from the ground up. In the early days while Sam was still in high school, he helped as well. As part of the family, he was obligated to do so.

We'd always put God first in everything we did, and the B&B was no different. God chose to bless it. Our odds for success in that location were little to none. Nobody expected it to succeed, but it did.

> But seek ye first the kingdom of God and his righteousness: and all these things shall be added unto you. Matt. 6:33

While Rachel was on the road nursing, one of the weddings we did was a second marriage for a woman in her early fifties. Her adult son attended the wedding, and we were quite impressed with him. He was a kind, polite young man and reminded us of Rachel. Neither one of us wanted to utter the words, "He's perfect for Rachel." But eventually one of us broke the silence.

I remember Joe standing at the kitchen sink as I entered the room with an arm full of sheets that I'd just stripped from the guest rooms. I was headed to the laundry room when I stopped. I said, "Joe, I hate to say this." He turned and said, "I know, that guy was perfect for Rachel." I responded, "He was like a male Rachel." The feeling was so strong. We felt like we knew him when we didn't.

The reason we hated to utter those words, was because of how things had gone for Kelly. We didn't want to encourage one of our daughters to get involved with anyone. It hadn't gone well for Kelly and we never wanted the same outcome for Rachel.

The young man left us a lovely thank you note for providing such a great service for his Mother. We didn't hear from him again.

Joe couldn't get Uriah, the young man, off his mind. He felt strongly that this was someone Rachel should meet. So, when Rachel came home to help with the restaurant, he kept hoping that somehow Uriah would show up again, but that didn't happen.

Joe finally gave in to his instincts and phoned Uriah's mother. Between the two of them they worked out a time for Uriah and Rachel to meet. This wasn't easy. It was a two-hour drive, and he wasn't looking for a relationship. They were both very shy and neither wanted to make the effort to meet a stranger. He was an airline pilot and had a crazy schedule. Rachel was working at the restaurant from early in the day till late at night. She was a great cook and manager, but this arrangement was really putting a strain on her financially.

It was December twenty-first when Uriah finally came to meet Rachel. That turned out to be significant since it was my Mom and Dad's anniversary date. He and his Mother had dinner at the restaurant, so with a little coaxing Rachel came from the kitchen to meet him. They were both quite nervous. He agreed to wait around until Rachel got off work to visit with her. We didn't close till nine o'clock, and by the time she did the cleanup it was around ten PM.

To break the ice, he pulled out a wooden puzzle he'd made. He loved working with wood, and made custom furniture when time permitted. We'd seen some of the pictures of custom furniture he'd made in his free time. No one had been able to figure out his puzzle by taking it apart and putting it back together again. However, Rachel took it in her hands, dismantled it, and then reassembled it again. He was impressed! Then she took out a marble game called Mancala that she had mastered. He beat her at it the first time around. They clicked immediately. The drawing element was that they were both fascinated with each other's intelligence.

They exchanged phone numbers, and just a few days later Uriah sent Rachel a dozen beautiful, long stem roses. No one had ever done this kind of thing for Rachel, and she just didn't know how to respond. She said, "I feel like he's stalking me." I explained to her that many women would love to have such a gift, and all she had to do is to email him a thank you response. It took her all day to be able to sit down and to compose a thank you note. She was out of her element. No one had ever treated her so special.

Little by little Uriah was winning her heart. By New Year's Eve she stayed on the phone with him for hours. Joe and I never heard her laugh so much or sound so happy. They'd find a way to be together every chance they got.

We could see how stressed Rachel was financially and we really wanted her to go back to travel nursing. She had a car and a house payment to make. She needed a better income than the restaurant could provide for her.

Instead of a blessing the restaurant had become an albatross. It was costing us at least five hundred dollars a week just to keep the doors open. We knew Rachel wouldn't abandon us, so one night after dealing with all kinds of customer issues, Joe came home and said, "I'm done." He closed the doors after eleven months. We never opened for even one more day.

He once listened to a teaching called, "Fail Forward Fast!" That's what he was doing. Counting his losses and refusing to lose any more. I never give up that easily. I'm a die hard. To me closing the doors meant failure and that wasn't something I was comfortable with doing. I certainly couldn't run the restaurant alone, so I got on board with his decision.

Rachel finally felt free to leave again. Uriah's work provided plenty of travel opportunity so he could be in whatever city Rachel resided. He was patient with her in every way. As a matter of fact, she kissed him first. She was twenty-seven years old and had never been with a man. For the first time our little girl was no longer alone. She waited for God's timing. Now He was rewarding her. She'd met her match.

> But if we hope for what we do not yet have, we wait for it patiently. Rm. 8:25

She had waited on the Lord and He had provided

They could've been married anywhere they wanted, but they chose to have their wedding at our Bed and Breakfast. By then Kelly was back home and she worked long hot days in the gardens to get them ready for Rachel's special day. She remembered how Rachel had worked to make her wedding great and she wanted the same for her sister. She added hardscapes and court yards with fountains, lovely pathways and hundreds of roses and flowers everywhere. Kelly was a master at this stuff. She wanted her little sister's day to be perfect. It was. We set up a large white tent outside with round tables, draped fabric, and twinkle lights all over the gardens. It was spectacular!

The time for my girls to be close had passed. Rachel became a self-reliant adult while Kelly was struggling through a miserable marriage to Ken. Kelly's return came at a time of Rachel's departure. Once married Rachel moved to Texas and she and Kelly would be like two ships that passed in the night. They lost their chance to rekindle their closeness. Something they both regretted.

> A brother offended is harder to be won than a strong city. And contentions are like the bars of citadel. Pr. 18:19

Kelly was married to Ken for twenty years before she returned home. Rachel was wounded and gun shy. She couldn't reconcile having been cut out of her sister's life. The closeness the girls once had would take a miracle to restore. They both wanted that, but the physical distance between them wouldn't make it possible. They really did love one another, and never wanted it to be this way. They both got busy with life and just didn't find the time to re-establish their sisterly love.

Off and Running

After the wedding Uriah was transferred to Texas. There they purchased their first home together. They never quit improving. They loved working together on it. They spent eight years there perfecting every aspect of it. Eventually they decided to sell and build in the country, as they planned for a family. Rachel's heart's desire was to be a Mom.

211

She went to work for the medical Examiner's office in Houston as a forensic nurse. She loved this position, and as usual, she attacked it with a passion for excellence. The crazy Houston traffic eventually convinced her to take a position in a free-standing ER closer to home. Once again, her management skills and intuition paid off greatly.

She instinctively knew what was wrong with a patient when they entered the ER. The same way she knew things ahead of time when she was a little girl. This drove some of the doctors nuts because she'd say, "You have a patient in exam room four with such and such going on. I've already started an IV." Some of them resented her for this, others just loved it. She'd done the work for them before they'd ever seen the patient.

She and Uriah included Joe and I in everything they could. I don't know if part of this was because Rachel saw how painful it was for me to lose Kelly or not, but they seemed to sincerely enjoy our company. They never planned a vacation without including us, and we enjoyed going with them.

Rachel wasn't perfect, and neither was Uriah. She could be bossy. There were times it felt like she was trying to control our lives, even from a distance. He was a loner and loved having Rachel to himself. It wasn't that he didn't share, but it needed to be on his terms.

Even though Rachel could complete a term paper with little planning while in college, that seemed to change. She'd become quite the planner as she began working and running a household. I guess the apple didn't fall far from the tree, in that aspect. She always made sure everyone on her shift at work had food to get through the day or night. There was usually a crock pot of some delicious food stewing in the break room. The smells swirling through the ER often made staff and patients both wanting to stay for a meal, even if their shift was over. She routinely kept her locker filled with little stuffed toys, crayons, and color books for her tiny patients.

She routinely decorated and entertained for the holidays, even though that wasn't Uriah's cup of tea. She made sure the people in her subdivision had at least one block party every year. She was serious about building support systems in her life. She was determined the neighbors should get to know one another. They lived in Houston which suffered more than one hurricane while she lived there, and she was a survivalist at heart. Even when she was a teen, she had backpacks of supplies ready in the event we had a Midwest earthquake. When those Texas storms hit, she and Uriah were there to help their neighbors.

After selling their Houston home they were free to build what Rachel called their "Forever House." The new house had to have space for homeschool rooms. Rachel had been homeschooled and didn't want any less for her children, which she didn't have yet. The whole house was built with lots of faith that one day she'd be a Mom.

They chose a seventeen-acre plot of land in rural Texas and began their project. The Houston Woodlands house sold the first day on the market, even before the sign went up in the yard. To save funds, they rented a one-bedroom apartment not far from the new construction site, while they were building.

Joe and I had retired to Florida in our RV and were greatly enjoying the warmer weather. Rachel stayed in touch with us, phoning often. I always knew I could count on her cheery voice calling every Friday evening to say, "Shabbat Shalom." We weren't Jewish, but we did honor the Sabbath. Rachel didn't adhere to the convictions of our faith walk, but she always respected them and kept an intimate relationship with God.

While the construction of their house was going on, the four of us took a cruise out of Houston together. This gave Joe and me the opportunity to see the progress on their new home. It was a huge house, with two bedrooms and baths on the second floor. In the middle was a large open space, designated as the Home School area. On the first floor were two more bedrooms and baths, with an extravagant kitchen designed to do online cooking shows. That was one of Rachel's passions and she hoped that once children arrived that she might be able to phase into another career. The walk-in pantry was huge. It was certainly large enough to store all the freeze-dried stash Rachel had accumulated for "a rainy day."

She had a history of not having menses, but now they had returned, and she was excited about the possibility of conceiving.

In January of 2014, the house was complete. They emptied out all the storage units and their apartment and finally moved into their

Forever House. They didn't have the funds to do the landscaping at the time, so they put it off till the next year. They convinced Joe and I to make a trip to see the completed house and to help with the landscaping. We'd done that for them once before when they were selling their first property. We exhausted ourselves working with them to get it ready to sell. When we were finished, it was beautiful. They were hoping to get the same results on the new house.

It was spring break 2015 and we couldn't get flights to Houston. They were all booked by college students on break. I wanted to wait till the next week, but Rachel had already arranged to have time off work. So, Joe and I drove from Florida to Texas to spend a week with Rachel and Uriah. We hadn't seen the house since it was completed so this was a lovely trip, getting used to where everything was in their new home and helping with the landscaping.

It was extremely hot outside even though it was still spring. We were doing a lot of digging and planting. Occasionally Rachel sat down to rest. We all needed to do that from time to time. While we were there it was Joe's seventy first birthday, so Rachel made him a German chocolate cake from scratch, and the four of us celebrated together.

We left on Thursday to get home in time for a gathering we wanted to attend on the weekend. We weren't even completely unpacked the following Wednesday when we got a call from Uriah. He was panicked and crying. He said, "Rachel has had a heart attack and if you want to see her alive, you have to come right away!"

I said, "Uriah, slow down, tell me what happened." He said I was in the barn and Rachel was in the field taking pictures of all the wildflowers. She had been admiring the landscaping and was so happy that the house was finally done outside. She came to the barn and said, I don't feel right." I asked her, "Do you want me to call an ambulance?" She said, "No just take me to the house."

Because she was a prepper, Rachel had a stash of medications for emergencies. As she got into the golf cart to head toward the house, she collapsed. Uriah lowered her to the ground and tried to help her. He phoned 911 immediately. He stayed on the phone with them until the ambulance arrived. The dispatcher told him not to do CPR as long as she was still breathing. It took eleven minutes for the ambulance to arrive. Rachel took her last breath as they drove in the driveway. They worked to revive her and were able to get a faint heartbeat and blood pressure by the time they arrived at the hospital.

I stayed amazingly calm and confident. I told Uriah," She will live and not die. They'll revive her, and she'll pull through this." Not for one minute did I believe Rachel would die. God wouldn't allow it! Joe and I began to pray as we headed to the airport. Uriah was inside the ambulance with her when he phoned us, so I could hear all the activity as paramedics tried to keep her alive. Uriah just kept saying, "Hold on Rachel, hold on baby, Rachel I love you, Hold on."

The airport was about an hour away. We purchased airline tickets on the cell phone as we drove. In route, the phone rang. It was Uriah, he said, "There's no hurry, Rachel is with Jesus." He was crying and sobbing through every word. I said emphatically, "No! that's not true!" He answered, "It's true, Sharon, she's gone. She's with Jesus. The police won't let me in to be with her because they are treating it like a crime scene!"

Rachel was only thirty-eight years old and since she was so young, her death was being investigated. It seemed so odd. Rachel used to do the crime scene investigations for others, now it was being done for her.

I couldn't wrap my mind around all this. We'd just spent a week with her, and she seemed fine. I just spoke to her on Monday. She was leaving the doctor's office where she had a complete physical and received a clean bill of health. He told her, "You are in great health, go make babies." She was so thrilled with the prospect of finally being able to have children. How could this be happening now?

If I were there with her, I would be praying for God to raise her from the dead. I knew that even when I arrived in Houston, I wouldn't be permitted to see her body. She was just gone.

In fact, because Rachel had donated so much of her body, I was never able to see her again. There was no closure in seeing her dead body. It never seemed real. She wasn't REALLY gone.

The airline flight was awful. We'd managed to get the last two seats on a tiny plane and sat in the last seats squashed in like sardines.

My stomach was so upset, and I couldn't stop crying. I felt like I was dying with her. It was just unbelievable. I was in shock. My mind and my body couldn't handle this news. I kept asking God, "Why? How? I'm your friend and You didn't even warn me! How can this even be possible?"

Uriah met us at the airport. He was so distraught that he couldn't drive. He had a friend that was kind enough to help us all in our time of confusion. We embraced and just held each other and cried for what seemed like a long time. For days we needed to just stop and hug one another while we cried. To each other we were ALL that was left of Rachel!

A person's mind plays tricks on them in times like this. I'd imagine that Rachel wasn't really dead but had faked her death and was hiding on some remote island waiting for Uriah to join her. Yet rationally, I knew this wasn't true. I had trouble sleeping, just trying to reconcile how this could happen without a warning. The autopsy showed no heart attack, no clot, no clogged arteries, no aneurism. In my mind I was screaming, "**Then, how did it happen**?"

Kelly arrived in Texas the next day and she helped greatly with the things that needed done. Uriah was kind to us and considered our feelings with every decision. We made them together.

Jeff wasn't able to fly in from Alaska because of his teaching position, but he sent money to help us with unexpected expenses. Sam didn't show up until a week later when we had the memorial service.

Joe and I were both searching for answers, just trying to understand. The autopsy came back negative, she just simply died. There was no explanation. Being in the medical field I demanded answers but there were none. I questioned the medical examiner to be sure she didn't overlook anything. Rachel's doctor friends went over the ambulance and ER reports, as well as the autopsy. Her closest physician friend finally said, "Sometimes people just die, and we never know why."

That was *NOT* an acceptable answer. There had to be a reason. My mind and my body continued to play tricks on me and for the first three months after Rachel's death. I was in the ER three times with anxiety attacks. My heart rate and blood pressure shot up so high, that everyone was afraid I was going to have a stroke. I couldn't reconcile in my mind that a perfectly healthy person just dropped dead. What I knew from my training and what I knew about my God and in my spirit just didn't line up. I couldn't make sense of it, any of it.

I reasoned; I'm a Christian. I have the mind of Christ. I shouldn't be having these episodes of anxiety. I needed to know why I was having so much trouble with *letting go.* This was a different kind of *letting go.* I had worked through and learned so much with the other children, but I wasn't ready for this!

The memorial service was at two PM the following Wednesday. We didn't expect a large turnout, because so many people were working at that time. I was wrong. It was overwhelming. We had posters full of pictures of Rachel everywhere. Kelly and I worked for a couple days putting them together once Uriah chose what photos he wanted to use. The huge meeting room at the senior center was filled with people. There were doctors, patients, and friends from everywhere. They all had something wonderful to say about Rachel.

I walked up on a conversation with four or five physicians talking about her. One said, "She always wanted to tell me what was wrong with my patient even before I saw them." Another doctor answered him, "Well, was she ever wrong?" He replied, "No, she wasn't." These were some of the physicians that wanted to sponsor her to go on to medical school. She loved being a nurse and the close connection she had with her patients. She was concerned about losing that if she became a doctor.

I had no idea how many lives Rachel had touched in her short life. This was the girl who had trouble making friends, or at least that's how she saw herself. I was proud to have been her Mom. She not only saved lives, she changed lives forever.

I felt like I'd poured myself into my kids. I taught her to read, I taught her about God, I shared every important moment of her life with her, and now she was gone. I truly felt like she took part of me with her. Part of my heart had been ripped out. I know Joe felt that way as well.

Here are my questions for this chapter:

1. How do you keep living when your child dies?
2. How do you move on?
3. How do you stop those grief attacks that hit you when you least expect it?

I never had to pray for Rachel to be independent or self-reliant. The truth is, she was born that way. However, I would learn I still had to *Let Her Go.* I couldn't do it alone, I needed God to teach me.

I had a terrible time leaving Texas after Rachel's memorial. I felt like everything that was Rachel was in her house and Uriah was all I had left of her. There were no grandchildren, no little Rachels running around to remind me of her. I didn't want to lose her forever. My heart sank as I drove away. How would I live through this? How would I *let go?*

Chapter 27
Only God can Truly Heal

I started this book four years ago, about six months after Rachel's death. This book has been part of my healing process. Hopefully along this journey, I've helped others. These chapters about Rachel are the reason I procrastinated. I just wasn't ready to put it all in writing. The thing is, I don't normally put things off. I'm one of those people who has a thing about completing whatever I start.

Do you remember my question about what do you do, when things are completely out of your control? Rachel's death was completely out of my control and I had to learn to reconcile it with my faith, what I knew and believed about God.

Rachel's death effected the entire family. It changed everyone forever. It left Sam wondering, "Am I next?" He couldn't help but ask if it was genetic. My sister's daughter Dana died just one year before Rachel at about the same age. Now Sam was approaching that age, and all these events left him wondering if he was vulnerable.

God began to sovereignly touch my life, to take my hand and begin to heal my heart.

The week after Rachel's memorial, Joe and I were back in Florida. He had a doctor's appointment in Gainesville, which was about a thirty-minute drive from where we had the RV parked. We were on our way back home going north on highway 75, when I began to doze. Joe was driving when I sat straight up in my seat and exclaimed," OH My God! OH My God!" Joe was alarmed, and said, "What? What?" I answered, "I just saw Rachel get her glorified body." I was between that awake and asleep state and God gave me a vision.

I saw Rachel standing in front of God. She had her back to Him, and He was towering over her. She was wrapped in a velvety like purple robe, with a fur collar up around her face. Within the fur were all kinds of colored jewels, large and glistening. The robe was so beautiful, but it looked heavy.

In an instant, God put one hand on each of her shoulders and whisked the heavy robe upward off Rachel's body and it disappeared! In the same moment, he wrapped her with a shear flowing shimmering white garment! Even though it was shear and light weight, it wasn't see-through. It had sparkles of light like glitter running throughout the garment. As soon as she was clothed with this, she began to move upward and in a swirling motion. She was smaller and able to move freely in every direction, wherever she desired to go. She wasn't held by gravity; it was the most beautiful thing I'd ever seen!

Thank you, Jesus! Thank you! I knew Rachel was blessed. I knew she was in The Father's presence.

Maybe this doesn't fit with everything you've been taught about life after death, but this is what I saw. This image brought me spectacular comfort and peace. No more weight problems, the heaviness of the flesh had been lifted off her. No more skin issues, she was clothed with a body of light. No more restrictions in her movements. She was free to travel the universe, to explore and to see the vastness of all God's creations. She still had that beautiful long red hair. It had always been her most lovely feature, and it remained in her new body. I had no problem recognizing her. Beyond a doubt, it was my Rachel. Hallelujah! I shared this with Uriah.

He experienced the deepest grief I'd ever seen in my life. Rachel die in his arms and he felt helpless to do anything to save her. The entire thing had been recorded on his security camera. It would be years before he could ever turn them on again, fearful that he might get a glimpse of what they'd captured. He wondered why God would show me Rachel when he hadn't had that privilege. In time, he too would see her in a dream and be comforted by God. That story, my friend, is for another book.

This would be just the beginning of learning to *let Rachel go*. God had given me a new image of her. When we see through the eyes of God, everything changes.

That wouldn't be the end of my grieving for sure. Prior to Rachel's death, she'd asked numerous times for us to move to Texas. She wanted us to help with home schooling her children, while she continued her career.

After Rachel's death Uriah needed us. Maybe the truth is, we needed him for all of us to heal. He flew to Florida and helped us to make the trip back to Texas. We stayed on his property in our RV for over a year.

In that time, I began to question God as to why my body was betraying me with anxiety attacks. I'd think I was doing ok and without a warning my physical body would be doing its own thing again. It was responding to the stress of the loss. How was I going to overcome this?

As I sought the Lord, I began to realize that this grief felt somehow familiar to me. I finally asked, "Father What is this? Where is this coming from?"

Then a deeply buried memory began to come to the surface. At age five my grandmother died suddenly. She was killed by a hit and run driver. His car drug her body for ten blocks. My grandma was the first person I remembered ever telling me about Jesus. She was my father's mother. I took her death so hard that I was rushed off to the ladies' parlor to curtail my hysteria when I saw her dead body at the funeral home. That little girl didn't know how to deal with the pain of losing her Grandma. The cell memory of that had stayed in my body, and I'd been carrying that unresolved pain for sixty years without knowing it.

As the memories of that pain and loss began to come to the forefront of my mind, I could see Jesus standing before me. He said to me, "Take the grief of your grandmother and the grief of your daughter and wrap them up together. Put it in a box and lay it at My feet. Then begin to download the grief and pain of loss of those you love into Me." He wanted me to allow Him to take the pain for me. He said, "You were never meant to carry this."

> "I was wounded for your transgressions and bruised for your iniquities. The chastisement of your peace was upon me and by my stripes you are healed." Is. 53:5

I was a trained counselor. I'd been taught this process from the teachings of "*Heart Sync Ministry." I'd ministered this with others to help them with brokenness and unforgiveness, but now it was my turn. With the Holy Spirt leading me, I downloaded my pain and grief to Jesus.

This is just like your computer. Sometimes it takes a while for it to download. The pain came in waves as I just kept letting it flow to the cross. Then there was a moment when I knew I had been set free. I saw Jesus pick up the box that I'd laid at his feet. As He lifted it up with both of His hands, He directed it towards His chest. Suddenly the box with all my grief and sorrow disappeared into His bosom. I remember saying out loud, "Whoa…. What was that?" As I saw it disappear, He said, "It is now in the sea of forgetfulness." He had taken my grief and my sorrow. Once again, the pictures in my mind were changing.

> Let this mind be in you, which was also in Christ Jesus. Phil.2:5

I was learning to *let go*. The anxiety attacks stopped. Joe and I decided to attend grief counseling for a short while. I also learned a process called "*tapping." It calms the fight or flight response and works to get fear or anxiety under control. As a trained medical professional, I needed it in my arsenal of weapons to use along with my spiritual weapons for any future attacks.

We encouraged Uriah to go on with his life and in a year, he was beginning to date again. It was hard for all of us, but especially the guys. Uriah relived the day of her death over and over and questioned what he might have done to save her. The answer was nothing. He has become a son to me, and I am so grateful that he still includes me in his life.

In a loving gesture for her Dad, Kelly purchased a motorcycle for Joe's Father's Day present. He and Uriah would go for long rides in the countryside and that gave Joe some escape from the pain of losing Rachel.

Rachel didn't choose to leave this life. I don't believe the devil killed her. It was almost like she was raptured. She was, and then with no explanation, was not. Just gone. She was an *old soul*. In some ways, she lived half her life before she was born. In my heart, I trust that she ran her race and finished her course. The Apostle Paul said it this way:

> I have fought a good fight, I have finished my course, I have kept the faith: Henceforth there is laid up for me a crown of righteousness, which the Lord the righteous judge, shall give me at that day and not to me only, but unto all them also that love his appearing. 2 Tim 4:7-8

She changed lives, especially Uriah's. In ten years of marriage, I never once heard Rachel complain about him. She loved unconditionally. I don't think many people have that ability. I don't. Maybe I will someday.

I couldn't save Rachel. I couldn't rescue her. I had to *let her go.* Just like I had to trust God with Jeff and Kelly, I trust Him with Rachel. He knows the end from the beginning.

> Declaring the end from the beginning, and from ancient times the things that are not yet done, saying, My counsel shall stand, and I will do all my pleasure: Is. 46:10

I have no doubt that I will see Rachel again. We'll be reunited in the presence of God and I will always thank Him for sending her to earth to be my daughter. I'll always love and miss her, but I have learned to *let* her beautiful spirit *go.*

I am confident that she is still very much alive. She has just changed addresses.

Chapter 28
Lady Wisdom or Lady Folly
Which is it?

The book of Proverbs is known for being filled with wisdom. Often it talks about two types of women. The first kind is seen in Chapter eight where wisdom is depicted as a woman calling to a young man to choose her. She says her ways lead to life, truth, instruction, and knowledge, that riches and honor are in Lady Wisdom. In verse twenty-one she says she causes those that love her to inherit substance and she will fill their treasures. So, Lady Wisdom is a giver, one who blesses.

On the flip side, in Proverbs nine it speaks of a foolish woman (Folly). She is simple, clamorous and she knows nothing. It says the simple turn into her, but they know not that the dead are there; that her guests are in the depths of the grave. Lady Folly is a taker, one who brings curses.

The choice seems simple. Unfortunately, mankind is prone to choose the wrong lady. Without Christ in a young person's heart, according to James, they will be led astray by their lust.

> But every man is tempted when he is drawn away and enticed by his own evil desire. James 1:14

It doesn't matter if they are male or female, if it's sexual lust, financial gain, popularity, or power. There are many forms of lust that can trap a person, and you don't even have to be young. Hopefully, if you live long enough, you'll get smart enough to recognize good from evil. The truth is, for some people, they never get smart.

Today, we live in a world of instant everything. The answers to most every question can be found with a click of the finger or a voice command on the computer. Our children have been conditioned by American society to pass every grade if they do the work or not. They expect a trophy for every person on the team. It's no longer about endurance or skill. Young adults, just starting out in life, expect to have what their parents have worked a lifetime for. We're a self-indulgent culture, and unfortunately, as parents, we have been conditioned to be Santa Claus, or at least the bank.

From the time my oldest child was born in 1965 until the youngest was born in 1978, the world changed. An entitlement generation began to emerge. We were poisoned by psychologists and their new ideas on discipline, leaving Biblical principles behind. Self-esteem became the goal for children instead of problem-solving skills and maturity.

The personal goals of Madeline Murry O'Hara dictated to America that we couldn't continue to display the Ten Commandments or have prayer in school. There arose a *Just Follow Your Heart mentality*. That was soon interpreted as *I have a right!* A right to follow *MY* heart, no matter who else it might hurt. My feelings come first!

If a person has the Spirit of God within it might be safe to *Follow your Heart*. If not, it can be disastrous.

> The heart is deceitful above all things, and desperately wicked: who can know it? But those things which proceed out of the mouth come forth from the heart; and they defile the man. Jer. 17:9

This might explain why we hear unkind things and accusations being hurled at parents by children. They are things that older generations would never have considered saying to an elder.

Our hopes and prayers for our children are to recognize the difference between Lady Wisdom and Lady Folly, and that they choose wisely. Sometimes they choose Lady Wisdom. Sometimes they choose Lady Folly and sometimes they choose both.

Here are the questions:

1. What can you do to ensure that you and your children make the right choices?
2. What can you do if they don't?
3. Will you reward them anyway?
4. Can you trust God to pick them up when they fall?
5. Will you let them fall?
6. Will you catch them, or will you permit God to?

They might make it through this life without God, but they won't make it to the next.

What Really Matters?

Someone once asked me if the story of the Prodigal son was God's example of how to deal with our wayward children? My understanding of that passage of scripture is that the faithful son, who didn't appreciate the return of his wayward brother, is Judah. They have been faithful to preserve Torah. The wayward son is the lost tribes of Israel, which became the Gentiles.

> …I am not sent but unto the lost sheep of the house of Israel. Matt 15:24

In the prodigal teaching, the father provided for this son while he was under his roof. He blessed him at the time of his departure, but didn't continue to provide for him in his riotous lifestyle. When the Prodigal returned the Father greeted him with open arms. There's no evidence of financial support or blessing from the Father, until that son repentantly returned home. If this parable is our example, then it looks to me like, while a child is living a riotous life, there is no precedent of rescuing or supporting them. So, is the Bible our example when we are considering how to deal with a wayward child?

Yes, or No?

Chapter 29
A Son for Us

I wanted a son with Joe that would bring God honor all the days of his life. I had read Oral Robert's book and learned his mother had prayed for a blond-haired blue-eyed boy to preach the gospel. I knew God was no respecter of persons. If He did it for Oral Robert's Mom, He'd surely do it for us. Joe had so enjoyed being a Dad. I still desired a son to carry on The Cluck family name.

Before Sam was conceived, we prayed for him continually. Just like with Rachel, it didn't really matter what sex this child would be, we would love it dearly, but God gave me the desire of my heart. Of course, we wouldn't know the sex until Sam was born.

After my unpleasant experience with the hospital delivery with Rachel, I didn't want to relive that again. After much prayer and research, we decided to do a home delivery. We lived a long distance from the hospital. Home delivery wasn't a popular thing to do at the time, and I realized it could be a life or death decision. I didn't personally know anyone who had delivered their child at home, in my generation.

While pregnant with Sam, I experienced an extremely traumatic event. We were still living in an apartment complex prior to purchasing our home in Texas. Often, I went outside to do my praying. Across the courtyard was a couple and their two children that lived on the second floor. As I paced and prayed the husband sat in his lawn chair from his balcony and peered at me. I'd spoken to his wife and knew he was quite troubled.

Joe and I'd been active in the deliverance ministry for years but since we were in Texas, we hadn't made this known to anyone. I have always been sorry for that. We might have been able to help this man but didn't offer. Most people don't even know this kind of help is available, so it's not like they'd ask for what they didn't know existed.

And these signs shall follow them that believe; in my name

shall they cast out devils; ....Mark 16:17a

There would be no doubt that the Devil was behind what happened next.

One Sunday morning the man stood in front of his Catholic Church and declared he was Jesus. He was waiting to ascend, to be taken up into heaven. His behavior frightened his children greatly. By the end of the day, he had been hospitalized for mental observation. He spent three days being evaluated and then was discharged. He took several days to recover before going back to work. That morning he dropped his wife at her place of employment and then returned home instead of going on to his own job.

It was still early morning when we heard the blood curdling screams for help. Joe was off work, but he wasn't dressed for the day yet. When I heard the screams, I ran outside to see if I could help. My neighbor was yelling, "Help, please help, he shot himself." I ran up the stairs to the balcony where she was hysterically shouting. I tried to calm her. She cried, "Please go check on him, he may still be alive." I ran into her apartment to see if I could help her husband.

I had no idea what I was walking into. It was a demon infested pit; the spirit of oppression was tangible. On the coffee table laid a Playboy magazine opened to a picture of Freddy Fender with a crack drawn down the middle of his face. It was an article on how he put a gun in his mouth and shot his head off. The deception of that photo was gross. It led people to believe that suicide was a simple personal decision. It didn't reveal the carnage it leaves behind for everyone else involved.

On the wall in his apartment was a weird moving picture of the last supper. The eyes of Jesus kept looking at you as you moved around the room. We were told later that he spent hours a day in front of this picture, talking to it.

He'd been deceived into believing that he himself was the Messiah. He'd written letters to the US government telling them he was the President. He wanted them to know he was in possession of dangerous top-secret, intelligence information and they needed to contact him immediately.

When I entered the bedroom with intentions of helping a wounded man, I was gripped with the most ungodly, horrifying sight I'd ever seen. There's no need for detail. He'd taken a shot gun and reenacted what he'd read about in the magazine. I knew immediately he wasn't alive. There wasn't any need to check for a pulse. The image depicted on the cover of the Playboy magazine was nothing like what I was witnessing. It was an image that wouldn't leave my mind for many days.

I was strong in my faith, and yet I couldn't sleep because I kept reliving the scene. Every time I closed my eyes, I saw the expression on his face. The shock of what I'd seen was haunting.

This horrendous event happened in the first 6 weeks of pregnancy with Sam. Joe prayed with me frequently to help me overcome the shock I had encountered. Joe had been in combat. He'd witnessed this kind of body mutilation, and he understood how it was affecting me. In retrospect, I can see it taught me a great lesson about running into situations that I'm not equipped for. Up to that point, I thought there wasn't anything that I couldn't handle. I was still young in the Lord, I heard His voice, I had dreams and visions, and many answered prayers. I had cast out demons, but it was always on my terms, in settings I'd chosen. Had this happened after I completed nursing school; I'd have been prepared to address this with much more wisdom. This event was a surprise attack, and it left me extremely troubled.

Our neighbor was in shock. Joe, in his usual kind manner, offered to help her with the cleanup of her apartment. She and her children needed to move. They couldn't go back into that apartment again.

A few months after this event we moved to our new home in the suburbs. The rest of my pregnancy seemed to be normal. We were so happy with our new home. We lived in a delightful subdivision with a community pool. It was in a good school district and we busied ourselves with settling into our new surroundings.

Enter Sam

In early June we were blessed with our son Samuel. He was a joyful child with an incredible sense of humor. He was delightful in every way. As he grew, he had the wit and timing of a stand-up comedian. He was loving and affectionate. He enjoyed a cuddle and hugging. He wasn't at all like Rachel with her independent demeaner from birth. Sam was outgoing and social. He was smart and a quick learner. He and I built a strong bond from day one. He loved to laugh and so enjoyed teasing. He was creative. He'd invent ways to entertain himself and keep people laughing along with him. He was dealt many challenges but easily rolled with the punches. He never had a poor me attitude. He faced things head on and he had an early awareness of God.

The whole family was caught off guard, surprised when Sam was born with a cleft lip and palate. The doctors explained to us, that because of the trauma I experienced during my pregnancy, the growth process was interrupted temporary. When it kicked back in again, all the tissue (building blocks) were still there. It just hadn't connected properly.

We considered that Joe had been exposed to agent orange (a chemical used in the Vietnam war). Large numbers of military offspring had birth defects that were known to be related to it. Spiritually, I felt it was an attack of the enemy, designed to prevent Sam from reaching his God given destiny.

Many children with this birth defect have speech impediments, mental retardation, and other defects. Sam was blessed in that he didn't fit into the norm.

He was a very large baby at ten pounds, eleven ounces. The delivery was long and hard, but even with his imperfections, he was simply endearing. When he smiled, it spread across his entire face. He appeared imperfect to others, but to us he was a cherished possession. He just needed tweaking. My midwife proclaimed over him, that he'd be a comfort to me in my old age. I was thirty-one when he was born.

When he was about twelve hours old, we took him to the hospital. I needed help learning how to feed him. He wasn't able to produce enough suction on a nipple to use a baby bottle, or to nurse. When I told the nurse in the ER how old he was, she was surprised, because he was already so large. I laughed as they got a wheelchair for me and insisted that I sit down. I had sprung back from this home delivery like there was nothing to it. Not at all like the misery I experienced in hospital deliveries after being drugged.

I learned to feed Sam with a syringe and tube, which was a time consuming, long drawn out process. Eventually a proper type of nipple was found. It was specially designed to keep him from choking. In time, we worked through all the difficulties presented.

Sam was born with his first tooth already showing. It fell out in about ten days. It was protruding from a part of the cleft. So, for a short time we called him Fang. We'd never seen a child born with a tooth before.

At ten weeks Sam weighed enough to undergo his first surgery. It was to draw all the tissue together and close his upper lip.

We took Sam everywhere. Often, I'd notice a child staring at him, or hear them ask their mother questions about what happened to that little baby? I always used it as a teaching opportunity to reassure them that Sam was going to be ok. Someday he'd look just like everyone else. For the most part that brought comfort to little minds.

The neighborhood children made fun of Sam. Their parents said things like, "This is the result of a home delivery." Kelly and Rachel both took up the cause of defending their baby brother, and they took it seriously. When we walked him in the stroller in the subdivision, both sisters walked alongside him. They were ready just in case somebody said something about their baby. They'd be sure to set them straight.

After his first surgery, we began working on his speech. Rachel spent hours with Sam, saying over and over, "La, la, la, co, co, co." We heard it constantly as she tried to get Sam to say it after her, helping him to learn to speak clearly. She repeated over and over, "Docker fixxy Sammy's mouth." We'd been given speech exercises to do with him. At just two and a half, Rachel made sure it happened every day, all day.

I remember waiting in Sam's hospital room the day they repaired his upper lip. When they carried him back from surgery, he looked so different. I had bonded with him through his twinkling blue eyes and that huge smile. Now he looked like a different child. He looked like Joe. I just loved him so much. I was so thrilled to see him becoming whole, although I had to get used to his new appearance.

He was exuberant and outgoing. It was fun being his Mom. He loved everybody!

After the lip surgery he was fitted with a prosthetic plastic pallet, that made taking the bottle easier. In fact, without it, he couldn't suck properly. The milk would go up through his palate and out his nose. The prosthesis was held in with poly grip (a sticky adhesive). It became extremely messy when he began teething. We began asking God for a miracle.

We were attending church one evening, and they had a special speaker followed by a healing line. I went to the church nursery to get Sam to be prayed for. I stood in line with what seemed like a hundred people. The minister went down the line, just saying, "In The Name, in The Name" and touching each person. People were falling down under the power of the spirit all around me. I hoped I wouldn't fall with Sam in my arms. As the minister got closer, I could feel the anointing and I began to cry. Then he touched me, and just kept moving on to the next person. I didn't move from the spot. I knew God had done something. There's something so passionate about a mother's prayer and her desire for God's best for her child. I knew God was hearing my heart. After the prayer time Joe took Sam back to the nursery.

On the way home, Sam was on my lap. I decided to give him a bottle to help him fall asleep. He drank without difficulty, but the pull on the bottle felt different. I wondered why. So, I felt in Sam's mouth and the artificial plate was gone. It was a very expensive piece of equipment and Sam hadn't been able to eat without it. I exclaimed, "Joe, Sam's plate is gone!"

He answered, "Oh yeh, when I took him back to the nursery a while ago, it fell out. So, I cleaned it off and stuck it in my pocket. I forgot to put it back into his mouth." Wow! Sam was drinking without the plate in his mouth. He'd never been able to do that before. I just worshipped God. To me it was a miracle! I never put the plate back in his mouth again! I truly believed this was the beginning of a complete restoration.

We played scripture tapes in Sam's room all day, every day, and throughout the night. We put the TV in the garage, and just kept worship and scriptures going all the time.

Sam was still a baby when we moved to Arizona. The opening in the roof of his mouth was quite large. When I laid him down on the bed to change his diaper, he'd laugh, and I could see the opening. It was more than an inch wide and went all the way up between his eyes. He was old enough by now to have the palate surgery, but I was waiting for a miracle. That was a scary decision. What if

I was hindering my son, instead of helping.

But let him ask in faith nothing wavering…. James 1:6

My faith was really being tested! I didn't want to waver.

Then one morning I picked Sam up out of his crib and laid him down on Rachel's bed to change him. As usual, he laughed. He always woke up happy. I loved that about him. As I looked down at him, he laughed so hard that his mouth opened wide and I could see that overnight God had touched him. The opening had closed completely with just a small hairline crack that could still be seen in the tissue. I believed that eventually that would disappear. We were so excited. We'd gotten our miracle!

But to me, it wasn't complete. Sam was eating whole food and occasionally some liquid would escape through the crack in the palate and look like a runny nose.

So, I waited, and I waited. It seemed like forever, because I was being pressured by the doctors that said, "The longer you wait, the harder it will be for Sam to have clear speech." I was told that the tiny crack, still in the roof of his mouth, could let air escape and pressure letters like b's and p's wouldn't come out clearly. Sam was nearly two years old and the surgery had been approved for him at eighteen-months.

We were in our Phoenix home where I had the day care center. It was extremely successful. I never had to teach Sam to use the toilet. As soon as he could walk, he just did what all the other boys did. That was so nice since I had struggled through this process so long with Jeff.

I felt stressed and pressured that I needed to decide about another surgery. Joe always left these decisions up to me. It made me feel responsible for either hearing from God or missing Him altogether. I wanted Joe to offer more input, but for some reason, he felt it should be my decision.

I prayed continually about what was right for Sam. I didn't have a clear answer. Finally, we scheduled the surgery to complete the closure of the remaining crack in Sam's palate. I didn't understand why God hadn't done a complete work. It left me with questions about my faith, and God's wisdom in all this. The doctor was very upset with me for "waiting" so long. He basically scolded me for trusting God and told me I had subjected Sam to years of speech therapy to unlearn all the poor speech habits he'd developed prior to surgery. He did his best to put a huge guilt trip on me. I wanted to be "Mother of the Year." The doctor did his best to make me feel neglectful and unwise.

The morning of the scheduled surgery Sam woke with an earache. Because of that, the surgery was postponed till Sam was symptom free. I didn't understand. I had such a hard time making this decision, only to have it postponed. When your child is involved, every decision is a major emotional event. I never faced dealing with major surgeries for any of the other children.

Sam will never know the amount of time I spent in prayer just trying to make sure I was doing the absolute best thing for him.

The following week Sam's doctor attended a national conference on cleft and palate surgery research. It covered the latest techniques in treating Sam's condition. When the doctor returned from the conference, he had adopted a new method of repairing the cleft palate. He learned that when a child's palate is surgically closed at a young age, their face continues to grow but the palate doesn't expand with the child's face. This causes the face to cave in as the child grows. I began to feel like I understood the wisdom of God a little better. The new process allowed for an opening to remain in the palate behind the gum line for the child's face to expand properly. God knew exactly what He was doing!

Sam was nearly two years old before this surgery took place. He already had quite a large vocabulary and we had little trouble understanding anything he said. However, we were still getting accusations from the doctor. He insisted that the procedure still needed to be done.

Following the surgery was a difficult time for me. I wasn't at all sure that it was even necessary. Sam wouldn't eat or drink due to the pain he was experiencing. I continually held back tears as I observed his pain.

I was so thankful when Joe stepped in and took over. He stayed at the hospital with Sam and let me go home and get some much-needed rest. I'd been awake for many hours. He was able to get Sam to eat when I couldn't. Even though Sam was only two years old at the time of this surgery, he remembered lots of things about it. He even remembered the Sesame Street Big Bird that was on his pajamas.

When he came home, both arms were in casts. This was to prevent him from touching his face. His mouth was swollen so much that his speech was distorted. I began to wonder if the doctor was right. Had I waited too long? As the swelling subsided, Sam spoke completely clear.

During our follow-up visit with the doctor, he scheduled speech therapy immediately. I announced confidently to him, "Sam can say ball clearly." This was one of the words I was told he wouldn't be able to pronounce.

The doctor said, "That's not possible." So, I asked Kelly to go to the waiting room and retrieve a ball that was in the play area. When she brought it to Sam, he said loud and clear "Ball." There was no doubt what he was saying. Those b's and p's were never a problem. The doctor could barely believe it! Sam could speak as clearly as anyone else. God had been completely faithful.

When those casts came off, Sam got his first big cowboy hat, toy gun and holster. He loved wearing that hat. He looked like his big brother Jeff, who was going through his cowboy phase.

Sam was with me all the time in the Day Care Center, as I taught early reading skills. He picked it up right away and was reading at an incredibly young age. As he got a little older, he had a knack for spelling. If anyone had trouble spelling anything, they'd just say "Sam, how do you spell that?" We knew he would just instinctively know how.

On an afternoon with just family at home, Joe thought Sam was with me and I thought he was with Joe. When I missed him, I headed out to the pool. We always kept the door locked, but I found it open. My heart began to pound as I saw Sam in the pool. He was still conscious, struggling to breathe and to get above water. His eyes were already rolling back. I jumped in the pool and carried him out. I laid him on the ground face down and began to do back thrust, as I yelled, "Jesus, Jesus. Breathe in the name of Jesus! Breathe in the name of Jesus!"

Joe had climbed up on the roof to check the air conditioning. As he heard me yelling, he came to the edge of the roof and hollered,

"Sharon, stop that yelling." I replied, "I found Sam in the pool, come help me." Just then Sam began to expel gushes of water from his mouth and started to breathe again. We were both soaking wet when I picked him up, held him close, and rocked back and forth as I wept, thanking Jesus for saving my son. The whole thing left Joe and me quite shook up and looking for better ways to secure the pool area. We investigated ways to teach a toddler to swim and we started working with Sam right away to prevent ever going through a scare like that again.

How did I know to go to the pool when I did? I have a friend who's first born drowned. It was devastating! Why had God spared Sam?

> Moreover, man does not know his time; like fish caught in a treacherous net and birds trapped in a snare, so the sons of men are ensnared at an evil time when it suddenly falls on them. Eccl. 9:12

Just a few more minutes, and Sam would have died. God has a purpose for Sam he hasn't yet fulfilled.

Both Kelly and Rachel spoiled Sam every chance they got. Somehow, he doesn't remember this, but those of us who observed it do. He and I were always remarkably close. He was about four when he and his Dad had a game, playing it all the time. If Sam heard his Dad coming, he'd jump up on my lap, and wait till Joe came into the room. Then he'd tease Joe saying, "We're married." He'd hug my neck and give me a big kiss. Joe would pipe back, "Oh no you aren't, that's my wife." They'd banter back in forth until they both broke out in joyful laughter as they teased one another.

Once Joe worked in the oil fields for a short time. It was so cold that he grew his first beard. He sent a photograph home and I said, "He looks like a porcupine!" Sam caught onto that right away. He wanted to know what a porcupine was. I opened a book and showed him the prickly spikes of the pudgy little animal. He couldn't wait for his Dad to call so he could tease him about being a porcupine. He always laughed at his own jokes. This one had him rolling on the floor of the living room in riotous laughter, repeating "My Dad's a porcupine, my Dad's a porcupine."

When Sam was learning to read, he was asked to fill out a form with his name, address, and phone number. In the phone number slot, he wrote the word "birdie." I asked him, "Sam, why did you put birdie in where your phone number goes?" He said simply, "Well when the phone rings it sounds like a birdie." He reasoned, that must be what went in that slot.

While in Arizona, Joe and I trained with a Christian Publishing Company and were taught how to set up Christian schools. We began traveling with the children and working with different churches, to assisted them in establishing their Schools.

In Oklahoma I trained staff in the reading program and once they were doing well, I felt I could stay home for a while. I turned my first-grade class over to Ms. Shirley. Sam was her only male student and he was a year younger than all the others. One day while visiting the school, I passed Ms. Shirley's classroom. I couldn't believe my eyes. All the little girls had their heads down and were working on something, but Sam was standing up in his desk kind of dancing around. Later I asked Ms. Shirley why she permitted this behavior. Her answer was, "He's not hurting anything, he already knows the material and he doesn't bother anyone." That sounded crazy to me, but it was the way people seemed to approach Sam.

Often people thought he was older than he was, because he was so big. Because of that, they expected more from him than he was mature enough to give. Joe fell into this category. Others just had so much compassion on him that they'd let him by with way too much. Just like Ms. Shirley.

It was at this school that Sam had his first crush on a girl named Lynette. She was the Pastor's only child. They were cute walking through the halls at school holding hands. Sam told me he intended to marry Lynette.

I home schooled the children unless we were setting up a new school. Then they attended wherever we were working. When Sam was in the fourth grade, I went back to college, and I enrolled him and Rachel in a public school for the first time. That didn't last long.

Over the years Sam underwent a total of eight surgeries. Several to straighten his lip as his face grew. His lip would pull. He still looked different than other kids. Most the time he seemed confident, but this public-school setting was a new challenge.

As he waited daily for the school bus, there was a bully that kicked Sam's gym bag around and called him *pushup lip*. He yelled, "Stay away from him, he's got AIDS." So, the kids were afraid to sit next to Sam on the bus. It reminded me of how they yelled for the crowd to move out of the way in the Bible when a leper came near. The boy pushed Sam around, and tormented him constantly. Sam was like his Dad when it came to a fight. He avoided it at all cost. Both were people of peace. They didn't want to fight.

To make matters worse, Sam had a fourth-grade teacher who took one look at him and decided he couldn't keep up with the class. She insisted he be tested academically and then sent to speech therapy. She was prejudiced against a child that looked different. Sam passed all her required tests. The speech therapist met with me and said, "There are children in that class who need speech therapy. However, Sam's not one of them." She kept him in her class for two weeks and then gave him a certificate of completion to keep his teacher happy. His teacher expected him to be in there all year. Eventually I confronted her about her attitude, and it seemed to make a difference.

I finally spoke with the principal about the bully at the bus stop. It had gotten so bad that I started driving the kids to school each day. The Principal said, "We've had trouble with that kid before. I suggest Sam just punch him in the nose and get it over with, but don't tell anyone I told you that."

I relayed to Sam what the principal had told me. Sam wasn't thrilled with the prospect of a fight. Neither was I.

The next day I watched out the front window, hurting inside, while Sam underwent the same abuse. I prayed for him in the afternoon when I knew he'd be riding the bus home with the bully again. About four PM he came busting through the front door. "I did it! I beat him up." He was quite pleased with himself. It wasn't long before the bully's mom was knocking on our front door, with her crying son. She had no idea what her son was putting Sam through. That was the last time Sam had any problems with this kid. It was the one and only time Sam ever fought anyone, at least to my knowledge.

So, this is the crazy thing. As an adult Sam tells stories about how mean he was as a kid. How he beat up a bunch of other boys when we lived in a mobile home park. At the time, he was being homeschooled and was only eight years old. Never once did a parent or anyone else ever complain to me that Sam was a fighter. No one in the family ever remembers any of this occurring. But this is what Sam remembers about his childhood. It's his reality, part of his identity, how he sees himself.

After the public-school experience, we went back to home school. I tried him in public school two more times, and neither had good results. Once in the seventh grade and then again in high school.

Sam was in the fifth grade when we moved to a new city. He didn't have time to make friends yet. So, one evening at dinner time he showed up with a robot with movable parts. He'd built it with building blocks called Constructs. They were kind of like Legos. He sat the robot down at the end of the table and set a place for it to join us for dinner. I asked, "So Sam, who is this?" He replied, "That's my new friend. I haven't met any here, so I built one." What an imagination! It wasn't long before Sam was riding his bike all over town and making new friends.

When I enrolled in nursing school, I tried Sam in public school again. He was in the seventh grade. He didn't do well in this environment. He was required to change classes every hour and was faced with a new teacher in every class. By the time he settled into the classroom, the bell rang and he had to start all over again. For Rachel it was an easy transition. We couldn't figure out why this was so difficult for Sam. I left our first teacher conference in tears.

After I completed nursing school we moved to the little town where we eventually opened the Bed and Breakfast. Sam was in the eighth grade.

He was a site to behold, tall and lanky. He was six feet tall and a wiz on roller blades. This little town had never seen roller blades. Our house was on the same street as the school and so the whole summer before his freshman year he owned that street. He went up and down and back and forth maneuvering on those roller blades to perfection. The height of them added another four inches to his stature. He wasn't done growing, he still had three more inches to go.

In this town, basketball was king. They lived and breathed it. The coach took one look at Sam and thought with that height, we got us another player. Sam wasn't interested. There were some in this school that had an attitude about Sam right away because he had no love for the game.

In contrast, the art teacher realized that Sam was creative. After a few successful projects, he commissioned Sam to paint the school mascot, a panther over the entrance to the gym. That panther has been there for over twenty-five years now.

Sam had his last surgery when he was sixteen. He could've elected to have others but since they were considered cosmetic, he decided to opt out. He felt like people could take him or leave him. They could accept him the way he was or not. He just didn't care anymore. Caring for Sam through so many surgeries was influential in my deciding to become a nurse. Ultimately that decision would one day save my own life.

After the bully encounter, Sam never had trouble making friends. He fit in at church but at school it was with the *fringe* kids. Sam never drank alcohol while in high school. It reminded him too much of the anesthesia from all his surgeries. So, this group of kids loved having Sam around to be the designated driver.

It was obvious that public school wasn't the best place for Sam. In his junior year we met with Sam's high school counselor. He was a Godly man and we trusted his opinion. I told him Sam wanted to finish school at home. I was working as an RN so Sam would be required to complete his assignments on his own. The counselor felt it was a good choice for him. He told us that the previous year, Sam had started hanging with what he called *the wrong crowd*.

After studying at home for a while Sam took the GED test. He was one point from receiving a scholarship to attend college. We encouraged him to retake the test, but at the time Sam just wanted to go to work.

He'd met a girl. She was four years older than him, and he was quite taken with her. He felt if he could get a good job and nice housing that she'd consider a proposal.

He was so motivated, that he was working two jobs. With our help, he had even purchased a mobile home on a nice little lake. He was demonstrating very responsible patterns, and it was natural to want to help him. However, Sam seemed to lose interest in everything when his relationship to Natalia ended. She was a preacher's daughter, and she had led Sam to believe they had a future together. She and her brother took a vacation with our family. The whole time she behaved as if she were Sam's girlfriend. Her attention toward Sam continued when we returned home as well. She was quite young for her years. It seemed intellectually and spiritually they were a good match. Sam was more mature than she was.

She went out of state to a Christian college, where she started dating a *ministry major*. All along she kept Sam on the hook. She caught him by surprise when she came home with an engagement ring from someone else. Sam was active in church and even playing base guitar in the band.

We all felt she was trying to please her parents by choosing a ministry major. Sam had every intention of serving God together with her. The sad part is that once she married the guy, he didn't even go to church with her. It all sounds way too familiar.

Sam never came right out and said it, but his actions looked like he blamed God for this loss.

He was always quite talented. He was artistically and musically inclined. He picked up a guitar, looked on the internet and learned to play with no other instruction. He built dozens of custom guitars and at one time he even owned a music studio and did a few successful productions.

We never saw music as part of his future. Joe had no interest in music of any kind. By the time Sam was a young man we probably could have afforded lessons. Looking back, I wish we'd paid more attention to his God given abilities.

Unfortunately, being a parent doesn't come with an instruction manual. Often, we learn by trial and error. Sam had many skills, everything he put his mind to seemed to succeed, except relationships.

Even though he didn't drink in high school, that wasn't the case after Natalia. He was laid off work at Christmas time from one job, and then just quit the other. He didn't seem to care that he was out of work. He and his buddies stayed in his house, playing video games, smoking cigarettes, and drinking beer all day during the month of December. Then it was January, and then February. It wasn't long before he was behind on payments for his truck and his house. We tried to make him understand that he wouldn't be able to keep these things if he didn't pay for them. That didn't seem to register. He acted like he could just float a note at the bank indefinitely.

Joe and I finally sat down with him to discuss the alternatives. We were extremely disappointed. Sam had been so responsible in the past, that we saw him as a successful businessperson, owning his own property and being debt free at an early age. It was like he just changed overnight. Perhaps we spent so much time focused on his physical needs that we missed seeing that his spiritual condition wasn't what we thought it was.

We had co-signed for him, because we didn't learn our lesson well enough with Jeff. The mortgage for our home and Sam's were at the same bank. When Sam defaulted, the bank threatened to call the note on ours as well. Joe and I made our living from our home where we ran the B&B. Sam was about to lose his house and that put ours in jeopardy as well. It was like Sam just didn't grasp the gravity of the whole situation. We didn't want him to lose his home. Together we decided to sell Sam's home before it went into foreclosure. No parent wants to be put in that position. We couldn't allow Sam's loss of interest rob the whole family of everything we had worked for. We loved our son, and we could see he was slipping away. He became even more bitter. He acted like it was our fault that he lost everything. We always prayed for Sam, but now we were doubling down.

> Do not guarantee another person's debt or put up security for someone else. Pr. 22:26

It's astounding that we don't learn these lessons the first time around. What's crazy is how the same kid that is willing to put their parents in a financial bind, will be the most critical when you do it for another child. They can see that it's not wisdom when it's done for someone else, but not when it pertains to them.

Sam found a little apartment a few towns away but seemed to be behind on the rent most of the time. He entertained a lot of people, and we were extremely uncomfortable with the company he was keeping.

> Walk with the wise and become wise, for a companion of fools suffers harm. Pr.1:20

Chapter 30
Hope for a Turn Around

One of the guests visiting the B&B was a gentleman representing an auto body school located in Tennessee. He told us this school was known for building race cars. He was in the area to sell their program to the local high school. He eagerly shared some details with us about their program. It sounded interesting, and we thought Sam might think so too. We were hopeful. It might give him a new interest and perhaps change his direction. Indeed, he was interested, but only on his own terms.

Together we packed the car and took a trip to tour the school. It was quite a long trip, so we had lots of time to talk, coming and going. Once on campus, we were given more details. Sam and I discovered that the tuition had to be paid in full for the entire five semesters training up front. That wasn't the worse part! They had a policy that if a student got caught drinking or smoking pot, they'd be suspended and forfeit the entire tuition. Sam was doing both.

Sam was all hyped up about building NASCARs. As we looked further into their program, we found that the pictures on the walls at the school were of their *one and only successful student* they could boast of. I researched employment of the general population of their graduates. They were making about ten dollars an hour as a beginning mechanic in shops and dealerships all over the country. Sam was already making twice that installing satellite systems!

Sam and I talked all the way home. We discussed his willingness to stop drinking and smoking pot. His answer was that he wouldn't stop. He just wouldn't get caught.

I was a psychiatric nurse, caring for young men that had court appointed incarceration sentences. I dealt with them every day on my job. When we worked together to set goals for their release, it was nearly always the same story. Their goal was to go back on the streets, doing the same crimes that gotten them into trouble in the first place. The rote answer was "I'm too smart to get caught." My reply was "Then explain to me how you got here in the first place. If you're so smart, why are you sitting across the table from me, in custody?" Sam's answer about not getting caught wasn't realistic.

Joe and I were talking about spending twenty-five thousand dollars for a five-semester vocational course. When Sam finished, he'd make half as much an hour as he was currently making. That was if he was even able to complete the course without being caught. We didn't have the money. To finance this school would've required taking out a loan. It couldn't be paid a semester at a time to see if it were something Sam really wanted to do. It had to be paid all at one time. It was a crazy gamble with exceptionally bad odds!

Once again Joe and I had a decision to make. One that'd be difficult with years of consequences. We knew Sam was drinking too heavily to stop cold turkey. He was also smoking pot. We just couldn't borrow that much money with the chance of losing it when Sam broke the rules.

He was angry with our decision. He said, "You paid for Rachel's college, why not mine?" We didn't pay for Jeff's education, he did. We hadn't paid for Kelly's, she did, and we had only helped Rachel with a small portion of hers. Uriah ended up paying off Rachel's student loans after they were married. Not to mention, I was still paying off mine from nursing school.

We spoke with Sam about re-taking the GED exam. He was only one point away from a scholarship. He could've had his education paid for. He had made up his mind. It was the mechanic school or none.

We'd spent most of our lives in the ministry, and unlike the stereotypes of wealthy ministers, we never fit into that category. The truth is many ministers spend their lives in near poverty as they make one sacrifice after the other to fulfill their call. We always trusted God to provide for what we needed. This school appeared to be more of a rip off than a blessing. I wished we'd never suggested it to Sam. He never understood that the trip to tour the school was a fact-finding mission. It wasn't a commitment to attend.

It was the mid-nineties, and $25,000.00 was a huge amount for us to consider. Had the school permitted us to pay by the semester we'd be able to tell how serious Sam was about completion. Over and above tuition was the cost of housing, transportation, and shop fees. He'd be responsible for providing all his own tools and they dictated what brands were required. The total cost was way above just the amount of tuition. When we checked the graduation rate, it was not impressive at all. So, this school was collecting full tuition for five semesters when just over half of their students ever completed the course.

Sam had bought the sales pitch, believing that when he graduated, he'd be able to join the successful builders of NASCARs. There just wasn't any evidence of that being true.

The wedge between us was getting deeper all the time. He never forgave us for not paying for his education. In his mind we'd paid for all of Rachel's. What we'd uncovered about this school, and their graduates, made no difference to Sam. He couldn't accept the facts or our reasoning. He wasn't willing to give up his drinking. He simply assured me that he wouldn't get caught. We weren't willing to take that chance.

> Hope deferred makes the heart sick, But when it comes it is a tree of life. Pr. 13:12

Sam had his hopes dashed. Even if he'd been willing to abide by the school's policies, we still didn't have the ability to pay. It had only been a year since we nearly lost our home because we co-signed a note for him. Other schools allow tuition to be paid per semester. Few people would ever attend college if they were required to pay for their entire education up front.

Sam took this very personal. He reminds me several times a year, every year, how we'd helped Rachel but not him. She spent every weekend and summers working for nothing to help build the family business, while Sam was partying. All we really managed to do for Rachel was to purchase books for the year and pay lab fees. We wanted to do more, but that was the extent of our ability to pay. Over the years we offered to pay for college courses for Sam if he had the interest. Anytime he found himself between jobs, the blame would be laid at our feet for his lack of education.

He was gifted and creative beyond the average person. He always had the ability to make a good income, but our decision to not pay for the mechanic school, wounded Sam. He is still hurt to this day.

Sam is my only child that was never saddled with years of debt from student loans.

Questions for the chapter:

1. Are you a bad parent if you can't afford to pay for your child's college education?
2. Is every child cut out for college?
3. Does it a take a college education to be successful in life?
4. Are there ways for your child's education to be paid for if not by you?
5. Is it necessary or even Biblical to treat all your children equally?
6. Does your child really need to go to a private college, or will a state school do?
7. Is it an embarrassment for your child to go to a local junior college?
8. Is it possible for someone to work their way through college?
9. Does my child have a passion to go to college to pursue a career, or is this just the next thing to do?

I added these questions, because as I type, the world is in the middle of a pandemic. Unemployment is unprecedented for our lifetime. Many parents are going to find themselves in new circumstances. They may not be capable of providing for their children in the manner they have in the past. It's not your fault! Parents and partners will need to learn to be kind to themselves, not condemning. The devil will use every opportunity to accuse you and remind you of your inability to provide. You may not be able to supply those you love with the luxuries or even necessities that you once did. We all hope and pray this situation will pass. That we'll be able to enjoy the lush economy we were spoiled with again. But, what if we can't? Guilt is not your friend. The enemy will use the lack of finances to drive a wedge within families. It's a time to trust God. A time to yield to His leading, and to resist the condemnation of the enemy.

Revelations 12:10 tells us where accusations come from:

....for the accuser of our brethren is cast down, which accused them before our God day and night. Rev. 12:10

This is the devil's job. Day and night, he throws darts at God's people to accuse them. Don't let him use those weapons against you. Don't let him steal your peace. The future will have enough challenges without guilt being added to your stress.

Facts:

1. One-third of all billionaires have no degree.
2. There are many ways to obtain an education, like online, one course at a time.
3. There is funding available from many sources, like grants and scholarships.
4. Student loan debt is a burden that will hang over a person's life for decades.
5. There are Pell Grant funds that go unused every year, because not enough people apply.
6. Tuition for a private school is approximately $48,000.00 per year.

References found on page 269

Chapter 31
The Cruise

Sam had just turned twenty-one when Rachel planned a cruise to the Bahamas for the family. He had a terrible attitude about America and was quite verbal about it on this vacation. Since he was old enough to legally drink, he ordered several cocktails each night at dinner. Joe and I had a room and Sam and Rachel shared a room. Prior to leaving the states Rachel was cutting up an expired credit card when Sam said, "Hey, don't cut it up, give it to me." She explained it wasn't any good. He replied, "That's ok, at least if I have one in my wallet, chicks will think I have a credit card." So, Rachel let him have it. There was no way of knowing how crucial this was going to be.

Once the ship docked in the Bahamas, Joe and Sam went one way and Rachel and I went to get our hair braided. We agreed to meet back at the ship at a certain time. I returned to our room before Joe. When Joe came into the cabin, he said to me, "I don't know where Sam is." I said, "What do you mean?" He answered, "Oh, I left him on the street with some drug dealer." I came unglued!

He told me, "Sam saw some guy wearing a Bob Marley shirt selling roach clips, and drug paraphernalia. I told him to come on several times, but he wouldn't listen, so I just left him there." I was outraged! "How could you do that?" He said, "Sharon, he is twenty-one, I can't control what he does and doesn't do."

> A wise man will hear and increase in learning. And a man of understanding will acquire wise counsel. Pr. 1:5

Oh, that I would have a wise son. I went into prayer mode. "God, what do you want me to learn from this? Is my son going to spend years in some foreign prison?" I had heard about those prisons. I told God, "If you want me to sell everything I have, to pay for a lawyer to get him free, I will." I was so afraid for him, and angry that Joe had left him there. My brain was swirling as I wondered how *I could fix this*!

I was a supervisor over twenty-nine employees at the hospital and it was my job to *fix things*, but this wasn't looking like I had the power to fix anything. Even so, as I paced and prayed, somehow, I felt God had a plan. Was this a lesson for me or for Sam? Maybe it was for both of us.

It was already past the time for the boat to disembark. I went into Rachel's room so I could watch out her window on the boarding side of the ship. I was pleading with God, with everything I had in me! I was so afraid Sam would be left behind. Just then, as I looked out the window, I caught a glimpse of Sam's long-legged figure. He was panting and huffing, running as fast as those legs could take him. I broke into tears thanking The Lord, "Thank you, God! Thank you, God! Thank you, God!" That was all I could say.

> May your father and mother rejoice: may she who gave you birth be joyful. Pr. 23:25

I wasn't joyful because I had an obedient son. I was joyful that God loved me enough to not let my son get stuck in a foreign country, in jail, or dead!

Sam wasn't able to hold a conversation the rest of the trip. All he wanted to do is get back to America. Every time I asked him what happened, he'd get up and walk away. The drinks at dinner came to a halt, and there was a soberness to the rest of the vacation. When we arrived back at the port in America, Sam knelt and kissed the ground. Suddenly, he loved his homeland. Funny how his attitude changed so quickly.

It'd be a while before we learned what had occurred on that island. Sam had been lured by the smooth-talking salesperson and some of his buddies. They took Sam back into a deep ghetto area, where they threatened to kill him. He gave them all the money he had, but it wasn't enough to appease them. They saw Rachel's credit card in Sam's wallet and agreed to let him go if he'd give it to them. He was more than happy to do so. Remember, it was expired. He had come extremely close to losing his life, but the Heavenly Father had made provision for Sam's ransom ahead of time. He made sure he'd be set free before any of this even happened.

The blood of Jesus has been shed for us once and for all. His provision is there for us all the time. His love is so complete and remarkable that He is making a way for us when we don't even know that we need a way.

For God so loved the world that he gave his only begotten son, that whosoever believes on him should not perish but should have eternal life. John 3:16

My Big Test

You can see from Sam's story that it's different from the other children. There aren't any angelic sightings, hearing the voice of God or knowing things in the future. What there is, is the prayer of a mother asking for this child to be born. There is evidence of the sovereign hand of God in saving his life and providing miraculous healings. God has an investment in Sam, if he knows it or not. He's God's property and the enemy can't have him!

After the cruise, Sam lost yet another job and was staying with us. One day he and Joe were walking across the yard together when Joe asked him, "Why do you feel it's necessary to party every night?"

His answer was, "Well, Dad, that's what people do in their twenties." It sure wasn't what Joe did in his twenties.

Sam was like the Pied Piper. We had a picnic table outside on the back deck of the B&B and in the afternoon, a group of young people gathered around him at this location. He would play his guitar and smoke and they all visited together each day.

Years later, I asked Sam what the draw was for all the young people. He told me he was the *Candy Man*. He was selling pot, which was still illegal. That would have never been permitted on our property had we known.

Joe really wanted to see Sam grow up and be more responsible. He decided to have a serious conversation with me. He felt that I enabled Sam.

Here it was. One more time I'd be required to *let go*. To give up control.

We'd been studying a teaching series called "The Calling Out of Sons." In that teaching we learned that many other cultures expect their boys to become men at a much younger age than we do in this country. It asked questions like what constitutes becoming a man? Is it when you get your first muscle car? Conquer a woman? Graduate high school? What does that look like in our society?

In the bush countries, a boy is taken from his mother's tent at age thirteen. She knows he won't return as a boy but as a man. Her days of nurturing have passed. The boy is put through rigorous training on how to hunt, fish, trap, and become a provider for his future family. He's taught how to survive all kinds of difficulties. They have a year of training in the wild with other men of their tribe. When that year is ended, they return to the village. The boy has become a man and is ready to take a bride.

In Jewish cultures a young man has a bar mitzvah. There's a specific time he is declared to be a man. He has studied and prepared for this transformation, and then he is celebrated for his accomplishments. However, in our American culture, our boys just stay boys and never become men. Their toys just get bigger and more expensive. There's no such passage for our sons. No one ever tells them, "Today you've become a man, and you're expected to demonstrate that."

Joe began talking to me about how I protected Sam. He felt like I had overcompensated with him. That because he was born with an imperfection, that I was always trying to make life fair for him. As if I was the great equalizer. Basically, Joe was asking me to quit babying Sam and to require him to grow up. I'd guarded and protected him all his life.

Even though Sam was living with us, when Joe expected him to pitch in and help, I made excuses for him when he didn't do what his Dad asked him to. I always felt Joe expected too much from Sam. Joe and I didn't fight ever, but if we did disagree on anything it would be on Sam. Joe wanted me to make an agreement with him to *let go*. He wanted Sam to come to him for every situation. He felt I was holding him back from being the man he was destined to be. I felt Joe was asking too much. Sam and I had always been close. I had stepped in to protect him so many times in his life and I felt like it was my responsibility. He'd endured a lot with all the surgeries and recovery periods, and I saw myself as his ally. I didn't think I should abandon ship at this point. Sam and I had this great bond, I just wasn't willing to let that go. It was too valuable to me.

The Dream

I told Joe I would pray about it. That night I had a dream. In the dream, there was a huge steam roller rolling into our little town. It was one of the largest pieces of equipment I'd ever seen. It took up the entire roadway. When it turned in front of our house, I could see that Sam was in the steam roller trying to guide it, but he was too short to see where he was going. In this dream he was still a little boy. It was moving recklessly all over the road.

I'd been working in the gardens in front of the house and for some reason I had my purse with me. The steam roller turned into a parking lot next to our house and I breathed a sigh of relief, thinking Sam would be ok now.

I kept working and suddenly I realized the steam roller was on the move again. This time it was on tracks. It passed by me in front of our home. I could see Sam struggling unsuccessfully to control it. He was all alone in this massive piece of machinery. It was headed straight downhill on those tracks. It picked up speed and was moving at an extremely rapid pace. It was rushing right into a quaint shopping strip at the bottom of the hill, where there were hundreds of people shopping. I could see the steam roller, with Sam inside, about to crash into all those people. It seemed he'd be killed and so would many others.

In the dream, I started to run toward the direction of impact. I headed out the garden gate yelling for Sam to jump off before it crashed. Then I said to myself, "Take your purse. You'll need it to get Sam out of this mess if he lives."

The dream was so real. I awoke in disbelief. That was crazy! Why did I go back for my purse? After all I am a nurse. Why wasn't my first instinct to save lives?

This dream troubled me greatly. I prayed about it for days. Then the Lord began to speak to me. He said, "You still see Sam as a child, and you think Sam's life is a train wreck looking for a place to happen. You don't trust Me with his life, and you don't even trust Joe to help him to become the man he was meant to be." Even in the dream I thought I could fix things. I wanted to rescue Sam at any cost. That's why I needed my purse.

You'd think after what I had learned with the other children that this would have come easy. It didn't. I wanted the best for Sam, and I wanted to do it my way. We were so close, and I'd been his protector so many times before. He was my baby, and I didn't want to give up that closeness. I spoke with Joe about the dream. He concurred that it was from the Lord. Here I was again being chastened by the Lord, for *my* need to be a provider and protector for my son, for not trusting God to be God. I had something to lose here. I loved having Sam's loyalty. I loved the closeness I had with him. I didn't know if I could ever *let that go*. I had to love him enough to do what was best for him, even if it meant I'd lose this precious relationship.

We had an old friend that we respected greatly, named Gary. We hadn't seen him in years. That afternoon, he just happened to be in our county doing some sales work. So, he dropped by. Joe was not around, so Gary and I had coffee together and I shared my dream with him. I didn't tell him about "The Calling out of Sons" teaching we'd been studying. When I finished sharing my dream, Gary said, "Well, it sounds like God is telling you that you're a rescuer. Perhaps you need to leave that up to God." That was a huge confirmation to me. Once again, *I was in God's way*. Would I ever learn?

I made an agreement that day to surrender my claim on my son. After all God had already told me that my children were only on loan to me. I'd stop rescuing him. I'd turn him over to the Lord and to his Dad. Joe was never as close to Sam in the way I was. Yet I wanted a son in the first place so Joe would know the joys of having a natural born son. I'd been corrected again.

> Blessed is the man whom You chasten, O LORD, and whom You teach out of Your law. Ps. 94:12

I might be slow to learn sometimes, but I'm not stupid. I know when God is dealing with me, and this was one of those times.

Every time after that when Sam came to me for anything, I'd say, "Take that up with your Dad." He was so used to coming to me for everything that he got resentful and acted like I'd deserted him. This was hard for me, but I agreed it was best for him. There were times I felt I'd been robbed of my son's affection, and it hurt. I believed I was being obedient even though it wasn't easy for me.

> Whoever heeds discipline shows the way to life, but whoever ignores correction leads others astray. Pr. 10:17 NIV

I wanted Sam and his Father to finally bond, for them to have a close relationship. I felt Joe could mentor Sam and bring him back to fellowship with God. I wanted that more than I wanted Sam to think I was his ally and rescuer.

What ended up happening was that Sam looked for hurtful things to say to and about me. Things he knew weren't true. Joe and Rachel would stick up for me and tell him he knew better, but it was his way of getting back at me. Someday his heart will turn toward me again. The dream was from God. I'd been corrected. I had to be obedient despite the cost.

I never suggested that serving and obeying God would be easy, but it will pay big dividends in the long run. It takes courage, guts to do this God's way. His ways are higher. He knows the end. He will not fail us.

Chapter 32
So, How's That Working for Ya?

Sam landed a good job installing satellites and was getting paid very well. He was good at what he was doing. He and another worker were about five hours from home one evening. They were in a work van when they got pulled over by the police in a little town, for a burnt-out taillight. The police searched the van and found one of Sam's souvenirs from the Bahamas. The only thing he got away with besides his life, a pot pipe. It had never been used but it was considered drug paraphernalia. Sam always got out of every difficulty and he figured he'd get out of this too. Instead, he was taken to jail. Initially he made light of it. It was just a little tiny county jail house and all his friends and co-workers promised to raise the money to get him out and to hire a lawyer. After several days passed, he realized these were just empty promises.

Then the unthinkable happened. The little jail was scheduled to be exterminated for bugs. This required that all prisoners be moved, including Sam. They were stripped and dressed in orange prison uniforms. Both their hands and feet were chained while they were being transported to the *Big House*. They didn't know how long they'd be in this new location. Quickly the situation had changed, and Sam was feeling desperate. He was going to a real prison, with actual criminals, he decided it might be time to pray!

He had nowhere to turn. It was time to phone Mom and Dad. He was already in the little jail three days but was trusting his buddies to get him out. Joe had told Sam if he got arrested not to call, we wouldn't rescue him. I felt badly that he had been in jail and didn't feel he could call us for help. Per our agreement the decision to help would be Joe's. We agreed to send bail money by Sam's older brother Jeff, who lived in the same vicinity. They hadn't spoken in an exceptionally long time. They had a huge argument years earlier and had never made amends. I understood Sam's anger with Jeff, but the unforgiveness was eating him up. Jeff, who was always evangelistic, agreed to go bail his brother out of jail. We knew that

Jeff would preach to him until Joe could pick him up. His van had been impounded and he had no way home. He had spent his last thousand dollars on a lawyer to help get the charges dropped.

Now Sam was without work and asked if he could move home. Joe and I agreed, but it would have to be on our terms. He'd have to abide by house rules and participate in family chores and functions. He was waiting for a court date and in the meantime, he didn't have a driver's license.

Together, the three of us drew up a contract, stating what we expected of him. Sam agreed and signed it. That way we all understood what was required. Behavior contracts were something Joe and I had learned in our medical training. We knew Sam hadn't honored contracts in the past, but we hoped this one would work. He was in his mid-twenties by now.

What Sam had laughed about, and thought was a simple little matter of losing his license, turned into a major event. The attorney he paid the thousand dollars to was disbarred. Sam lost his money and when he didn't show up to court, there was a warrant issued for his arrest. He believed his attorney, who took his money, was representing him in court. The idea that he might go back to jail was more than a little frightening.

He didn't want to abide by our house rules. None of this made any sense to me. This was a child that was well behaved in high school, didn't drink, went to work and was a responsible individual. What happened?

The contract we drew up forbid staying out all night. Well, that was the first thing he did to try us. He gave the excuse that he didn't have a car and went with friends that decided to stay in another town overnight. He couldn't get home. We let that one slide, but then it was a bunch of little things. He was going to try every aspect of that contract.

He began to skip family devotions. When I told him, he wasn't abiding by his word, his answer to me was, "Yeh I know, and you can't make me do it." I replied, "You'll find yourself outside with nowhere to stay." He didn't believe me. He arrogantly touted back, "I have a key."

He went downstairs to shower, thinking this conversation was over and that he'd won. I asked Joe to go into the bathroom and get the key out of his pants pocket. While he was in the shower, I packed everything he had in large black trash bags, and placed it on the back deck, with his guitar.

Sam came flying up the stairs. He was six foot three, and he could take the stairs in about four leaps. He yelled, "Where are my things and who took my key?" He was angry. He couldn't believe we'd put him out. This was his house too. He reasoned, Rachel still had a key, even though she was living in another state on assignment. How could we take his key? He was highly insulted.

He hung around on the back deck playing his guitar until dusk, and eventually a friend picked him up and he stayed the night with him.

I didn't want this to happen. He thought he could manipulate and control us. That he could do as he pleased in our house. This was not only our home, but our business. We had paying customers coming and going all the time. Sam felt he had the right to use guest amenities without consideration of the guest. He and his buddies would converge on the outside hot tub at one or two in the morning. They got so loud that they'd wake the guests as the water echoed the sounds of their laughter. I didn't want to put my own son out. He forced our hand with his defiant attitude. This was the last time Sam ever lived in our home.

It took years for him to get over losing the house key. In his mind, it meant he was no longer a member of the family. That wasn't the message we intended to send, but that's what he says that it meant to him. We haven't lived there for years and he still complains about losing his key.

When we asked around town how he was doing, one of his acquaintances said, "Why are you living up there in that mansion and your son is down here in some dumpy little run-down trailer?" My reply was, "All Sam has to do to come home is to abide by the house rules. He wasn't willing to do that, so where he is living is his own choice." I really hoped his friend would tell him what I said. He might decide to come home.

The whole issue of Sam's license and the court date was still hanging over his head. So, Sam and his Dad wrote to the judge to explain the situation. The court was understanding, and he was given a new court date. Joe agreed to drive Sam the six hours to the hearing.

On the way to Kansas City to his court date, Sam was asleep in the front seat of the car. It'd been raining and recently stopped. Joe was driving in the left lane. There was a semi-truck in the right lane that must not have seen them when he started to change lanes. The truck hit and shoved them sideways into the median. If it hadn't been raining and the median muddy, the force would've pushed them over into oncoming traffic. As it was, they got stuck in the mud in the median. To God be the glory!

Sam shot up from his sleep and yelled, "What the hell just happened?" Joe explained that they'd been hit by a truck and that the driver didn't even stop to see if they were ok. Once again, God had intervened. They both walked away unharmed but obviously shook up.

The day Sam finally got his license back he wanted to drive to San Francisco with his sister Rachel. She was taking a new traveling nurse assignment. He hadn't driven for months and convinced her she would enjoy his company. If you remember, Rachel hated eating alone, and she and Sam had been remarkably close for years. He was supposed to drive her out and then take a bus back home, but that never happened. Sam loved the liberal California life.

When Rachel moved on to Sacramento, Sam worked installing satellites again and did well with it. He often found himself in the homes of well-known celebrities. He had a wealthy clientele and frequently he was given side jobs installing expensive sound systems in elaborate homes. He liked getting to know people of influence.

From one of these side jobs he met Jennifer. She was my age, and extremely wealthy. She decided to hire Sam as her personal assistant. She was a philanthropist, and Sam did research to help her to determine where to give her money away. She spoiled him rotten. He was able to work any hours he chose. She paid him extremely well and she treated him like a son. This was the only long-term job Sam ever kept. Sam spent his days reading newspapers and doing research. He felt all this knowledge made him smarter than most people and he wasn't humble about it. He worked for Jennifer until she became ill, and unable to have people around her for health reasons. Sam had been spoiled by this job, and he found it difficult to deal with the reality of a nine-to-five job like everyone else.

Truth on Trial

One evening Sam phoned home. He said, "Mom, I've been dating this girl named Lori. She's German born and both her parents are scientists. I really like her, and we're having so much fun together. I just don't think it can work out because she's an atheist." We talked for a while and he assured me he was going to break it off, because it just couldn't go anywhere. They were too far apart on how they felt about God.

Sam knew what was right.

> Therefore, whoever knows the right thing to do, yet fails to do it, is guilty of sin. James. 4:17

However, he didn't do it. He stayed with Lori for four years. They fought often. Twice he broke up with her after she laughed and made fun of him at parties in the presence of many friends. She tormented him about being stupid because he believed in God. She frequently belittled him over his home education and lack of college hours. It was her way of magnifying her self-importance. By the time Sam finally found her cheating on him and ended the relationship, he had been totally robbed of his faith.

It was while Sam was with Lori that Joe and I visited him in San Francisco. I was so impressed with Sam. He was still such a kind man. When we entered shoppes to browse, he asked each owner for permission to look around, and he never left a store without graciously thanking them for allowing us to look. When we rode the trolly, he called to the driver from the back as we got off at our stop. He said, "Thank you for getting us here safely, Good Job." I was so pleased with his thoughtfulness.

I commented on his politeness and encouraging words, even to the trolly driver. He said, "Mom, these guys are here in this country just trying to make a living for their family, doing the best they can, and no one ever thanks them. I feel like that is my job."

Sam took us to his recording studio, and we had a blast. We wrote songs together. It only took five minutes to make up a quick song and then we began to record. He started with a rhythm, then added

263

a keyboard, then a guitar, then our voices. It was so much fun to do this together as a family.

Lori was still in school working on her master's degree, and so we were able to be alone with Sam. In the evenings she made sure we realized how much she hated the Jews and anything Christian. We tried to reason with her, but she wasn't open to any other view. She was hard core Pro-abortion. It was just so hard to see what Sam saw in her. She was exceedingly impressed with her education and had an intense sense of superiority. It felt like she had some dark secret about Sam that kept him in her clutches. One day Sam will look back and see how happy he was serving God and how miserable it is to be without Him.

This one thing I know! *Everyone has a GOD!* It may be the god of money, sex, power, alcohol, or *self.* Whomever they serve *is their god.* Whatever they pursue or live for is their god.

Some worship the god of Science, instead of the God of the Bible!

For all my children, you can see that who they included in their lives changed who they ultimately became. At one time, Joe and I prayed Sam out of San Francisco. There isn't space to tell that whole story here. He went to Florida for two years and picked up a great building trade. He learned to be a skilled carpenter, building hurricane proof homes for the wealthy on Jupiter Island. Eventually he returned to San Francisco and learned to build earthquake proof homes there. Sam has never liked working for a *boss.* Most of the time he feels he is smarter than they are.

He and Rachel grew apart once she was married. Their life views and values differed greatly, but once she was gone, he missed what he'd lost in her. The night of her memorial he stayed out late drinking with some of the people he'd met that day. He spent no time with Joe, Uriah or me. We were all hurting and needed each other. He has no relationship with Jeff or Kelly, even though Kelly has made numerous attempts to reach out to him.

In 2016, just thirteen months to the day of Rachel's death, Joe died suddenly. Joe's death was as unexpected as Rachel's. He and I were blessed to have forty-one wonderful years together in a marriage that everyone envied. Sam expected an inheritance after his father's death. It's still hard for him to grasp that any inheritance he might receive won't happen until after I die.

Over the years God has seen Sam through at least eight surgeries, nearly drowning, a head-on with a semi, being side swiped by a semi, a motor-cycle accident, a gang beating, escaping death in the Bahamas, a short time in jail, and who knows what else? Obviously, he's here for a purpose.

My hope for my son is that Lady Wisdom keeps calling and that her voice gets louder and louder until Sam can hear her again. I hope that Lady Folly will be defeated in his life once and for all.

I spoke with Sam for a long time this week. He was blessed to be able to keep working during the pandemic. He told me, "Mom, there is one scripture I always remember, *Silver and Gold have I none, but such as I have give I thee*. If I have it and someone else needs it, I'm always willing to share." Sam is a kind man at heart. I see God in him, even when he cannot see God in himself. He has been helping neighbors that are without and has still been able to save a little for what might be coming. He's working on another music studio. I'm pleased he is following his passion.

He asked me, "Mom, how can you have a science degree and still believe in God?" What I believe about God is based on faith. However, science is proving God's Word to be true more every day. He said, "I asked God to show me if He is real, but there is just nothing. He never answers, so He must not be real."

> Behold the LORD'S hand is not shortened, that it cannot save, neither his ear heavy, that it cannot hear: But your iniquities have separated between you and your God. And your sins have hid his face from you that he will not hear. Is. 59:1-2

It's just a matter of repentance. When a person is able to say, "I'm sorry God. I've tried to be my own God. I'm sorry I've left You out of my life and I want that to change." That's when God turns His face back to them. It's just a simple turning of one's heart to bring God close enough to hear and to answer.

I asked God to give me this son. I named him Samuel, which means, "God has heard."

I see God in my son. One day he will see the same. I have learned to *let go* of Sam. To let him be who he is. When both Joe and Rachel died, I felt Sam and I needed one another. He doesn't want to be part of the life I've chosen, and I can't be part of the life he's chosen. The rest is up to God. I keep loving, I keep praying, I trust.

Lessons Learned

I told you in the beginning this book isn't about my successes as a parent, or the victories of my children. It's about my God and all that He has taught me. I had to learn to *let go* of every one of my kids, in one way or the other.

Not long ago, Sam phoned me, very excited. He was dating a woman and she was pregnant. They'd decided together to raise the child and share responsibilities. Sam wanted more than that. He wanted to be a dad. He told her, "My parents weren't perfect but at least every day when I woke up, my Dad was there. I don't want to be a part-time dad. I want to be married and raise this child." There it was! A glimpse into who he really is, what he really wants in life, and that is to be a husband and a dad. Sadly, she didn't agree to his terms. He's alone again, but at least it gave me insight that I didn't have before.

I cannot change my son, but I can choose to love him as he is. God is the one who has this assignment now. He loves my son more than I do. He gave His life for him. He died in his stead. What Sam does... is not who he is. We are designed to bring God glory with our lives. I trust God that I've done what He's instructed me to do.

> Train up a child in the way he should go: And when he is old he will not depart from it. Pr. 22:6

It's not over, until God says so. I may not see the fruit of my labors in this lifetime. However, even after I am gone the Word put into my son's life will continue to produce.

> God is not a man, that he should lie: neither the son of man, that he should repent; hath he said, and shall he not do it? or hath he spoken, and shall he not make it good? Num. 23:19

God's working even if we don't see it. He's sending people, dreams and maybe even visions. Whatever it takes to open Sam's eyes. When he returns, he'll be welcomed with open arms by a loving Father. *Get out of the way.* Trust God. Stop trying to be Him! *Let Go.*

Chapter 33
To Be Continued

It's time to compare your answers from Chapter One. I pray my story has helped you to reach deep inside to better understand why you do what you do. Be honest, listen to The Father. *Let Go!*

1. Might this struggle be for someone's good?
2. What if this is what it takes for God to gain this person, for them to discover their purpose in life?
3. Why would Paul tell us to endure hardships?
4. Is it right to bail a child out of *every* difficulty?
5. Should a person learn to suffer consequences for their actions?
6. Do they need rescued?
7. Do you reward or comfort when discipline is what's needed?
8. Were there difficult things you had to figure out for yourself growing up?
9. Did it make you stronger or wiser in the long run?
10. Think about your friends, did tough times ruin them?
11. Do difficulties produce character by learning to overcome?
12. Are hardships a normal part of growing up?
13. Will it kill my child if I don't *fix* what's wrong?
14. Will it kill me if my child gets angry with me?
15. What *exactly* am I afraid of?
16. What's driving my decisions concerning my children?
17. Does God have a plan for my child that might not be mine?
18. Am I getting in God's way?
19. Do I have preconceived ideas how God should answer prayers?
20. *Why* can't I let go?
21. Am I a rescuer?
22. How do I respond when things are totally out of my control?
23. Can I trust God with my child's future?
24. Will this situation build character in my child?
25. Do *I insist* on being in control of most everything?
26. Do I try to force God's hand? Or attempt to Manipulate?
27. Am I willing to *let* my child fall/fail?
28. Is it a reflection on me personally if my child isn't a success?
29. Is there anyone as capable of doing things as well as me?

30. Do I take responsibility for my own actions?
31. Can I say I'm sorry even if I'm not the one in the wrong?
32. Will a struggle strengthen or destroy my child?
33. What is the long-term goal?
34. Does God love my child more than I do?
35. What are the benefits and pitfalls of promoting independence?
36. *Do I know my own heart?*
37. *Is God in this trial?*

There are ten more really good questions in Chapter 11. I suggest you look back at those as well.

These questions are like truth serum for the soul. If you will take the time to be truthful with yourself, you might learn a lot about who you are and how you relate to God. My story is not over, it's to be continued.

I shared earlier that I started this book four years ago. I hoped that it would have a different ending by the time it was complete. Additionally, I wasn't ready to write about Rachel's death yet. What I've come to realize is that my ending probably sounds a lot like many of yours. We're waiting for just one more miracle. For God to do His perfect work and to restore all the broken or strained relationships.

What we know is that even if we don't see others change in our lifetime, that doesn't mean they won't. What's important is that *WE* change. We quit being manipulating, or manipulated, rescuing, or fixing. *We let God be God* and get out of His way. Just maybe, you might even get a good night's sleep, and you might stop worrying.

Being a parent is the most important job I've had in my life. We never stop being parents. We never stop loving, even the unlovable. We leave a legacy to our children and our children's children. Let that be one of strength, decisiveness, and Godliness. Allowing God to be the fixer, and not throwing the lifeline, unless we're completely sure our instructions are from The Lord. May you be free of the fear of rejection and receive power to do what The Father is saying.

To be continued.

I am praying for you.

References

1. EmpoweringParents.com, p.13
2. "A Promise of Hope" by Autumn Stringam; p.22
3. Affection Deprivation: Google for numerous articles, p.153
4. Heart Sync Ministries/Heartsyncministries.org; p.221
5. Tapping; The Tapping Solution by Nick Ortner, p.222
6. Wealth-X, Billionaire Census; p.250
7. Nerd Wallet (College money left on the table) 9/2017; p.250
8. MU30 Millennial Financial Independence Survey; p.250

About the Author

Sharon Cluck is a licensed RN with years of medical and psychiatric nursing. She is a trained counselor in the Heart Sync Method and has also trained with Family Foundations International.

She has been writing articles for the past five years for an independent Christian Magazine. You can find some of those articles at www.mindofmessiah.com

She and her late husband have co-pastored two churches. They pioneered the Home School movement in the late seventies and traveled to establish Christian Schools in the Midwest and southwestern United States.

Sharon has a history of ministry in deliverance and has a deep understanding of God's Word. She is a knowledgeable and passionate speaker.

She may be contacted for speaking engagements at:

Mind of Messiah Ministries

573-482-0756

Sharoncluck@mindofmessiah.com